THE S. MARK TAPER FOUNDATION

IMPRINT IN JEWISH STUDIES

BY THIS ENDOWMENT

THE S. MARK TAPER FOUNDATION SUPPORTS

THE APPRECIATION AND UNDERSTANDING

OF THE RICHNESS AND DIVERSITY OF

JEWISH LIFE AND CULTURE

The publisher and the University of California Press Foundation gratefully acknowledge the generous support of the S. Mark Taper Foundation Imprint in Jewish Studies.

Luminos is the Open Access monograph publishing program from UC Press. Luminos provides a framework for preserving and reinvigorating monograph publishing for the future and increases the reach and visibility of important scholarly work. Titles published in the UC Press Luminos model are published with the same high standards for selection, peer review, production, and marketing as those in our traditional program. www.luminosoa.org

The Eternal Dissident

The Eternal Dissident

Rabbi Leonard I. Beerman and
the Radical Imperative to Think and Act

———

Edited by

David N. Myers

To Yana,
with best wishes,

UNIVERSITY OF CALIFORNIA PRESS

University of California Press, one of the most distinguished university presses in the United States, enriches lives around the world by advancing scholarship in the humanities, social sciences, and natural sciences. Its activities are supported by the UC Press Foundation and by philanthropic contributions from individuals and institutions. For more information, visit www.ucpress.edu.

University of California Press
Oakland, California

Suggested citation: Myers, D. N. (ed.) *The Eternal Dissident: Rabbi Leonard I. Beerman and the Radical Imperative to Think and Act.* Oakland: University of California Press, 2018. DOI: https://doi.org/10.1525/luminos.50

Library of Congress Cataloging-in-Publication Data

Names: Beerman, Leonard I., 1921–2014, author. | Myers, David N., editor.
Title: The eternal dissident : Rabbi Leonard I. Beerman and the radical
   imperative to think and act / edited by David N. Myers.
Description: Oakland, California : University of California Press, [2018] |
   Includes bibliographical references and index. |
Identifiers: LCCN 2018000546 (print) | LCCN 2018005632 (ebook) | ISBN
   9780520969797 () | ISBN 9780520297456 (pbk. : alk. paper)
Subjects: LCSH: Beerman, Leonard I., 1921–2014. | Reform Judaism—United
   States—History—20th century. | Jewish leadership—United
   States—History—20th century. | Social action.
Classification: LCC BM755.B382 (ebook) | LCC BM755.B382 A25 2018 (print) |
   DDC 296.8/3410973—dc23
LC record available at https://lccn.loc.gov/2018000546

Manufactured in the United States of America

25 24 23 22 21 20 19 18
10 9 8 7 6 5 4 3 2 1

CONTENTS

ILLUSTRATIONS

ACKNOWLEDGMENTS

My first debt is to Leonard Beerman himself. He was a remarkable mentor, friend, and inspiration. My conversations with him were unfailingly spirited, challenging, and profound. Only in the last months of his life did he agree to work with me on a volume of his sermons and writings. I am sorry that he did not live to see this volume take concrete shape—or to know how seriously his ideas were taken.

Profound thanks are due to his wife, Dr. Joan Willens Beerman, who is also a close friend. Joan opened her home to my frequent intrusions, allowing me to make my way up the spiral staircase to Leonard's study to pore over his papers for hours on end. I'd also like to thank Leonard's daughters, Judith, Eve, and Elizabeth, who supported the project from its inception and permitted me to make use of their father's papers and photographs. I'm delighted that the Beerman Papers will be housed at the UCLA Department of Special Collections, where Genie Guerard and her colleagues will attend to them with their customary care.

One of the distinctive features of this book are the commentaries that follow each selection. I'm most grateful to the distinguished roster of commentators who have graced and elevated this volume. Invaluable research assistance was provided by Lindsay King, Nadav Molchadsky, and Kathy Rubio. Talia Graff invested a great deal in this project and contributed significantly as both researcher and proofreader. Thanks are due to the University of California Press editorial team including Eric Schmidt, Cindy Fulton, and Jolene Torr, as well as to Marian Rogers for her meticulous copyediting.

Finally, I would like to express thanks to David Hoberman, a deep admirer of Leonard Beerman, who instantly provided generous support to allow this project to get off the ground.

Introduction

David N. Myers

Capturing the multifaceted personality of Rabbi Leonard Beerman (1921–2014) is not a simple task. He was a deeply inquisitive thinker who posed probing philosophical and theological questions from his early to his last days. He was an impassioned preacher who lavished attention on his weekly and seasonal sermons, which alternately dazzled, moved, and angered his congregants. After his retirement from Leo Baeck Temple, he continued to give a much anticipated and often controversial sermon every Yom Kippur, delivering the final one two and a half months before his death on December 24, 2014.

Leonard Beerman was also an indefatigable activist for social justice whose renown extended well beyond Los Angeles to the wider nation. His commitment, like his life, was forged in a time of dramatic historical change. Beerman's early years were marked by the profound economic uncertainty of the Great Depression, out of which emerged his empathy for the less fortunate. As an adolescent, he encountered racism, xenophobia, and antisemitism in America, while developing a nascent awareness of the rise of murderous totalitarianism in Europe that culminated in the Holocaust. And in the first decades of his professional career, he devoted a great deal of energy to combating the scourges of McCarthyism, racial injustice, and later, nuclear arms.

Beerman was not alone in these commitments. During this tumultuous period in American history, the rabbinical profession was propelled forward by powerful new currents in American society such as progressivism and the social gospel movement.[1] Towering figures such as Stephen S. Wise, Judah L. Magnes, Abba Hillel Silver, and later Joachim Prinz and Abraham Joshua Heschel reimagined the rabbinate as a vehicle for broad social engagement, consistent with their vision of an ethical Judaism rooted in the ancient Hebrew prophets' demand for justice. By the 1950s, the American Reform movement at large was assuming an increasingly activist and public stance, issuing books, guidelines to congregations, and proclamations that echoed the famous charge from Deuteronomy, "Justice, Justice Shalt Thou Pursue," as a 1953 rabbinical proclamation was titled.[2]

Leonard Beerman came of age in this charged midcentury era as a Reform rabbi inspired by predecessors such as Wise, Magnes, and Heschel (who was not a Reform rabbi, but whom Beerman met at the Reform seminary Hebrew Union College in Cincinnati). At the same time, he was very much his own man. The sight of injustice of any sort induced a raw pain in him. He was especially vigilant and outraged when he believed that fellow Jews were complicit in causing injury, either through direct action or indifference. Never content to settle for the easy path, Beerman challenged and chastised his fellow Jews—and himself—with fiery intensity. He was willing to alienate, indeed, to afflict the comfortable in order to comfort the afflicted, as the well-known phrase has it.

Leonard Beerman was an unusual mix. He was a thinker, a vastly literate reader, and a scholar manqué who was somewhat hesitant to commit his spoken word to pen. And he was a doer, who proudly lived the Heschelian principle of praying with his feet by frequenting and leading protests against injustice. In both of these domains of activity, Beerman was animated by a deep humanity. He loved people in the abstract, and he loved people in the flesh. He loved his fellow Jews, and he loved human beings in general. He knew the healing powers of love in personal relationships. And he knew, as his brother-in-arms, the legendary civil rights activist the Reverend James Lawson, put it, that "love in action" was the defining force of social justice.[3]

It would be easy but inaccurate to suggest that Leonard Beerman's personality was free of tension. He was filled with love, but also anger at injustice. He was a bold pacifist, but also an unrelenting fighter. He marched, demonstrated, and was arrested with people in South Central, but served a wealthy congregation in upscale Bel-Air. He was his own kind of Jewish particularist and an unbounded universalist.[4] These dissonances and disjunctures reflected a spirit of restlessness, a constant fear of inadequacy, and a fair measure of inner turmoil. But they also gave real force to his sense of prophetic vocation. Like his rabbinical forebears, Beerman looked to the Hebrew prophets for inspiration. They were his models for thinking and doing in the world. It was they, he declared in a sermon from 1983, who "address our condition of being Jews and yet at the same time being citizens of the larger society."[5]

What especially spoke to Beerman's sense of mission in the prophets was their courage to remonstrate, to fight against inequality, to look inside themselves with critical eyes. This captured for him the essence of what it meant to be Jewish. Beerman articulated this sentiment already in his first major sermon—the one that every graduating rabbinical student gives at Hebrew Union College. In his "Chapel

Sermon," of October 1948, Beerman stated: "Israel is the eternal wanderer and sufferer, like man himself, fighting against thistles and thorns, shadows and abstractions. Israel is *the eternal dissident,* the great disobedient child of history."[6] This had more than a trace of autobiographical insight, for Leonard Beerman was himself an "eternal dissident," fighting against convention and comfort not in the name of tearing down, but rather with a deep belief in the possibility of repairing the world.

The roots of this distinctive commitment extended back to early childhood. Leonard Beerman was born on April 9, 1921, in Altoona, Pennsylvania, the eldest of three siblings. His father Paul (1896–1983) belonged to the great wave of Jewish immigration to the United States that commenced in the late nineteenth century, moving to this country at the age of three from Kovno in Lithuania. His mother Tillie (1896–1982) was born in New York to Hungarian Jewish parents. Neither of his parents went to school beyond seventh grade; both were needed to care for their families. In Altoona, Beerman and his parents lived in close proximity to his maternal grandparents, Rose and Jacob Grossman, who kept a kosher home and introduced Beerman to Jewish rituals.[7] Life in Altoona was not easy, especially in economic terms. His father moved from peddling fruits and vegetables on a horse-driven wagon to selling notions, small objects, and toys.[8]

When Beerman was six and a half, his father took a more stable job as a department store manager in Michigan. The Beermans were one of seven Jewish families in their small town, and Beerman was one of two Jews at his high school. The town itself was, as Beerman remembers it, "ultra-Republican."[9] His oppositional tendencies were evident already at this early stage. In a student poll at his high school in 1932, twenty-nine of thirty students voted for Herbert Hoover; one, Leonard Beerman, voted for FDR. Not only did the local newspaper, the *Owosso Argus-Press,* regularly inveigh against Roosevelt and Communists, but the Ku Klux Klan was a presence in town. Antisemitism was also part of the general milieu; his father would regularly tune in during the 1930s to the weekly broadcasts of Father Charles Coughlin, the rabidly anti-Jewish Catholic priest from Detroit.[10]

Beerman learned from his father that it was possible and even necessary to hold to unpopular positions. Paul Beerman had returned from his service in the US military in World War I as a pacifist. Beerman recalls: "He didn't believe in war. I mean, he didn't make a big deal of it but that was what he was. He basically was a man of peace and gentleness."[11] Paul was also a person who identified with the plight of the workers, as would his son throughout his life.

Beerman's teenage years were challenging ones, and inculcated in him a life-long empathy for the underdog. In the first instance, he was unusually short, 4'10", paired with a partner on the high school tennis team who was 6'3". This led to a certain lack of confidence, as he remembered: "Puberty really didn't come to me until I was about 16, and that was a problem, a big problem in my glands and in my mind."[12] Compounding these difficulties was the fact that his father was forced to take a major pay cut in 1937, at the tail end of the Depression, sending him into a depression that culminated in the loss of his job—and then a nervous breakdown. After a period of rehabilitation for Paul in a sanatorium, the cash-strapped family was forced to move back to Altoona to live with Rose Grossman. Beerman remembers being very angry that he had to leave his Owosso high school after his junior year to commence his senior year in Altoona.[13]

One year later, the family again picked up and moved from Altoona for State College, Pennsylvania, where Beerman was to begin his college studies in the fall of 1939 at what was then the Pennsylvania State College. To make ends meet, the family took in boarders in its new house. Penn State was extremely important in Beerman's formation in several regards. There, he joined the local Hillel chapter, and began to develop a much richer connection to and intellectual interest in Judaism. An important guide was the Hillel director, Benjamin Kahn, a Conservative rabbi whom Beerman respected and learned from.[14] At that point, though, he had given no thought to becoming a rabbi himself. Rather, he was coming into his own intellectually, discovering a passion for serious study, especially in his three favorite subjects: literature, history, and philosophy. He also took mathematics and physical education virtually every semester and was enrolled throughout his time in college in ROTC.[15] At Penn State, he found contemporaries with whom he could converse in stimulating fashion as well as a talented faculty that challenged him. One professor, the medieval historian Francis Tschan, thought highly of Beerman, but was apparently no lover of members of the Mosaic faith. While giving him a ride home once, he said approvingly: "Beerman, you're not like those Jews from New York."[16] Another faculty member, a Jewish biochemist with whom his parents were friendly, encouraged Beermam to go into that field. In the same period, he took a test designed to identify career options at Penn State. The person who administered it said that it revealed that Beerman had the aptitude to be a professor in the humanities, but added that it was virtually impossible for a Jew to attain such a position in the year 1941.[17]

At that point in the summer of 1941, with few prospects awaiting him, though close to completion of his course work, Beerman left school and began to hitchhike around the country. Eventually, he landed in Flint, Michigan, where he got a job at the AC spark plug factory, which had been repurposed to make guns for the war effort. Beerman worked on the assembly line seven nights a week. In this setting, he stood out. In the first instance, he was an intellectually inclined and curious college student. In the second instance, his political instincts tended toward socialism, which was hardly popular in the jingoistic war years. And finally, his religion set him apart. He recalled that he once was socializing with a group of coworkers at the YMCA where he lived when he told them that he was a Jew. They responded:

> "If we had known you were Jewish, we never would have had anything to do with you." Another one said, "In fact, we're not going to have anything to do with you," and they walked out of the room.[18]

Given his later trajectory, it is surprising that this and other encounters with anti-semitism as a youth and young man did not turn Beerman inward or render him defensive toward the world. On the contrary, these experiences seemed to heighten his own sensitivity for the plight of other victims of group discrimination. At the same time, he was learning and reading more about Jewish history and thought, working his way through the Judaica section of the Flint public library. This led him to develop a stronger sense of Jewish identity, and he began to think for the first time of a career as a rabbi.[19] Soon thereafter, Beerman returned to Penn State to complete his studies. This was a period of further intellectual growth and exis-tential tumult. He spoke with a close friend at Penn State, Leonard Feldstein, who would later become a psychoanalyst in New York, about his thoughts of becoming a rabbi. Feldstein immediately blurted out: "You can't become a rabbi; you don't believe in God."[20] Indeed, Beerman harbored his own serious theological doubts, even as he was deepening his knowledge of Judaism. He felt some measure of solace when he discovered the great Dutch thinker of Jewish origins, Benedictus Spinoza (1632–1677), who helped give him a philosophical and theological han-dle on the world. He was particularly drawn to Spinoza's notion that God was essentially equivalent to nature (*Deus sive natura*): "The god of Spinoza, I thought, could be my god, and that's the god I think I could believe in and affirm, so I was comforted by that."[21] Indeed, this intense engagement with Spinoza became the philosophical foundation of Beerman's lifelong agnosticism, which lent his rabbin-ate a curious quality, but also a tension-filled authenticity.

Throughout his life, Beerman asked tough questions of himself, refusing to accept pat answers or easy resolutions. He was a man of courage and boldness, but not of certainty. Moreover, he took steps in his life that were as much a chal-lenge to his value system as an affirmation of them. One such step came after he returned to Penn State in the summer of 1942 to complete his degree. He finished his requirements in the fall semester and was awarded a bachelor's degree with Phi Beta Kappa honors on December 17. He then decided immediately thereafter to enlist in the Marine Corps, prompted both by his need to fulfill his ROTC obliga-tion and, in choosing the US Marines, by the desire to overcome his own sense of physical inadequacy.[22] He shipped off to Parris Island, South Carolina, spent three months in grueling training camp, and emerged, as he recalled, with "a butch haircut, very lean, muscular."[23] Because of his intellectual aptitude, Beerman was recommended for Officer Candidate School, but could not pass the final physical test required of new recruits. Faced with a variety of options, he took an honorable discharge after only seven months.

Over the course of his time at Penn State, Beerman had discussed the option of rabbinical school with Rabbi Kahn, the Hillel director. Because Beerman did not have a strong background in Hebrew or other traditional Jewish subjects, Kahn recommended that he consider the Reform movement's seminary Hebrew Union College (HUC), where the fact that he was not familiar with traditional

Jewish sources would not be a disqualification. And in fact, Beerman had written to HUC's president, Dr. Julian Morgenstern, before heading off to Parris Island. As he remembered it, Dr. Morgenstern told him that he'd be happy to admit him if he returned in one piece from the Marine Corps.[24] Accordingly, after being discharged, Beerman made his way to Cincinnati, Ohio, and enrolled in the fall of 1943 in HUC.

There he took a wide range of courses, including Hebrew, the Bible, Jewish ritual, and rabbinic literature.[25] He studied with a number of leading Jewish studies scholars, including Israel Bettan, Jacob Rader Marcus, and Abraham Joshua Heschel. And yet it was a lesser-known faculty member who influenced him most, Abraham Cronbach, a Reform rabbi and scholar with radical pedagogical and political ideas. In his classroom, which was festooned with magazine covers expressing political views from Communist to Fascist, Cronbach did not allow argument. One had the right to express an opinion, but not to oppose another's. Cronbach himself was a deeply committed pacifist with strong socialist inclinations, whom Beerman remembered as "an absolutely brilliant man"—and one of the first to write on Judaism and psychoanalysis.[26]

Meanwhile, the students at HUC were informally divided by their various interests. Beerman remembers three such groups: the "*kavanah*" boys (including Samuel Dresner and Richard Rubinstein), who came together on the basis of their common desire to make prayer and liturgy spiritually meaningful;[27] the "theology" boys (including future luminaries such as Eugene Borowitz, Arnold J. Wolf, and Steven Schwarzschild), who were the intellectual vanguard of the student body and were searching for a more vigorous theology than what they were taught; and the "social justice" boys, who were committed to the prophetic spirit of bringing equality and peace to the world. Beerman had little to do with the first group, had strong ties to those in the second, but was a mainstay of the third, along with his close friend Robert Goldburg, with whom he shared a passion not only for activism, but for fine literature and rigorous intellectual exchange as well. The "social justice" boys read the texts of Marx and other Marxists, and engaged in their own forms of activism. For example, they undertook, together with a black student from the University of Cincinnati, a sit-in at a segregated restaurant in town, refusing to leave before being removed hours later.[28]

Beerman's participation in the informal social justice group gave expression to an ethical-political commitment that had been developing in him for years. It reflected his view that to be a Jew was to act in the world for the betterment of all humanity. It is thus somewhat curious that he decided that he would travel, along with his wife, Martha, and his fellow HUC student, Ezra Spicehandler and his wife, Shirley, to Palestine to study at the Hebrew University in Jerusalem in the fall of 1947. Although the American Reform movement had moved away from its unequivocal opposition to Zionism (in the Pittsburgh platform of 1885) to a position of qualified support (in the Columbus platform of 1937), many Reform rabbis remained opposed or agnostic about Zionism. Given Beerman's own universalist rendering of Judaism and disdain for all forms of chauvinism, one might think that he would simply sidestep Zionism and avoid Palestine. But Beerman was insatiably curious and liked to learn for himself. Palestine was a source of intense controversy even then, and it was important to go to visit. At the same time, he harbored within him a vestige of his grandparents' world, traces of a certain Jewish ethnic bond, as well as pride in the fortitude and accomplishments of the Zionist settlers. Notwithstanding his profound concern and frequent criticism, Palestine (and later Israel) held a special place in his heart.

And in fact, Beerman's time in Palestine proved to be formative. He settled in Jerusalem, and quickly went about meeting people and making new friends. He planned to enroll at the Hebrew University in the fall semester, though there is no record of his actually taking courses.[29] That said, he did seek out and forge in this period a connection with one of the most controversial Jews in Palestine, who happened to be the president of the Hebrew University and a Reform rabbi: Judah L. Magnes. The American-born Magnes (1877–1948) had served congregations in the Bay Area and New York before taking a most unusual step for an American Reform rabbi in 1922: he immigrated to Palestine. He became a leading force behind the efforts to create a new university in Jerusalem, and presided over the opening of the Hebrew University in April 1925 as its founding chancellor. Beerman was drawn to Magnes not only because of his role in creating the Hebrew University, and not only because he was a Reform rabbi. Magnes was also one of the most notable Jewish pacifists in Palestine and was heavily involved in efforts to achieve peace between Jews and Arabs from the time of his arrival in the country. Magnes did not hesitate to voice his political opinions, which were decidedly out of step with the sensibilities of Jews in Palestine during the British Mandate period (1922–1948). Even at the Hebrew University, whose faculty included a number of well-known liberals and progressive, Magnes's words were not always well received. For example, students hissed at his speech at the opening of the winter semester in 1929, three months after the murderous Western Wall riots. On that occasion, Magnes declared:

> If the only way of establishing the Jewish National Home is upon the bayonets of some empire, our whole enterprise is not worthwhile and it is better that the eternal people that has outlived many a mighty empire should possess its soul in patience and plan and wait. It is one of the great civilizing tasks before the Jewish people to try to enter the Promised Land not as Joshua, but bringing peace, culture, hard work, sacrifice, love and determination; to do nothing unjustifiable before the conscience of the world.[30]

In virtually every regard, Judah Magnes was a model for Leonard Beerman: his pacifism, his commitment to Jewish-Arab peace, his vision of a prophetic Judaism defined by its ethical norms, and his willingness to brook controversy with his words. In fact, a recent biographer of Magnes described him in terms that could

FIGURE 1. Leonard Beerman (far right) with Judah Magnes, Ezra Spicehandler, and two unidentified people at the Hebrew University, Jerusalem (1947).

well suit Beerman: "American Jewish nonconformist."[31] Among other affinities, Beerman was drawn to Magnes's most controversial of stances—his opposition to a self-standing Jewish state in favor of a Jewish-Arab binational state.[32] And yet, he did not publicly endorse Magnes's proposal. As a matter of fact, he took another action in Jerusalem that is surprising in light of his own instincts as well as his new relationship with Magnes. Following the United Nations General Assembly vote in favor of the partition of Palestine into a Jewish and an Arab state on November 29, 1947, he joined the Haganah, the Jewish paramilitary force associated with the Labor Zionist Mapai Party. He renewed his knowledge of how to use a gun from his time in the Marine Corps, and was even sent out on a mission shortly after the outbreak of hostilities between Jews and Arabs that followed the approval of the United Nations partition plan on November 29, 1947. On that mission, which he undertook with his HUC friend Ezra Spicehandler, he recalled carrying but not detonating hand grenades in the Katamon neighborhood of Jerusalem.[33]

The experience of serving in the Haganah and countenancing the prospect of doing serious harm to another human being, along with his conversations with

Judah Magnes, solidified what would become an iron-clad principle for Beerman from this point forward: pacifism. He returned to the United States in the spring of 1948, and was invited to speak about his experience. In a speech entitled "I Saw Palestine Betrayed" at the Penn State Hillel chapter on April 30, 1948, he followed in Magnes's path by taking aim at the British, whom he scored for failing to prevent violence between Jews and Arabs. Unlike Magnes, though, he supported the idea of partitioning Palestine into Jewish and Arab states, but on the condition that "Arabs are given access to educational and cultural opportunities such as the Jews have."[34] While clearly drawn to the ideal of binationalism, he remained committed throughout his life to the principle of independent states for both Jews and Arabs. Over time, though, one notices a shift in his rhetoric regarding the relations between Jews and Arabs in the Holy Land. Soon after his return in 1948, he expressed the view of fellow Jews about the desire of local Arabs to "impose their feudal rule on the country and overturn the achievements of the Jews."[35] In later years, from the late 1960s onward, such sentiments gave way to frustration over the errant path of Zionism, especially in denying to Palestinians their national rights. Incidentally, Beerman never identified himself as a Zionist, though he felt a strong connection to Israel and, on a subsequent visit in 1964 while on sabbatical with Martha and their three daughters, even considered moving there—yet another evocation of the life path followed by Judah Magnes.

Meanwhile, back in the United States, Beerman entered his final year of rabbinical school in 1948. Although he tended to describe himself as shy and merely one of the pack, he distinguished himself enough to be elected student body president. Moreover, with his "Chapel Sermon" on October 30, he revealed himself not only as a skilled orator and explicator of the Bible, but also as a wide-ranging and fearless intellectual. Over the course of his time at HUC, Beerman always did well in his classes on public speaking, earning the grade of Excellent. As a general matter, the attention paid to popular speaking, and more particularly the sermon, in that era of the American rabbinate was high. For many congregants, it was the key measure of the rabbi's public performance as well as the center of gravity of the weekly Sabbath service.[36]

From the very beginning of his career, Beerman brought a formidable array of talents to the art of sermonizing: lyrical eloquence, a large library of philosophical and historical references drawn from his wide reading, a seemingly endless repository of poetic allusions, and deep psychological insight into the human condition.

This last quality was on display in his first major homiletical appearance, his "Chapel Sermon." He began by reflecting on children and their tendency to rebel against their parents. In fact, this impulse was not restricted to children, but applied to humans at large. Beerman's proof text was the series of early chapters of the book of Genesis describing Adam and Eve in the garden of Eden. He treated Adam's taking a bite of the forbidden apple (Gen. 3:6) not as a manifestation of man's fall from grace, but as an essential, if not fully complete, step toward individuation—indeed, as liberation from the state of infant dependency. Beerman analogized Adam to man in his time, who has taken a step toward liberation by gaining mastery, through technological advances, over nature. But like Adam, who took only a bite rather than consuming the entire apple, human beings have not gained mastery over themselves or society. They remain in need of "a sense of purpose, a sense of human dignity in the changed and different world in which we live."[37]

This incomplete state yields fear, frustration, and a lack of boldness. The resulting lack of rationality and emotional maturity led people to believe, Beerman observed, that "if there were no Russia and if there were no Communists, all the problems with which we and the world are troubled would vanish."[38] This statement announced his own steadfast resistance to the rabid red-baiting of the day. Beerman also pushed back against the grim view of human nature that he associated with neo-orthodox Protestant theologians, who held that man is evil and "the world is set against him in eternal conflict."[39] On the contrary, human beings are not evil nor condemned to ignorance. They are on a ceaseless quest for enlightenment and justice. What is required is not more conformity, but to "eat more and more and more at the tree of knowledge," to rebel against constraint and convention. The prototype for this transgressive pursuer of knowledge is Israel, the Jewish people, whom Beerman designates, we recall, as "the eternal dissident, the great disobedient child of history."[40]

This early sermon presciently captures a good portion of Beerman's lifelong vocation as rabbi—to believe in the goodness of humanity, but to be mindful of its enormous unrealized potential and not infrequent missteps. This is the credo that guided him in fulfillment of his role as eternal dissident. And it was a role for which he became known throughout his career. More than thirty years later, in the wake of Israel's invasion of Lebanon in the summer of 1982, Beerman's picture was on the cover of the local *LA Weekly* with the headline "A Dissident Rabbi Speaks Out." He and a number of colleagues had proposed a resolution critical of the invasion at the recent convention of Reform rabbis (the Central Conference of American Rabbis, CCAR), which was roundly defeated. In a lengthy interview in the *LA Weekly* to explain his position, Beerman reiterated his universalist and pacifist ideals: "My concerns as a Jew are not only for the survival of the Jewish people and the State of Israel, but for the ethical values of my Jewish tradition. Anything that involves the destruction of human beings of any race or nation is something that I consider to be a tragedy, an outrage against the principles that I, as a Jew, am committed to."[41]

Alongside this early and rather constant dissident stance, Beerman displayed another, somewhat opposing tendency as rabbi: as institutional partner and builder. At the end of the 1948–1949 academic year that began with his "Chapel Sermon," he graduated HUC. Soon thereafter he was interviewed by a small group of Reform Jews in Los Angeles interested in hiring a rabbi to lead their new community as of August 1, 1949. The group had first organized in 1947 as Congregation

FIGURE 2. "A Dissident Rabbi Speaks Out," *LA Weekly* (1982).

Beth Aaron, but decided that it should take its name from the famous German rabbi and theologian whom some members had heard speak in Los Angeles: Leo Baeck (1873–1956).[42] The new group did its due diligence, interviewing eleven candidates for the position. It chose the newly minted rabbi Leonard Beerman to serve as its spiritual leader at the fledgling temple located on S. San Vicente

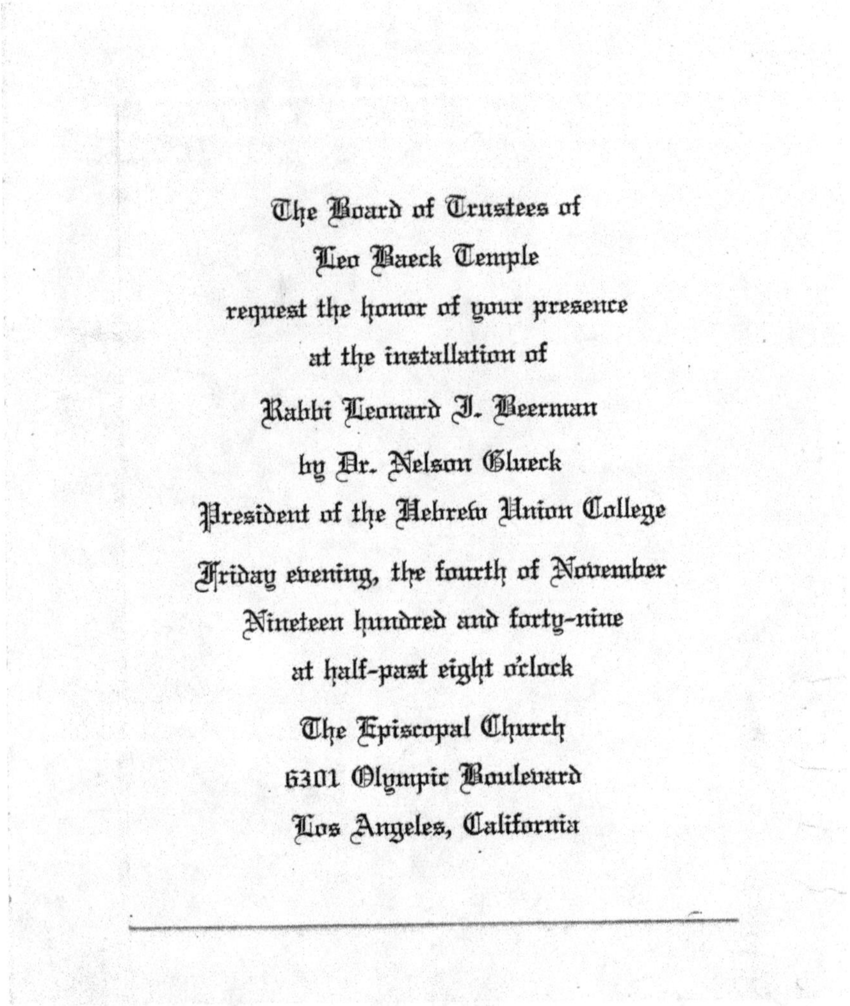

The Board of Trustees of

Leo Baeck Temple

request the honor of your presence

at the installation of

Rabbi Leonard J. Beerman

by Dr. Nelson Glueck

President of the Hebrew Union College

Friday evening, the fourth of November

Nineteen hundred and forty-nine

at half-past eight o'clock

The Episcopal Church

6301 Olympic Boulevard

Los Angeles, California

FIGURE 3. Invitation to installation at Leo Baeck Temple (1949).

Boulevard. It was a gamble for both sides: for his part, Beerman eschewed the easier path of working in an established congregation as an assistant rabbi in favor of a start-up experiment that could go bad; for the group, it was clear that Beerman was supremely talented, but also a person of deep and potentially divisive conviction. And indeed, over the course of his career at Leo Baeck Temple, he prompted some congregants to walk out in protest over his sermons.

And yet, Beerman built Leo Baeck into a major center of Reform Judaism in Los Angeles. This was one of the curious and impressive features of his personality.

FIGURE 4. Leonard Beerman and Dr. Nelson Glueck at installation (1949).

He was not merely a critic, but also a collaborator who became involved in the work of the local Jewish Federation and the local Board of Rabbis, of which he served as president from 1979 to 1981. He learned from an early stage in his professional career how to strike a balance between provoking and nurturing his flock to become informed activists.

It was not an easy task. The first years of his rabbinate at Leo Baeck coincided with the advent of the McCarthy era and the dangerous assault upon all suspected of

FIGURE 5. Leonard Beerman (*right*) with Dr. Leo Baeck (*center*) and Rabbi Phineas Smoller (*left*) (1952).

Communism. Although there were many otherwise liberal Jews who succumbed to the Red Scare, including more than a few in his congregation, Beerman frequently inveighed against McCarthy and the assault on democratic principles. Later in life, he recalled that on the Friday on which Julius and Ethel Rosenberg were executed, June 19, 1953, he inserted their names into the kaddish (mourner's prayer) at Friday night services. When confronted by a congregant as to why he would do such a thing, he recalled that he took the path of lesser resistance, for which he later felt regret, by saying that a member of the congregation was a relative of theirs.

Some months later, in October 1953, Beerman delivered a sermon at Leo Baeck intended as a tribute to one of his leading Reform rabbinical predecessors, Stephen S. Wise. It also provided him an opportunity to praise Wise and other noble figures such as Judah Magnes whom the McCarthyites, "pygmies of national shame" in his pungent language, had tried to brand and excoriate for their alleged Communist ties. In the course of his robust defense, Beerman articulated both a personal credo and a vision of Judaism that would last a lifetime. He declared to his congregants:

> As all men do, I hold opinions. My opinions may be right or they may be wrong. They may not always coincide with the majority. But because they are mine and because they are as honest as I can make them, I have the obligation to speak them. I have done so in the past and I hope to do so in the future.

This moral imperative to speak up derived from his broader sense of Jewish mission, rooted in the principle that "we have proclaimed our choice of virtue and goodness as our mission among the nations." He continued:

> Since the days of the prophets, we have borne the message that our God desires neither sacrifice nor burnt offering, but the doing of justice, the showing of mercy, and the pursuit of righteousness.[43]

At a mere five years' remove from HUC, Beerman gave eloquent voice to the guiding prophetic spirit that would remain the bedrock of his rabbinate. In the 1960s, he continued with his mix of building up and agitating for change. He worked together with the Leo Baeck board to raise funds and develop architectural plans for a new campus on the Sepulveda Pass. Leo Baeck moved from its San Vicente site to its current Bel-Air address in 1963, a convenient four months after the opening of the San Diego Freeway, to which it was adjacent. A year later, Beerman took an eight-month sabbatical, sojourning with Martha to Jerusalem via Europe, where they stopped at Theresienstadt, the Nazi concentration camp in which Rabbi Leo Baeck had been incarcerated. During this sabbatical period, Beerman studied Hebrew, met with scholars and politicians, and gave serious consideration to moving to Israel, but ultimately decided not to.

Upon his return to LA, he immersed himself in a variety of causes. As he charted his career throughout the tumultuous sixties and into the seventies, three major issues of social justice recur: the quest for civil rights, opposition to the Vietnam War, and a commitment to rid the world of nuclear arms. In the first case, Beerman joined many other Jewish leaders in taking an active role in the civil rights movement. One of the most notable examples was his German-born colleague Joachim Prinz, who delivered an impassioned address just before Martin Luther King Jr. at the March on Washington on August 28, 1963. There, Prinz declared that the Jewish experience of liberation from slavery created "a sense of complete identification and solidarity born of our own painful historic experience" with African Americans.[44]

In that spirit, Beerman channeled his lifelong resistance to any form of group discrimination not only into support for legislative reform such as the Civil Rights Act of 1964 and the Voting Rights Act of 1965, but into a far-reaching critique of the deep structure of racism in America. He was invited to speak in January 1967 at a symposium on Black Power, offering, as was his custom, a progressive Jewish perspective. He analyzed the psychological, as well as material, effects of racism before concluding with a stark candor that went beyond Prinz's powerful words:

> America is racist from top to bottom, and this racism is not a problem of human relations, but of a pattern of exploitation maintained actively or silently by society as a whole. And the rebuilding of society is not primarily a task of the blacks; it is the responsibility of the whites.[45]

FIGURE 6. Leonard Beerman (*top left*) getting an award from CLUE with others, including Rev. James Lawson (*bottom right*) (2004).

Critics, especially of his political stance on Israel-Palestine, would say that he never hesitated to blame himself or fellow Jews (or here, whites) for the ills of the world—and that such a tendency indicated a self-hating impulse. A more charitable reading would maintain that this impulse reflected Beerman's willingness to acknowledge his position of relative privilege and take stock of those upon whose shoulders it was built. It also reflected his deep powers of empathy, especially for the underdog or downtrodden, consistent with his Jewish mission as eternal dissident.

Beerman's work on civil rights brought him into contact with the Reverend James Lawson, the pioneering pastor, activist, and proponent of Gandhian non-violence who moved to Los Angeles in the summer of 1974. He and Beerman met shortly thereafter and recognized that the two of them, an African African minister and a Reform rabbi, were kindred spirits.[46] They met on a monthly basis as part of an interfaith group on human relations. They also joined hands in the struggle for justice on a dizzying array of causes: Vietnam, nuclear arms, El Salvador, Nicaragua, immigration, livable wages for janitors, the Persian Gulf War. Shortly after Rev. Lawson arrived, they agitated to expand opportunities for black students to gain admission to the UCLA Medical School. Beerman's position of support was at odds with some in the Jewish community who, from the 1970s onward, began to see remediation for past discrimination against African Americans (e.g., via school busing or affirmative action) as antithetical to their interests.[47]

Meanwhile, some years earlier, Beerman met another Protestant minister, who would become his closest friend. George Regas, a self-described country pastor from Knoxville, Tennessee, assumed the pulpit at All Saints Church in Pasadena in 1967. Under his leadership, All Saints became a national leader in progressive, church-based politics. The two men would remain extremely close to one another for the next nearly fifty years; following their example, All Saints and Leo Baeck Temple frequently joined together in support of social justice activism and to share occasions of celebration and protest. Indeed, so close was their personal and institutional relationship that Rev. Regas appointed Leonard Beerman Rabbi-in-Residence at All Saints in 1973, surely one of the few occasions in which a church had its own in-house Jewish cleric![48]

The Episcopalian and Jew first encountered one another in Los Angeles in 1967 at a site familiar to both, a peace rally, this time against the Vietnam War. Beerman was enchanted by the genteel accent and rhythmic cadence of Regas's speech at the rally, and they quickly found a common path in progressive politics. That said, the two men pursued distinct theological routes. George Regas was a man of deep faith in Christ and commitment to prayer. Beerman was an agnostic who believed in the great spiritual power of poetry and protest. But he recognized in Regas a similar prophetic passion. And like his friend, he was disinclined to remain silent when he saw injustice. To wit, he wrote a letter to President Lyndon Johnson on April 13, 1967 informing him that he and Martha wanted no part of the Vietnam conflict:

> That portion of our tax which helps to sustain the war in Vietnam has been paid involuntarily. We have no wish to support what we consider to be unjust. We should be happy to pay even a greater proportion of our income for works of healing and peace, but the acts of violence being perpetrated by our government violate our conscience.[49]

Beerman regularly used the pulpit to inveigh against the war or invite others to do so. One of the guest speakers whom he brought to speak at Leo Baeck on Yom Kippur was Daniel Ellsberg, the former defense analyst who gained renown in 1971 for releasing a huge trove of sensitive US government documents related to the war known as the Pentagon Papers. Even before that, on the eve of the Jewish New Year in 1970, Rabbi Beerman decried the "militarization of American life, the war in Indochina, the orgy of wasteful production and distribution," which, he lamented, "are all a part of a gigantic hoax that we are trying to perpetuate on our children."[50] There was in his words a daring, at times transgressive, quality that mesmerized and challenged his audience, always drawing from a deep well of moral outrage. He often accompanied and tempered his jeremiads with poetry, in this case, concluding his sermon with a poem from 1910 by the Briton Wilfred Owen, who anticipated the impending mass bloodshed of the Great War by making reference to the biblical binding of Isaac. In the closing lines of the poem, Owen's Abraham declines to substitute a ram for his son:

> But the old man would not do so, but slew his son,—
> And half the seed of Europe, one by one.

The mix of moral indignation and poetry made for a powerful listening experience, solidifying Beerman's reputation as a formidable and controversial preacher who not only talked the talk but also walked the walk of social activism. His resulting prominence, at both local and national levels, was not without its costs. In 1971, Beerman was proposed for the position of vice president of the CCAR by its nominating committee.[51] The group's annual meeting that year in St. Louis featured impassioned debate among the rabbis over whether they should be permitted to officiate at mixed marriages.[52] Beerman was already serving as executive secretary of the group, and had he ascended to the vice presidency, he would have been in line to become president of the CCAR, the youngest person ever to assume the post in its history. However, an unusual development jolted the CCAR assembly on its last day, as it went through the formal act of voting on the unanimous recommendation of the nominating committee. For the first time in its history, a rabbi-delegate proposed from the floor a different candidate than the nominating committee's choice, Leonard Beerman. He argued that his preferred candidate, Rabbi Robert Kahn of Houston, had the benefit of age and wisdom, which trumped in importance the precedent of supporting the nominating committee. A delegate stood up to criticize Beerman for his stance on Israel, which prompted another delegate to cast Rabbi Kahn as a tool of the establishment. After more debate, a secret ballot vote was held, and Robert Kahn was elected vice president by a vote of 77 to 55.

Beerman returned from the conference in a state of shock and disappointment, averring that "I had my rabbinic nose rubbed in the dirt; I was clobbered in public."[53] But this disappointment hardly detoured him from jumping back into the fray. He continued to agitate on behalf of important causes. For example, in January 1973, he joined with a number of prominent Christian leaders on "a journey for peace" in Europe. The aim was to put pressure on the Nixon administration in advance of the Paris peace talks, which brought a formal end to the Vietnam War.[54] In that same year, a new voice on the American Jewish scene surfaced: Breira (Hebrew for "Alternative"), which called on Israel to recognize the national aspirations of the Palestinian people and make territorial concessions as part of an overall plan in favor of two states. Beerman became an active participant in the West Coast branch of the new group, which brought together prominent Jewish intellectuals and religious leaders in Los Angeles, including his close associates from Leo Baeck, Richard Levy (the former assistant rabbi) and Sanford Ragins (onetime assistant rabbi and, at that time, Leo Baeck's associate rabbi), as well as Rabbi Laura Geller, Rabbi David Gordis, Rabbi Chaim Seidler-Feller, and Dr. Yoav Peled. Members of Breira promoted an alternative narrative and set of activities to the mainstream consensus of the American Jewish community.[55] They were no longer willing to provide unquestioned support to the Israeli government, which made them frequent targets of denunciation by Jewish and even non-Jewish leaders (such as former Vice President Spiro Agnew, who specifically attacked Breira). Their early advocacy of a two-state solution earned them the designation "anti-Israel," a label that would be frequently and unjustifiably attached to Beerman. Already from his first visit in 1948, he was deeply connected to the issue of Israel-Palestine, and would remain so throughout his life. His increasingly vocal criticism of Israeli treatment of Palestinians in his last decades made him a lightning rod in the Jewish community, with some on the far right casting him as a self-hating Jew. As he made abundantly clear in his public speaking, Beerman was undaunted by his critics and continued to speak out without inhibition until his last sermon at Leo Baeck in 2014.[56]

But Beerman's concern for the world was never confined to Jews, Israel or Palestinians. His close friendship with George Regas rested, in no small part, on their shared diagnosis of a world beset by grave challenges and their commitment to repair it. They appeared together frequently, including at a forum at All Saints in 1975 to discuss the place of religion in an age of crisis. In an illuminating exchange that reflected their differing theological stances, Regas lamented the fact that in 1960, 84 percent of Americans thought that religion was "an important factor in shaping American society," but in 1974, that figure had plummeted to 14 percent. Beerman, for his part, thought that this might be a positive development in that a lesser role for religion could bring about greater openness and honesty in addressing major social issues.[57] Here he was reflecting his skepticism—in the spirit of his intellectual hero, Spinoza—about the unequivocally beneficial effects of organized religion. This somewhat counterintuitive quality, especially for a rabbi—not merely his theological agnosticism, but his skepticism regarding religion—reflected his difficulty in accepting the claims of certainty, whether they were of a religious or a political nature. Indeed, this skepticism was the philosophical underpinning of his lifelong role as dissident.

Undeterred, and perhaps even spurred on, by their differences, Beerman and Regas pushed forward with their shared work. In October 1979, Leo Baeck Temple and All Saints Church collaborated to host a joint conference attended by one thousand participants to protest the nuclear arms race. In framing the conference, George Regas declared: "Reversing the arms race with all its madness is a fundamental religious obligation; we cannot continue to pray for peace and pay for war."[58] This conference became the launchpad for the Interfaith Center to Reverse the Arms Race, which, with Beerman, Regas, and their friend Harold Willens as its driving forces, was the leading voice of protest against nuclear weapons in Los Angeles for a ten-year period.[59] At the beginning of this period, Beerman assumed the presidency of the LA Board of Rabbis, which was convincing recognition of the fact that, in the midst of his wide-ranging advocacy beyond the Jewish community, rabbinic colleagues held him in high regard even if they did not agree with some of his views. Meanwhile, to his fellow Jews, he sought to cast the battle against nuclear proliferation as a distinctly Jewish imperative. He declared to an audience at a New York synagogue in 1982 that "because of our recent experience in history, we as a people know that the unthinkable can happen."[60]

For Beerman, 1982 was a fateful year, signaling an inescapable return of focus to Israel. It was in the summer of that year that Israel undertook what many have described as its first war without a national consensus. Responding to an assassination attempt on its ambassador in London on June 3 as well as to its unstable border with Lebanon, Israel invaded its northern neighbor on June 6. The declared goal was to establish a twenty-five-mile "cordon sanitaire" north of the Israeli border, but Israeli defense minister Ariel Sharon, with the tacit assent of Prime Minister Menachem Begin, saw an opportunity to push on to Beirut and root out the Palestine Liberation Organization, whose headquarters were in the city and whose forces were scattered throughout Lebanon, including in the south near Israel. In the course of the Israeli invasion of Beirut, Christian forces allied with Israel undertook, beginning on September 16, a massacre of Palestinian civilians (with hundreds and perhaps thousands killed) in the Sabra and Shatila refugee camps.

Ten days later, Beerman delivered a sermon on the eve of Yom Kippur. He recognized that the role of the rabbi, at times, was like the biblical Aaron, who "took the gold, fashioned the calf, and gave the people exactly what they wanted." The animating challenge of his life as a rabbi was markedly different; it was not to submit to the will of the people, but to "guide his congregation on the path that leads to the acknowledgment of moral failure, the awakening of conscience, the path that leads to the repentance that this day calls for."[61]

He identified himself as one of the small minority of American rabbis who "believed, from the first day, that the war in Lebanon, the war of Begin and Sharon, was doomed to be a moral and political failure." He went on to chronicle the tale

FIGURE 7. Leonard Beerman with Israeli diplomat Abba Eban (undated).

of carnage wrought by the invasion, refusing to soften the blow for his congregants on the holy day: "340 Israeli soldiers dead; 2,078 wounded. 17,000 Lebanese Palestinians killed; 30,000 wounded. About 50,000 people altogether, not to mention the 100,000? 200,000? 300,000? homeless." He immediately followed up with a question that he would pose in slightly altered form on subsequent occasions, and for which he would become famous, or infamous, depending on one's perspective:

"What kinds of Jews are these who kill and injure so many thousands and cause such massive destruction as a reasonable technique for carrying out policy?"[62]

Even before his first visit to Palestine in 1947, Beerman was unsure about the Zionist goal of establishing a Jewish state in which the Arab majority would become a subordinate minority. His time in the country, including in the Haganah, deepened his connection to the people and place, but also his concerns about the dangers of power. As a general matter, and, specifically, in his 1982 sermon, he resonated with the words of the iconoclastic Jewish statesman Nahum Goldmann, who declared that the test of our time was the proportional and moral use of Jewish might: "For two thousand years we were powerless as a people, and without power we learned how to be the best visionaries, the best dreamers, the best idealists. But without power we could not implement our visions. Now the powerless have become powerful." Goldmann, and Beerman in his wake, were channeling a concern rooted in the Bible. What happens when "the servant comes to rule," as Proverbs warned, and fails to remember the experience of subordination and oppression to which he was once subjected?[63]

Beerman had used the occasions of Israel's previous wars to question whether Jewish political and military power was being used appropriately. While many Jews were swept up in a euphoric reverie in 1967, mesmerized by the lightning display of Jewish military prowess, he remained sober-minded. He recalled after a visit to the country following the Six-Day War that "I feel today a deep love for Israel, even a deep yearning for Israel, and yet I do not share the intense national feelings." Indeed, he could not call himself a Zionist then.[64] And the subsequent decade and half after 1967 did not alter his decision.

Fittingly, Beerman's message in 1982, a week and a half after Sabra and Shatila, was one of *heshbon ha-nefesh*, of moral accounting. He called out to his congregants on the eve of Yom Kippur to engage in repentance by supporting efforts to bring an end to the violence and to address both "Israeli security and Palestinian homelessness." For the remainder of his life, he would remain focused on the entwined questions of Jewish power, Israel's well-being, and Palestinian self-determination. This was not a matter of abstract philosophical interest, but of intense personal responsibility, which impelled him to reject the pat formulations and conformist tendencies of the organized American Jewish community. In 1988, after the outbreak of the first Intifada in the West Bank, Beerman joined a small group of academics assembled as the Jewish Committee on the Middle East that called for "an American Jewish Intifada" against the US government, American Jewish leaders, and the pro-Israel lobby in Washington. The group also advocated for a cut in both economic and military aid to Israel, which placed it well outside of the Jewish organizational mainstream in the United States—and demonstrated Beerman's willingness to brook controversy and be counted among the radicals.[65]

Then again, in 2006, when the Israeli military entered Lebanon a second time (after finally exiting from the first Lebanon War only six years earlier), Beerman once more took to the pulpit on Yom Kippur to discuss the unfolding conflict. He acknowledged that he had stood in the same place at Leo Baeck, discussing a similar issue, twenty-four years earlier. The struggle that mattered most to him, he said,

> is one taking place within Israel and within us as American Jews. It is a struggle for the heart and soul, one that has been taking place in Israel from its very beginning, and certainly since 1967, when it conquered all of the territory between the Jordan and the sea. So it has become a struggle about the future of Israel as a moral state.[66]

Beerman evinced no trace of romanticism for Israel's military foe in Lebanon, the Shiite Islamic group Hezbollah. And yet, the task at hand, on this Yom Kippur, was to look inside oneself, to examine one's own self. The obstacle to doing so, his friend the renowned Protestant minister William Sloane Coffin once said, was "the sin of self-righteousness." Beerman quoted Coffin, who admonished: "If only we wouldn't go on using the conspicuous wrong-doing of our adversaries as a means of nourishing our own self-righteousness, instead of permitting the wrongs to deepen our awareness that we are all in need of some repentance, some humility."[67]

It was this aversion to self-righteousness that Leonard Beerman constantly sought to inculcate in himself and others. It was the essential prerequisite, in Levinasian terms, to turning to face the other.[68] It was this fundamental ethical principle that allowed Beerman to reach out, as a Jewish leader, to Palestinians well before such a step became somewhat normalized in the Oslo peace process. As early as the mid-1980s, he met with Palestinian leader Yasir Arafat in Jordan.[69] And at the local level, he routinely reached out to Muslim colleagues, who may well have had a different view of Israel-Palestine than most American Jews, including in some instances, him. In fact, Beerman called attention in his 2006 Yom Kippur sermon to his colleague of twenty years, Dr. Maher Hathout (1936–2015), a leading Muslim intellectual in Los Angeles and chairman of the Islamic Center of Southern California. Notwithstanding the fact that many Jews harbored unfounded suspicions of Dr. Hathout, particularly after 9/11, Beerman, along with George Regas, forged a powerful interfaith alliance with him. In doing so, he sought to model the importance not only of refusing to succumb to the political passions and prejudices of the day, but also of extending a hand in friendship to the beleaguered in times of crisis. The three men worked on many causes together, from homelessness to immigrants' rights to peace in the Middle East (as reflected in their work in founding the LA-based Abrahamic Faiths Peacemaking Initiative). Beerman, for his part, always felt a special affinity for Muslims committed to social justice, and was honored for his interfaith leadership by the local Muslim Public Affairs Council in 2013.

Leonard Beerman's natural allies in the Los Angeles area were progressives of faith, people such as Jim Lawson, George Regas, Ed Bacon, Maher Hathout, and Laila and Salam al-Marayati, who came from religious traditions other than Judaism. At a national level, he made common cause with prominent Christian

FIGURE 8. Leonard Beerman with Yasir Arafat (undated).

leaders such as Bill Coffin, Harvey Cox, and Jesse Jackson. In fact, Beerman traveled to the Middle East with Jackson and other clerics in 2002, meeting there with Yasir Arafat a second time. Beerman's ecumenism and spirit of engagement extended to those with whom he disagreed. He was never afraid of hearing or exposing others to divergent ideas. He engaged in an annual ritual with a Leo Baeck congregant, the well-known Los Angeles lawyer Bruce Ramer, who typically disagreed with the tenor and substance of Beerman's sermons, especially when they dealt with Israel. Ramer, as we see in "Exchange of Letters with Bruce Ramer," would write an admiring but highly critical letter to Beerman outlining his disagreement; Beerman would write back, affirming both his stance and his respect for Ramer. This openness to divergence extended to the pulpit at Leo Baeck, which welcomed a diverse range of opinions.

Beerman's unique ability to combine politics and the prophetic imperative made him a sought-after leader for many groups. He served as a board member of organizations dealing with civil rights, human rights, homelessness, Jewish social justice, the Israeli-Palestine conflict, and the death penalty.[70] On the occasion of his retirement from Leo Baeck in 1986, after thirty-seven years as the congregation's rabbi, he did not step back for a second from public engagements, but redoubled

FIGURE 9. Leonard Beerman with Rev. George Regas and Dr. Hassan Hathout, brother of Dr. Maher Hathout (undated).

his commitment to activism. By this point, his manifold contributions were widely recognized. Accolades came his way from obvious and less obvious quarters, including three honorary doctorates, the first from his alma mater Hebrew Union College (1974) and two from small liberal arts colleges on the East Coast, Lafayette College (2001) and Washington & Jefferson College (2007). The commendation from Washington & Jefferson read: "You have shown that religion and faith do not have to divide. You have reached across theological lines to work with Christians, Jews, and Muslims in solving our most pressing social problems. You are an example to us all."[71] Leonard Beerman was indeed seen by many as a model of passion, eloquence, and, above all, courage. And as he advanced in age, his sharp-edged critique lost none of its potency.

In going about his work, Beerman drew deep inspiration from the words of the great British philosopher Bertrand Russell:

> Three passions, simple but overwhelmingly strong, have governed my life: the longing for love, the search for knowledge, and unbearable pity for the suffering of mankind. These passions, like great winds, have blown me hither and thither, in a wayward course, over a deep ocean of anguish, reaching to the very verge of despair.[72]

FIGURE 10. Leonard Beerman with Rev. Jesse Jackson (undated).

This aphoristic statement fairly sums up Leonard Beerman's life philosophy. His thirst for knowledge and compassion for human suffering were fueled by his boundless love. This love was both universal and deeply personal. Beerman loved humanity in all its wild diversity. He loved his friends, of whom he had legions. He was particularly close to the members of his "Tuesday Knights" men's club, which met every week for forty years; the group included prominent LA figures such as George Regas, Stanley Sheinbaum, Harold Willens, Fred Nicholas, Dick Gunther, and Mike Farrell.[73] These men were not only friends, but partners on a range of social justice causes. He was especially close to Sheinbaum, the well-known progressive activist and philanthropist, with whom he joined forces for a half century of activism on issues ranging from racial and economic justice at home to Jewish outreach to the Palestinians abroad.

Leonard Beerman found love of a more intimate, familial nature, in his first wife, Martha, with whom he had three daughters, Judith, Eve, and Elizabeth.

2012 East-West Awards

Dr. Reza Aslan   Zainab Al-Suwaij

Councilman   Rabbi
Eric Garcetti   Leonard Beerman

About the East-West Awards
The East-West Awards recognize the sustained efforts of outstanding individuals working in the United States to bridge political and religious divides that may exist between Americans and the Middle East/North Africa, whether through media, peace activism or interfaith unity.

About the Levantine Cultural Center
Founded 11 years ago as a grassroots nonprofit organization that champions a greater understanding of the Middle East/North Africa and our communities in diaspora, we are raising capital to build a new, more self-sustaining cultural arts center for the Middle East and North Africa in Los Angeles. Southern California is home to the largest community of people from the Middle East and North Africa in the United States. It is high time that we had a multidisciplinary arts center that will serve as a focal point and hub for our many cultures.

FIGURE 11. Announcement of award to Leonard Beerman from Levantine Cultural Center (2012).

He had the great fortune to find love a second time, following Martha's death in 1986, when he met Dr. Joan Willens, whom he married in 1988. He often chose to express his love for others in poetry, not his own, but drawn from his vast repository of knowledge, samples of which he would often bring and declaim at a lunch or dinner. He was a dedicated and ceaseless student of poetry, who, even in his last days, drew succor from having it recited to him.

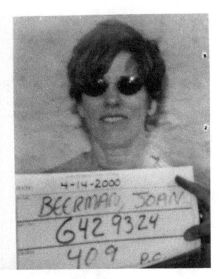

FIGURE 12. Leonard and Joan Beerman getting booked after arrest at "Justice for Janitors" protest in Los Angeles (2000).

In the final months of his life, as he recognized that his powers were waning, Beerman doubled down on his core commitments, to his family, to his close friends, and to the causes that burned so passionately within him. When he rose on the morning of October 4, 2014, to deliver his annual Yom Kippur address at Leo Baeck Temple, he had a clear sense that it might well be his last address there. For weeks before, he struggled over the phrasing of the sermon, even breaking from his decades-long practice by discussing it with a small handful of confidants before Yom Kippur. The subject was, tragically for him, a recurrent one: an Israeli military conflict, this time with Palestinians in the Gaza Strip in the summer of 2014. After opening with a refrain from W. H. Auden about being forgotten that he frequently quoted, he declared:

> And, here we are again, you and I. Another Yom Kippur. Another time to reflect on our lives and consider again who it is that we are and what we have become. Another Yom Kippur, another time to think seriously about whether there is anything in the way we are living that needs to be mended.
>
> Another Yom Kippur. Another war in Gaza. The outrages perpetrated by Hamas, the thousands of rockets deployed, thousands of Israelis rushing for shelters, living in fear, the many Hamas tunnels burrowing their way into the borders of Israel.
>
> Another Yom Kippur. Another 500 children of Gaza killed by the Israel Defense Forces, with callous disregard for their lives. I had thought about using the word "slaughtered" for what I was really feeling, and I lingered over it, wondering whether it was too provocative.[74]

Never one to shy away from provocation in the name of moral awakening, Beerman plunged in by excoriating the warring sides, and particularly the Israelis, for the unconscionable loss of children's lives. Drawing on a characteristically wide range of sources, including George Regas, the Japanese novelist Haruki Murakami, the Israelis Amos Oz and David Grossman, the American James Agee, and his own colleague at Leo Baeck, Rabbi Ken Chasen, Beerman returned again and again to the refrain: "Another Yom Kippur, another war in Gaza." He quoted the statement of principles that a small group of LA Jewish intellectuals had forged in opposition to the Gaza war, duly mindful of the fact that they were outliers in the organized Jewish community.[75]

There must have been a certain feeling of frustration and even despair as Leonard Beerman faced his congregants on the holiest day of the Jewish year, knowing that it might well be for the last time. After sixty-five years as a rabbi, he was addressing an all-too-common theme—violence and destruction through military force, made more poignant and painful by the fact that the greatest amount of destruction in this case came at the hands of the Jewish state. Neither flinching nor fading, Beerman once again assumed the role of eternal dissident, preaching a sermon that precious few of his colleagues the world over would dare to deliver.

His words were not nor could they be singularly negative. For all of his awareness of the human potential "to hurt and be hurt," he never lost faith in the potential for human good.[76] And so he concluded his Yom Kippur 2014 sermon, and parted from his congregation, with these words:

> Another Yom Kippur. It has come to us to remind us that our world, you and I, need desperately to be mended. Our world needs troubled people, Jews even, men and women who care, men and women who are not ashamed to be sensitive and tender. And our world needs men and women who have the courage to be afraid, afraid of all those forces which have removed our own humanity. And we need men and women who can resist all those, friends and enemies, who seek to prevent us from seeing the utter uniqueness and irreplaceability of our own and others' souls, and in the warmth we gain in joining souls together.[77]

When he finished speaking, the congregants of Leo Baeck Temple slowly rose, row by row, to applaud their founding rabbi for the first standing ovation in his career as a sermonizer. It was an acknowledgment not only of the courage of his sermon that day, but of the remarkable impact of his sixty-five year career. Beerman, for his part, would later say: "If this was in fact my last sermon, well, I spoke my truth."[78]

· · ·

As one can easily gather from the extraordinary quality of his sermons, Leonard Beerman was a great writer as well as a spellbinding speaker. But he authored no books and in fact harbored the view that he wasn't a very good writer. There was in Leonard Beerman something of the lifelong yeshiva student who felt incapable of writing anything because his mastery of the Talmud was not yet complete.

This was no instance of false modesty. It was a heartfelt sense of inadequacy. And it was jarring to encounter, given how powerful Leonard's words and deeds were. For several years, I had encouraged him to collect his sermons and publish them as a book; others had been making the same request years earlier. Leonard deferred, going so far as to question—to the utter incredulity of his listener— whether he had a body of work worthy of leaving behind. Only in the last few months of his life did he assent to working together or allowing someone else to collect his sermons.

This book is the result of that work of collection. Leonard left behind some eighty-three ring binders of sermons collected by year. The material was organized reasonably well, which is to say that the sermons were largely in correct chrono- logical order in the binders and sometimes included information about the date and occasion on which a particular sermon was delivered. Other writings, letters, and organizational documents could be found in files in filing cabinets, which, like the binders, were located in Leonard's beautifully appointed loft-study on the second floor of the home he shared with Joan and their dog, Charlie.

Selecting items for inclusion in this volume was no simple task. One is struck both by the remarkable range of Leonard's interests, reading, and sermonic themes as well as by a certain amount of repetition, unavoidable for a pulpit rabbi. This volume has attempted to offer a window into the thought and passions of Leonard Beerman by providing a sense of chronological development within distinct the- matic categories. It begins in part 1 with Leonard's first major address, his "Chapel Sermon" at HUC in October 1948, and concludes in part 5 with his final Leo Baeck sermon in October 2014. Part 2, following the "Chapel Sermon," offers an introduc- tion to some of Leonard's main intellectual inspirations. Part 3 deals with questions of faith and doubt, recurrent concerns for a lifelong rabbi who considered himself an agnostic. Part 4 includes selected sermons and writings on the social justice issues that were so central to Leonard's rabbinic vision. And part 5 traces the arc of Leonard's thinking and preaching about Israel-Palestine, the issue that vexed him like no other over the course of his life. A list of his own sayings that Leonard felt worthy of preservation and consulted and copied from time to time is included following part 5. The list is a fine summation of the 'ikarim, the guiding principles, of his lifework.[79]

Leonard Beerman was a great believer in the therapeutic power of dialogue. In evocation of that commitment, this volume seeks to preserve a dialogic quality. Each of the major pieces of writing is accompanied by a short commentary (usu- ally 250 words or so) written by a friend and colleague of Leonard's. Many of the commentators are well-known activists or thinkers in their own right, though for the purposes of this volume, all are profound admirers of Leonard Beerman.

I am very much that myself. I met Leonard Beerman shortly after moving to Los Angeles in 1988. We encountered each other as fellow travelers at gatherings of progressive Jews, acknowledging the other as a person of interest to get to know.

From early on, I recognized in him a rare mix of qualities: brilliant yet modest, a deep thinker and a tireless activist, and so very literate. Over the last decade of Leonard's life, we got to know each other much better; our wives became close, and our families were entwined. Leonard became, at once, an exemplar of goodness, a teacher, a comrade, and a dear friend. It was one of the great gifts of my life to have had the privilege to know and draw inspiration from him. This book is a modest gift in return to him—the eternal dissident, one of the great figures in the American rabbinate in the latter half of the twentieth century and a person who changed the lives of those he met.

PART I

First Sermon

Chapel Sermon

October 30, 1948

This first selection was Leonard Beerman's public debut as a preacher. Each graduating rabbinical student at the Hebrew Union College in Cincinnati, the seminary of the Reform movement, was required to deliver a "Chapel Sermon." Beerman began his talk by demonstrating his interpretive abilities, offering an explication of the biblical story of the garden of Eden. On his reading, which is informed by a deep interest in psychology, Adam is trapped between a sense of freedom gained by disobeying God's word and a tremulous fear of standing naked in the shadow of God's judgment. Beerman analogized this condition to modern man, who was caught between the gratification of material possessions and the sobering realization that he could not exert ultimate control over his physical surroundings Beerman introduced a theme that would reappear throughout his writings in the 1950s: that Communism and the Soviet Union were not the source of evil in American society. In the early years of the Cold War, as Americans, in general, and American Jews, in particular, were in the throes of anti-Communist fervor, the soon-to-be rabbi revealed more than a little courage by challenging this growing tendency in American society. In the next breath, he called out the lack of intellectual discernment of his fellow American Jews, as well as some of the theological presuppositions of neo-orthodox Protestant theologians. Rather than conclude his sermon on a pessimistic note, Beerman ended it by reminding his audience of the enduring moral vocation of the Jewish people, borne of Adam's original sin in the garden of Eden. "Israel," he declared, "is the eternal dissident, the great disobedient child of history."

There was once a time when children were supposed to be seen and not heard. Thanks to the contributions of modern psychology, however, our ideas have

FIGURE 13. Leonard Beerman (second from left in the second row) at Hebrew Union College graduation (1949).

suffered an alteration and while we do not go so far as to believe that a child who isn't permitted to smash everything he gets his hands on will grow up into an inhibited lunatic determined to smash everything in the world, we have learned that children must have free expression and that we should not expect a child to respond to his parents' commands like a well-geared machine. With all our erudition, disobedient children still create a problem and, in fact, are quite commonplace. But the classic story of disobedience is not found in any of the modern texts nor in any of the publications of a Spock or Gesell. It is rather to be found in the early chapters of the first book of our Bible.

Far removed as the writers of the story of the Garden of Eden may have been from a Sigmund Freud, they achieved nonetheless an amazing insight into human behavior. Man had been placed by God in this precious garden. He had been given a wife as a help-meet, and they lived together in harmony with each other, with nature, and with God. There was supreme peace for Adam, and, according to one version of the tale, no necessity to work. Man appeared to live an ideal kind of existence as a plaything of his Creator, who, in this very primitive picture of the Deity, came at the cool of the day to play with his children in their beautiful garden. But with all his privileges, man commits the supreme act of rebellion or disobedience.

He eats of the prohibited tree, the one thing denied him, and the overwhelming consequences of his act strike him with the suddenness of the wind that came up to cool him each day.

For Scripture states: "And the eyes of both of them were opened, and they knew that they were naked; and they sewed fig leaves together and made themselves girdles. And they heard the voice of the Lord God walking in the garden toward the cool of the day; and the man and his wife hid themselves from the presence of the Lord God amongst the trees of the garden."[1]

Adam understood what had happened. It was more than acting against God's command. He had actually severed the umbilical cord. Up to this moment in time he had been like a newborn child, who, though biologically separated from its mother through the process of birth, remained fundamentally one with her and dependent upon her for its existence for a long period of time. So Adam had been dependent upon his Creator and the Garden of Eden had given him security, a feeling of belonging, and a feeling of being rooted. Like a child he had been fondled by God and cared for. And yet he was not free any more than an infant is free. Yes, there had been no necessity to work. True, God had once flattered him by allowing him to give names to the beasts of the field, but actually there was not even a necessity to think. That tree in the middle of the garden, that tree which he had been forbidden to touch—that was the symbol of his lack of freedom. And with one touch of his hand he had committed—not sin, no, he had not sinned. God would punish him now. God would cast him out of Paradise—but he had not sinned. God would proclaim war between man and woman and man and nature. He, man, would work now, and sweat, which he had never felt, would roll from his face, and thorns and thistles would bar his way—but he had not committed sin— he had committed the first act of freedom. He had become human by becoming an individual, by tearing himself out of infancy, by breaking through his state of harmony with nature. Yes, he was free now but the freedom appeared as a curse, and although he was no longer a child, neither was he a man. He was free from the sweet bondage of paradise but he was not free to realize his individuality or even to govern himself. He had been released to another kind of bondage—the bondage of helplessness. He had lost the meaning of his existence and, being uprooted, could not find it in these new surroundings. He had taken only one bite of reason. Perhaps he had sinned after all. *Ochal mimenu* he ate *of* it. He should have devoured every bit of it—for now he could not cope with this new station in life— he was alone, naked, and ashamed; he was powerless and afraid.

The position of man today is somewhat akin to his ancient progenitor. Modern man, by virtue of eating of the tree of knowledge, has built a material world, which surpasses the most fantastic utopias. He has harnessed physical energies, which would enable the human race to secure the material conditions necessary for a dignified and productive existence—and now in the moment of his greatest greatness, at a time when he seems to have gained his freedom from all the tyrannies of nature—he, like Adam, feels his freedom to be a curse. In the process of advancement he discovers that he had produced a world so vast, and so complicated, as to be wholly unmanageable. He had not eaten enough of the tree of knowledge for he sees a world in chaos and cannot produce the light to interrupt it. His power over nature has reached his greatest proportions and yet he feels powerless in his individual life and in society. All of his accomplishments sit blushing in his face and a sense of futility overcomes him. He is powerless and afraid and would wish to hide himself if he could amongst the trees of his universe. And thus he poses our problem, our challenge, and our goal: to find a sense of purpose, a sense of human dignity in the changed and different world in which we live.

The reality of our own feelings of insecurity is a factor that many of us, for good reasons, prefer to ignore. But there are moments, perhaps when we lean upon the sills of evening, when the cool drafts of truth chill our minds. Quite fortuitously we become aware that we live in a strange, impersonal world. We need only recall the events of the period still fresh in our thoughts to discover that these events were strangely removed from their causes and wrapped in remote confusion. 365 days of the year we have consumed the news printed and broadcasted of drug affiliations, ax-murderers, police beatings, lynching, stonings, riots, revolutions, tortures, and sodomies—and they are as meaningless to us as the great disorders of nature, the hurricanes and earthquakes over which we have no control. Even the thoughts we have are as impersonal and mechanical as the world we live in. The art we enjoy is a mechanical vocabulary of electrically animated images without touch or smell, or electrically vibrated words only recently endowed with faces and bodies. We have watched wars precipitated without the motion or the knowledge or the consent of the millions of people who will be caught up in them, and today we see the nations heading for a battle arena from which not even the strongest may emerge alive. There seems no place to make a stand, nothing for us as individuals to do about it. A nerveless sense of fatality occupies our subconscious and we feel that this is our destiny and destiny is being imposed upon us. It is true we are richer and stronger as a nation than we have ever been. Our national income is far above the figure economists once dismissed as fantastic, and our military strength is supported, for the moment at least, by a monopoly on the most formidable weapons ever devised by man. But strangely enough, these facts do not bring us much comfort for they are coupled in America with a peculiar demand for conformity and national discipline. We are supposed to believe, at the risk of disloyalty, that if there were no Russia and if there were no Communists, all the problems with which we and the world are troubled would vanish—and this thought is supposed to possess the validity of a geometric axiom. A tiny nibble at the tree of knowledge reminds us that before Marx, Lenin, Stalin, and the Soviet Union there were wars and depression and insecurity and fear, and we might even be led to conclude, at the risk of being un-American, that the problems we face are much more deeply rooted than we are supposed to believe and that the fault is not only in the Russians but also in ourselves. The antagonism against Communism here and against Capitalism abroad is not really an affirmation of a faith in either one of them; it is nothing more than the expression of our mutual fears and frustrations, which stand like double-tongued adders barring the path to peace.

"Israel is the heart of all the nations," in the words of Yehudah Halevi, the heart that suffers whenever any part of the body is ill. For the Jew, the words "suffering," "fear," "insecurity," are weak symbols of the terrible frustration which have become a part of us and our brethren. It seemed for a time that our collective agony was more than we could bear. The enormity of the crime against our people is but an element of this feeling and if the Christians really believe that the body of Jesus is wounded each time a man wounds his fellow, his body must indeed look something like the picture of Dorian Gray. These are not new things with us—there is a crimson cord of blood that knits our history and makes it whole. Whatever comfort we derive from the victory of our people in Palestine and the fulfillment of their dreams, we cannot ignore the simple fact that a dream doesn't come true of itself— it takes work and much effort and still more pain. If the Jews of the new Israel have shown us that it is not nobler in the mind to suffer the slings and arrows of outrageous fortune but rather by opposing them to end them, their success only gives us pause to meditate on our own weaknesses. We are great as a defensive team. We can amass millions to help others fight battles and even live in decency, and we should not detract from this virtue of ours. But what positive virtue can we show world Jewry? Have we, even we, progressive Jews, produced an American Judaism dynamic and sustaining? Have we yet been able to attain that goal for which we strive—the harmonious blending of the best of the old with the best of the new? A casual visit to the Jewish State will only confirm us in our doubts as to the glories of Judaism and Jewish life in America. In our efforts to assume the coloration of the society in which we live, haven't we produced a generation that has lost that sense of intellectual discrimination that made the Jew a civilized being whether in Imperial Rome, the Church, or the Mosque dominated society? We remember that Philo the Jew lived in Alexandria but he was not a *ger*, a stranger in the land. He borrowed generously from the culture of his time and simultaneously maintained his identity with Jewish tradition, and the same may be said for Maimonides and Mendelssohn at a later date. Our own failings are quite obvious and the huge controversies that rage in contemporary Jewish thought give subtle confirmation to them.

There is a good reason to be apprehensive, but we need not drown ourselves in the current of our times. It never was, and neither is it today, wise or desirable to borrow everything from the environment, and so we need not succumb to our feelings of weakness. It is true, the time is short and the work may be great, but we are not free to desist from it. The whole burden of the community, we are taught, rests upon us. Wherever there be wrongs, we must intervene, we must raise our voice in protest. There are apostles of degradation among us; among them the neo-orthodox Protestant thinkers and their secular comrades, the men of the "New Look" that is not new. They come to us with the face of innocence and call us brothers and friends. See, they say, man is naked and ashamed and powerless—and we agree. See, they say, quoting the words of a New England Primer, in Adam's fall we sinned all. Man is evil; the world is set against him in eternal conflict; man must bow in submission. And then we understand that they are our enemies, as old as Time, that they are not our brothers and our friends, and we protest. True, we may be powerless, but our lives are not so cheap, nor our existence so meaningless, that we will tutor ourselves to this submission; there are none of us so base or cruel that we shall not protest. Adam's was the first act of freedom, and we are here, every one of us, to make that freedom real, to restore man to dignity. We will eat more and more and more at the tree of knowledge of ourselves, our society and our universe until this is fact.

"Israel is the heart of all the nations." Israel is the conscience, the raw, exposed nerve. All emotion passes through it. Israel is the eternal wanderer and sufferer, like man himself, fighting against thistles and thorns, shadows and abstractions. Israel is the eternal dissident, the great disobedient child of history. Israel is the servant of God, made like all men in His image, and nothing can deter him in his effort. The peoples will yet understand and will yet come to say:

This day we shall not be afraid, but we must be silent, for the house of Israel is at prayer. And its prayer is not for itself alone, but for all the children of men. We shall be silent, so that God may hear it. AMEN

COMMENTARY BY RABBI SAMUEL KARFF

As an admirer of Leonard Beerman, I relished his "Chapel Sermon." He reveals himself as a first-rate intelligence, a passionate moralist, and an elegant stylist.

Characteristically, he interprets Adam's disobedience not as a sin but as a claim to his humanity. However, with freedom come overwhelming challenges and the threat of meaninglessness. Even as a young man, Beerman embraces his lifelong view that the people Israel's role—and a major source of life's meaning—is to combat injustice and affirm the dignity of all.

Even as he celebrates Israel's recent rebirth and the rejection of Jewish powerlessness in a post-Holocaust world, Beerman anticipates challenges ahead and would be among the Jewish state's loving critics when he felt the absence of a good-faith pursuit of a two-state solution.

His sermon, delivered in the early years of the Cold War, attributes its causes not only to the Soviets but to our own nation. Some of his judgments in this sermon could stand revision in later years, including his dismissiveness toward the "realism" of the neo-orthodox theologians. I think of Reinhold Niebuhr, one of the more illustrious among them, whose realism was consistent with a robust social conscience. Rabbi Beerman might also have revised his blanket depreciation of the attainments of the American Jewish community vis-à-vis Judaism in the State of Israel.

Above all, even this early sermon reveals signs that he was destined to be one of America's great rabbis.

PART II

Inspirations

Sigmund Freud

May 11, 1956

This address on Sigmund Freud, which appeared in draft form in Beerman's binder of sermons and was likely delivered at Friday evening services at Leo Baeck Temple in Los Angeles, reveals the young rabbi's capacious interest in modern intellectual history, as he chronicles major innovations in the West since Copernicus. History was one of the holy trio of disciplines, along with philosophy and literature, that Beerman most favored and believed to be the key to an informed and enlightened life. In this sermon, he focuses his attention on Freud, arguing that the Viennese master followed Darwin and Marx in advancing our understanding of the physical, social, and psychological development of humankind. In the first instance, Beerman was struck by Freud's profound impact in teaching humanity "to probe for the truth hidden in the unconscious." He was also drawn to Freud's recognition of childhood as a self-standing stage in human development—and indeed, as the source of traits and conflicts that continue to shape men and women later in life. Beerman's interest in Freud, which belonged to a broader interest in psychology among Jews in midcentury, also had a deeply personal dimension.[1] He saw Freud as a man of great courage, who was willing to defy established norms and expectations. Moreover, he traced Freud's courage "to an aspect of his Jewish inheritance," thereby anticipating later scholarship that challenged an earlier claim that Freud had a diluted connection or wholly negative attitude to his Jewish identity.[2]

4,000 years is a relatively brief span of time in the history of man, and yet if we attempt to comprehend the revolutionary changes which have occurred in that period, our minds are almost overwhelmed. It is not only that the face of the earth has changed, but also that the heart and mind of the earth have changed as well.

A little more than four hundred years ago historians refer to as the medieval world, a world that was closed and certain and secure. The earth, and man its finest creation, was the center and substance of the universe. Everything was ruled by the laws of God and there seemed nothing new to be discovered, no blank spaces to fill in. But around the year 1500 this secure and closed and unified world was broken asunder. Man was suddenly uprooted from his central place. Everything about him and even he himself suddenly became a problem, something to be questioned, something to be discovered. The first tremor to strike medieval serenity was the discovery by Copernicus that the sun is the center of our planetary system. This discovery has led to a knowledge of the skies in which the sun is only one among a million suns, in a galaxy that is but one of a million galaxies. Copernicus began a train of insights, which culminated more than four hundred years later in the theories of Einstein and others as to the nature of space, energy and matter. Man learned that his senses deceived him about the relative position of the sun and the earth, and ours deceive us about the physical environment, which surrounds and supports us as well.

All the new discoveries, as we reflect on them now, seemed to follow the same basic pattern—the desire to arrive at the forces which lay behind observable phenomena. First the discoveries were about the world of nature, but gradually they encompassed MAN himself. Slowly men came to understand that immediate sensory experience, common sense, tradition—these were not guarantees of the truth—that to understand reality, outside and within man—we must know the nature and direction of forces which are not directly visible. Darwin hurt man's vanity by showing how he had developed under a law of natural selection from distant animal backgrounds. Marx showed that man's social systems and part of his thought and culture are determined by social and economic forces which operate behind his back. Then Freud completed the process by showing that the conscious thoughts man has about himself and about others are only a fragment of what goes on with him.

Freud taught us to be objective and to be humble; to be skeptical toward our conscious thoughts; to probe for the truth hidden in the unconscious, rather than to be satisfied with what we consciously believe to be true. And thus we see that Freud's discoveries are part and parcel of the progress made in the past four hundred or more years of seeing the world, nature, our fellowmen and ourselves as they are, not necessarily as we want them to be.

His ideas present such a continuing novelty and freshness that he seems to belong to us and to our time more intimately than to the quaint and curious world of the nineteenth century in which he was born and against which he rebelled. His ideas have established themselves so very firmly in our culture. It is not only that the modern practice of psychiatry is chiefly based upon them. His ideas have had a decisive influence upon our theories of education and child-rearing. They are of importance to anthropology, sociology, literary criticism. Even religion has taken account of them.

There is hardly an area of human experience which has not been touched and transformed by ideas which emanated from his work. There is hardly a Broadway play or even lowly soap opera which does not make use of some Freudian idea which the audience can be counted on to comprehend. Freudian terms are now part of our thought. We all, at one time or another, look for motivations, compensations, repressions, inner conflicts, anxieties, neuroses, and when someone has a headache, even before we give the aspirin, we ask what's troubling you.

And yet behind all of these words and concepts, used and misused, was a man, a human being, a profound and remarkable human being. And if we go back to his works we are struck by the original power and force of his ideas, whether we accept, modify, or reject them. He was a man of courage, for the ideas that we accept so glibly today met with powerful resistance when first offered to the world. For the publication of his sexual theories, he was branded as filthy and immoral and had to suffer ten years of organized professional isolation. The courage and stamina to withstand this kind of rebuff Freud attributed to an aspect of his Jewish inheritance. The passion of his ancestors, he called it, who defended their Temple.

He was a Jew, sensitive and aware of his Jewishness. He was not an observant, religious Jew in the commonplace use of that term anti-Semitism. Freud and Jung (Abraham)[3]

And yet in the sense that we use the term religious, Freud was a profoundly religious man. The whole purpose of his work was to enable man to see the truth about himself, to enable man to love, to become a free and responsible human being, to help men to find out who they were, to find themselves when they had become lost.

He was the first to conceive of human happiness and unhappiness as being matters of scientific research, whereas previous[ly] these had been left to the philosophers and theologians. In a sense he gave a scientific framework to the highest and noblest elements of religious aspiration. And yet because he experienced only authoritarian and dogmatic religion in his own lifetime, he saw religion at its worst, and understood [it] entirely as a force which prevented the full realization of man's capacities.

It would be impossible for me, a layman in this field, to attempt a discourse on Freud's scientific contributions, or even to deal properly with elements of his thought I personally view critically. But one aspect of his discovery I should like to mention, because I feel it is unassailable and because I feel it means so much for the advancement of civilization. That has to do with the importance of childhood as constituting the formative years of an individual's development. The idea, the insight, first advanced by Freud, that whenever in the formative years of a person's life, an intense emotional conflict is left unresolved, it does not disappear, but remains as a festering element that later takes the form of a severe emotional disturbance, or of a pervasive uneasiness in the handling of life.

What this insight comes to, is that an individual does not grow beyond a problem that has deep significance for him, until he understands it, accommodates his life to it, or resolves it entirely. By focusing our attention on the needs of the child as well as the dangers that beset the path of emotional maturation, Freud brought about a seriousness about how life should develop . . . Impt. insight.

World of technologies miracles, battle over nature won

Inner life, disharmonies, war,[4]

COMMENTARY BY PROFESSOR PETER LOEWENBERG

In what appears to have been a sermon on the centenary of Freud's birth, it is clear that Rabbi Leonard Beerman, whom I knew as "Lenny," "gets" Freud and his role in our culture. Freud was a famous twentieth-century atheist who knew and rejected "authoritarian and dogmatic religion." Lenny adopts Freud's explanation of blows to Man's narcissism by Copernicus, Darwin, and himself. His insight, which shook civilization, was that our ego is not the master of our minds—Man does not control his inner world (*Standard Edition*, 16:284–85; 17:139–42). Lenny was elegantly appreciative of Freud's discovery of the importance of childhood and the imprint of the formative years of life on later development.

In his daily life and actions Lenny lived his principles of social justice and racial equality. I encountered Lenny in my first year at UCLA in 1965–1966. A call came to the History Department from Martin Luther King Jr.'s Southern Christian Leadership Conference (SCLC) asking for tutors to prepare the African American children of Grenada, a city in north-central Mississippi, who were far behind educationally, for school integration. We put together an interracial team of ten tutors to teach history, government, English, math, science, art, and dance. I called on Lenny, whom I knew had marched in Selma, for financial aid in meeting our expenses for travel and teaching resources. He secured the substantial sum of $1,000 from his congregant, Dr. Leonard Comess, a psychoanalyst. When he informed me, Lenny modestly said: "This doesn't always happen!"

3

Bertrand Russell's Autobiography

Three Passions in Life

Rabbi Beerman retained this fragment from the philosopher Bertram Russell's auto-biography on a typed piece of paper on his desk. He kept it close to him because it embodied three of his animating passions in life: love, knowledge, and concern for the suffering of others. Beerman was a deeply devoted family man and friend whose patience and loyalty were legendary. He also was a ceaselessly curious intellectual who loved to engage in rigorous debate. And perhaps his most profound sense of service in life was to alleviate the suffering of others. In this sense, the excerpt from Russell represented a life credo parallel to—and even in lieu of—the well-known refrain from the Ethics of the Fathers (Pirke Avot 1:2) that "the world rests upon three things, Torah, avodah *(worship), and* gemilut hasadim *(deeds of loving-kindess)." Indeed, Beerman was as informed by contemporary literary and philosophical sources as he was by classical Jewish texts and precepts.*

Three passions, simple but overwhelmingly strong, have governed my life: the longing for love, the search for knowledge, and unbearable pity for the suffering of mankind. These passions, like great winds, have blown me hither and thither, in a wayward course, over a deep ocean of anguish, reaching to the very verge of despair.

I have sought love, first, because it brings ecstasy—ecstasy so great that I would often have sacrificed all the rest of life for a few hours of this joy. I have sought it, next, because it relieves loneliness—that terrible loneliness in which one shivering consciousness looks over the rim of the world into the cold unfathomable lifeless abyss. I have sought it, finally, because in the union of love I have seen, in a mystic miniature, the prefiguring vision of the heaven that saints and poets have imagined. This is what I sought, and though it might seem too good for human life, this is what—at last—I have found.

With equal passion I have sought knowledge. I have wished to understand the hearts of men. I have wished to know why the stars shine. And I have tried to apprehend the Pythagorean power by which number holds sway above the flux. A little of this, but not much, I have achieved.

Love and knowledge, so far as they were possible, led upward toward the heavens. But always pity brought me back to the earth. Echoes of cries of pain reverberate in my heart. Children in famine, victims tortured by oppressors, helpless old people a hated burden to their sons, and the whole world of loneliness, poverty, and pain make a mockery of what human life should be. I long to alleviate the evil, but I cannot, and I too suffer.

This has been my life. I have found it worth living, and would gladly live it again if the chance were offered me.

COMMENTARY BY DR. JOAN BEERMAN

These were the first words Leonard read to me in the earliest days of our loving each other. He was introducing himself with words that he cherished—that touched his soul. Not until later did I speculate as to why someone else's words, rather than his own, seemed to him better able to reveal his deepest self. For they do, of course. He could have written those words himself, and anyone who knew him would have agreed that these were his values, his yearnings, and his joy.

Language had such great power for Leonard, and he labored hard over every elegant and stirring word he chose. But I suspect that he never fully understood his extraordinary gift, and so preferred to present himself to me—as a loving man, as a questing man, as a Jew—through the words of Bertrand Russell.

When, many months later, I first heard Leonard's own words in a Yom Kippur sermon, I was awed. I had never heard someone speak with such passion, turning the thoughts of his deep intellect and profound moral sense into poetry. What I learned that day, and over the years that we were together, was that Leonard did not need Bertrand Russell's writings—did not need anyone else's writings—to reveal himself. He was seamlessly that person—in his public life and in his private life: one who passionately loved, one who tried to make sense of the world, and yet finally one who could never escape suffering for the pain and injustice that he witnessed.

4

———

Looking at Kafka

January 8, 1982

Alongside his interest in history and philosophy, Beerman was a great lover of litera-
ture and a voracious reader. The demands of the rabbinate—administering, officiat-
ing, counseling, and preaching—did not prevent him from pursuing his manifold
intellectual passions. In this sermon, Beerman shared with his audience his interest
in the tragic figure of Franz Kafka, the great author from Prague, through the sharp
lens of Philip Roth. Roth wrote a counterfactual essay on Kafka in 1973 in which the
writer did not die of tuberculosis in 1924, but survived the disease—and escaped the
scourge of Nazism by making his way to the United States in 1938. Roth conjures up
an unlikely image of Kafka as a Hebrew teacher in Newark, the site of much of the
action in Roth's earlier writings. In this rendering, Kafka is no less tragic than the
actual figure who died in Prague. The fictional Kafka is alone in the world, a misfit
for his new vocation, and involved in a liaison that may have gone awry because
of his behavior. Perhaps most significantly, Kafka left behind none of his writings.
Beerman, for his part, raised the unsettling proposition that had the real Kafka not
died prematurely, perhaps the author would have followed through on his desire to
burn his literary corpus in toto. Beerman frequently returned to Kafka throughout
his career. Whereas other rabbis drew inspiration from biblical or rabbinic charac-
ters, Beerman found something consoling in Kafka, and, to a great extent, Roth, who
understand well and represent the deep tensions that define the modern Jewish and
human conditions.

In his earliest stories, written when he was in his twenties, Philip Roth attempted
to transform into fiction something of the small world in which he had spent
the earliest years of his life in Newark, N.J. Roth drew from the experience of his

highly self-conscious Jewish neighborhood, a neighborhood squeezed like some embattled little nation in among ethnic rivals and antagonists, groups of people proud, ambitious, xenophobic, and baffled about being fused into a melting pot. It was here—this little Israel in Newark, so much like a volatile Middle East—to which Roth turned for the material of his beginning writing career. Out of such experience came the highly acclaimed *Goodbye Columbus,* and, ten years later, when he returned to the same neighborhood of desire and confusion, his controversial *Portnoy's Complaint.*

In some of these stories, the earlier ones, Roth departed from the customary stories of Jewish life on which he and many readers like ourselves had been raised. Instead of telling of a Jew who is persecuted by a Gentile because he is a Jew—a subject treated in such books as a *Gentleman's Agreement* by Laura Hobson, in *Focus* by Arthur Miller and in some of the works of Bellow and Malamud—in [his] stories [Roth] told about a Jew persecuted for being a Jew by another Jew. In so doing he turned the subject of anti-Semitism somewhat on its head, so that in writing of the harassment of a Jew by a Jew rather than Jew by Gentile he was pressing Jewish readers to alter an entire system of responses to so-called "Jewish fiction." Small wonder that Roth was accused of anti-Semitism and self-hatred. It was almost too much to expect that only fourteen years after Buchenwald and Auschwitz, with a great many people still frozen with horror by the Nazi slaughter of European Jewry simply too much to ask people to consider, with ironic detachment or comic amusement, the internal politics of Jewish life. It was indeed, in most instances, asking for the impossible.

Such was the demand placed upon readers by Roth's story "Defender of the Faith" when it appeared in 1959, a story told by Nathan Marx, an army sergeant just rotated back to Missouri from combat duty in Germany. There, in Missouri, he is made first sergeant in a training company and immediately is latched on to by a young recruit who tries to use his attachment to the sergeant to receive kindness and favors. The young recruit, Sheldon Grossbart, comes to demand not mere considerations but privileges to which the sergeant doesn't think he is entitled.

Portnoy's Complaint was a great hit and a great scandal. Going wild in public— that's what Portnoy did—was the last thing in the world that a Jew was expected to do by himself, by his family, by his fellow Jews and by the larger community of non-Jews. Jews were simply not expected to make a spectacle of themselves. Portnoy was seen by many Jewish critics as the crudest and most venerable stereotype of anti-Semitic love, displaying, said another, a fanaticism in the hatred of things Jewish.

Four years after *Portnoy,* in the year 1973, Roth published in *American Review,* volume 17, an essay on Franz Kafka, written with much sympathy and appreciation, written as he looked at a photograph of Kafka at the age of forty in 1924, the year Kafka died. Kafka's face in the photo is sharp and skeletal, pronounced cheekbones, a familiar Jewish flare in the bridge of his nose, and on his face a gaze of startled composure, full of fear, full of control. "Skulls, chiseled like this one," Roth wrote, "were shoveled by the thousands from the ovens; had he [Kafka] lived, his would have been among them, along with the skulls of his three younger sisters." Kafka died too soon for the holocaust. Had he lived, perhaps he would have escaped with his good friend Max Brod who found refuge in Palestine. Had he lived, perhaps his books would never have been published, for he had ordered his friend Brod to dispose of them at his death—Kafka may have destroyed them himself. But had he lived, had he come to America in 1938, he would have been a frail bookish fifty-five-year-old bachelor, formerly a lawyer for a government insurance firm in Prague, retired on a pension in Berlin—the author of a few obscure stories, stories no one in America had ever heard of and only a handful in Europe had ever read.

A year before he died, in 1923, Kafka finally finds the resolve to leave Prague and his father's home for good. Never before had he succeeded in living apart, independent of his mother, his sisters, his father, nor had he been a writer other than in the few hours when he was not working in the legal department of the Workers Accident Insurance Office in Prague; he was a dutiful, scrupulous employee, though he found the working tedious, enervating. But having been pensioned from his job because of illness, he meets a young Jewish girl of nineteen, Dora Dymant, at a seaside resort in Germany. Dora has left her Orthodox Polish Jewish family. She and Kafka—she is half his age—fall in love.

With Dora to love him, Kafka at forty is at last delivered from self-doubt and self-loathing. Kafka consents to the publication of a volume of four of his stories. With Dora's help he resumes the study of Hebrew (his Hebrew teacher a woman, now living in Israel, wrote recently a memoir about Kafka as her student). He studies Hebrew; despite his illness he travels to the Berlin Academy of Jewish Studies to attend lectures on the Talmud. He is transformed into a writer, à Jew, a lover, something of a father.

Was it Dora Dymant, or was it the approach of death that made all this possible? Whatever, the prospect of Dora, of a wife, a home, and children, was no longer the terrifying, bewildering prospect it would once have been. Yes, there is ease and happiness with a woman, with this young adoring companion. Kafka, who had tried unsuccessfully to marry twice before, is determined to marry Dora; he writes to her Orthodox father for his daughter's hand. The request of a dying man, a man dying of tuberculosis is denied. Dora's father consults with the man he admired most, the Gerer Rebbe. The Rebbe put the letter to one side and said nothing more than the single syllable, "No." A healthy young girl should not be given in matrimony to a sickly man who spit up blood, a man twice her age, yet.

Still he has Dora with him. In those final months of his life he studies, he writes. That last winter in Berlin he wrote a story called "The Burrow," the story of an animal with a keen sense of peril, whose life is organized around the principle of defense, whose deepest longings are for security and serenity. The ending of this story is unfortunately lost. The burrower has constructed an elaborate and intricate system of underground chambers and corridors designed to afford some peace of mind, until he begins to hear some subterranean noises—could it be a great Beast itself burrowing in [his] direction?

On June 3, 1924, a month before his forty-first birthday, Kafka died of tuberculosis of the lung and the larynx.

Then suddenly Roth's essay on Kafka returns to Newark N.J. in 1942. Roth is nine. He has a Hebrew teacher whose name is Dr. Kafka. Dr. Kafka is fifty-nine. Kafka would have been fifty-nine in 1942, had he lived. To the little boys who attended Dr. Kafka's class from four to five every afternoon he is known as Dr. Kishka. Two boys vented their resentment on him, their resentment of having to learn Hebrew at the very hour when they could have been screaming their heads off on the ball field.

How the boys in the Hebrew class liked to imitate him with his precise professorial finicky manner, his German accent, his cough, his depressed look. Doctor Franz, Doctor Franz, Dr. Franz Kishka. Who was always giving assignments, like the one to make up an alphabet of their own, out of straight lines and curved lines and dots. "That's all an alphabet is," Dr. Kafka had explained to them. That's all Hebrew is; that's all English is, straight lines and curved lines and dots.

Dr. Kafka lived in a room, not an apartment, a room. The Roth family invites him to dinner one Shabbos, and with him Aunt Rhoda. For years Roth's parents had been introducing his mother's baby sister to Jewish bachelors and widowers of north Jersey, but at forty Aunt Rhoda had still not been successfully matched.

Before long Rhoda and Dr. Kafka are seeing each other regularly. Dr. Kafka encourages her to renew her interest in acting by reading her the famous Chekhov play, read it to her from the opening line to the final curtain, all the parts, and actually left her in tears.

Rhoda becomes a changed person. Kafka sits in the back of the theatre watching in his hat and coat, all of her rehearsals.

But one weekend they go off together to Atlantic City. Something untoward occurs, never clear, but Rhoda comes back crying, inconsolably; she refuses to see Dr. Kafka again. The nine-year-old Philip Roth is confused by it all; begs to know the reason. His older brother, the Boy Scout, with a leer and a sneer on his face explains it all with one word, "Sex."

Years later, a junior at Harvard, Roth receives an envelope from home containing Dr. Kafka's obituary, clipped from *The Jewish News*. "Dr. Franz Kafka, a Hebrew teacher at the Talmud Torah of the Schley St. Synagogue from 1939 to 1948, died on June 3 at Deborah Heart and Lung Center in Browns Mills, N.J. Dr. Kafka had been a patient there since 1950. He was seventy years old. Dr. Kafka was born in Prague, Czechoslovakia . . . and was a refugee from the Nazis. He leaves no survivors."

He also leaves no books; no *Trial*, no *Castle*, no *Diaries*. The dead man's papers are claimed by no one, and they disappear.

No, this Kafka, who leaves nothing, could not ever become "The Kafka"—why, that would be stranger even than a man turning into an insect. No one would believe it.

Kafka remains the poet of the ungraspable and the unresolved, to use Roth's words, the poet whose belief in the immovable barrier separating the wish from its realization is at the heart of his excruciating visions of defeat. Yes, Kafka's writing refutes every easy, touching, humanish daydream of salvation and justice and fulfillment with densely imagined counter dreams that mock all solutions and escapes.

COMMENTARY BY PROFESSOR SAUL FRIEDLANDER

Leonard Beerman loved Franz Kafka's writing. He quoted him; he even published a short essay about him. Let me add a few lines about this common interest and briefly reflect on Kafka's attempts to define the meaning of Jewishness for him. For the generation of Hermann Kafka, Franz's father, keeping a Jewish identity devoid of any particular content sufficed. For Franz's generation—more precisely for the young Prague intellectuals of that cohort—such meaninglessness seemed unacceptable and often led to a search for very diverse alternatives: a return to religion (mainly reformed Judaism), as in the case of Kafka's friends the philosopher Hugo Bergmann and the writer Max Brod (in an extreme form in the case of another Kafka friend, Georg Langer, who became an ultra-Orthodox follower of the Hasidic Belzer Rebbe); fervent adherence to the new established Zionist movement (Bergmann, Brod, and the philosopher Felix Weltsch), socialist political activism, diverse esoteric quests, or, as happened with one of Franz's uncles, Rudolph, conversion to Catholicism.

5
___

The Legacy of MLK

January 15, 1982

Beerman's address on Dr. Martin Luther King Jr. was delivered a year before the United States Congress voted to create a day in honor of MLK (and four years before the commemorative day was formally inaugurated in 1986). Beerman felt a deep bond of identification with Dr. King for various reasons. They were both clergymen who labored hard to meet the demands of their congregants. They were both preachers who understood the power of rhetoric to inspire. They were both tireless advocates who sought to realize the prophetic imperative to social justice. And they were both drawn to the principle of nonviolence, which King and Beerman learned about from Rev. James Lawson, who introduced nonviolence to the civil rights movement after studying it in India in the 1950s.

Beerman's own commitment to racial and social equality began as an adolescent in Michigan and was fortified during his time as one of the "social justice boys" at Hebrew Union College. As a young rabbi, he gained a reputation for speaking out on behalf of racial equality. Throughout the 1960s, he was one of the most prominent rabbinic voices on the West Coast in support of the civil rights movement, not only calling on his congregants to protest injustice, but joining forces with black colleagues on the streets. In this regard, Beerman's activism paralleled that of the well-known East Coast rabbis Abraham Joshua Heschel, who marched with his good friend Martin Luther King in Selma and elsewhere, and Joachim Prinz, who spoke at the March on Washington in 1963 just before Dr. King. King would remain a source of inspiration to Beerman throughout his life, and he devoted a sermon to the civil rights leader's life every year.

Martin Luther King, Jr. would have been fifty-three years old today—still a young man. It seems difficult to believe that almost fourteen years have gone by since that day in April 1968, when he was assassinated in Memphis, Tennessee. So much has happened to us, to this country, and to the world since 1968. So many dreams have been broken and trampled upon and so many have been at least partially realized. One thing for certain: here in the state of California little black children have a holiday in honor of someone who looks like them. If for no other reason than this the celebration of King's birthday is a notable occasion. For fifty-three years after his birth, fourteen years after his death, twenty-eight years after Brown vs. Board of Education (the Supreme Court decision ending segregation in the public schools of America) far too many little black kids grow up without knowing what to do with themselves. Now in the beginning of what even President Reagan has called a Recession more than twenty-five percent of the young blacks are unemployed. Their government is not extending them much concern; it is indeed a dark time for these darker People, and there is no Martin King to inspire them.

There is simply no way for them to experience the strength and the courage that came from being part of the mass movement that he led, no way for them to be among those who once sang in the meetings, sang in the streets, and sang in the jails, nor to be among the 200,000 who stood before the Lincoln Memorial and heard King say, "I have a dream . . ."

King's life is inextricably intertwined with the great moments in the civil rights movement: Montgomery, Birmingham, the March on Washington, Selma. A dedicated leader, an eloquent advocate of nonviolence, he was awarded the Nobel Peace Prize in 1964. And he was a pastor, there in the Ebenezer Baptist Church in Atlanta. And with academic degrees, first from Morehouse College in Atlanta, then from a theological seminary, Crozer, in Chester, Pa., he, after some studying at the U. of Pennsylvania, and at Harvard, eventually received a Ph.D. from Boston University. And in addition to that, some 200 honorary degrees by colleges and universities here and throughout the world. A magical quality about him, none of us who lived through that era will ever forget him. All the efforts to denigrate his character, some fomented by the FBI, cannot cancel half a line of his greatness as a Black leader and as a powerful moral symbol.

King was not born to greatness, he had to be nudged into it. Montgomery, Alabama, provided the ground from which King vaulted into national prominence. The Montgomery of September 1954 may have seemed like an unlikely place for American history to rise to high drama. 80,000 population, 50,000 Negroes, and to most of the 30,000 Whites the Negro populace were essentially instruments to be dominated, and endured. The Black population had been subjected over the years to many indignities, like hundreds of cities throughout the South. Particularly annoying to Black leaders was the Montgomery City Lines, a northern owned bus company. The blacks provided seventy percent of the company's revenue. As in practically all Southern cities bus passengers in Montgomery seated themselves on a segregated, first come first served basis with Negroes seating themselves from the rear forward and whites taking seats from the front backward. In Montgomery, however, unlike some of the more enlightened Southern cities, the first four seats were reserved exclusively for the white patrons. What was especially galling to many Negroes was that the driver was empowered to order Negroes sitting in the foremost section to yield their seats to white customers. This was a flagrant reminder of white supremacy, as if the Blacks could forget. Moreover, it was not uncommon for drivers to require Blacks to pay their fares at the front door, get off, and re-board the bus through the rear door. Some of the Black leaders like E. D. Nixon of the NAACP had tried to arouse the populace against these abuses, but they were unsuccessful. The Negroes were just slumbering, passively, placidly.

So it was that in September 1954, M. L. King Jr. came to become pastor of the Dexter Avenue Baptist Church in downtown Montgomery. A new man and a new movement unknown to one another were about to coalesce. Mr. King unpacked his books, and he and his wife Coretta moved into a big white frame parsonage. From the beginning, King stressed social action, organized a social action committee in his congregation, which urged every member to become a registered voter, and a member of the NAACP. King was no radical; he leaned toward the gradualist approach as fostered by the Alabama Council on Human Relations, an interracial group. In these early months of his Montgomery ministry, King was working on his doctoral thesis, writing several hours every morning and every night. He also worked on his sermons so that within nine months of his coming to Montgomery he had earned a reputation as a fine preacher. Into this relatively quiet, conventional, ministerial life philosophic reading in the morning, visits to the sick, marrying, baptizing, burying—came a day in December, a warm day for December. At the Court Square where in the days of the Confederacy Negro slaves had been auctioned, a Montgomery City Lines bus passed by and pulled to a stop. There were twenty-four Blacks on the bus, Rosa Parks among them, she was sitting behind the white section which was filled with twelve white passengers. Six whites boarded the bus and the driver left his seat and asked the Negroes in the foremost section to get up and give their seats to the white patrons. It was an ancient custom and aroused no comment. Three of the blacks rose immediately, but Rosa Parks remained seated. The driver asked her again to yield the seat, and Rosa Parks, a rather sweet-tempered woman, again refused. The driver then summoned police officers who arrested Rosa Parks for violating the city's segregation ordinance.

Why did she do it? Why did she refuse to move? "I don't really know," she would say later. "There was no plan at all. I was just tired from shopping. My feet hurt." That was where the Negro rebellion had its beginning, that intersection of the pain of feet and a deeper pain, the pain of the heart, and perhaps something else, the receptivity of the moment, as Wm. James called it. E. D. Nixon, the Pullman porter, took the lead in the first phase of the controversy; it was he who provided bail for Rosa Parks and he who suggested that SOMETHING must be done. First, after a lot of telephoning to the local clergy it was decided to stage a one-day bus boycott. The mimeograph machines pumped out their instructions: "Don't ride the bus to work, to town, to school, or any place Monday, December 5 . . . come to a mass meeting." The Montg. Improvement Assoc. was formed and M. L. King, Jr. was elected president. Why King? For two reasons: He was new in the community and was not identified with any faction in a divided leadership. King was named because almost no one wanted to be identified publicly as the leader.

That day the Blacks walked, rode mules, drove wagons; the boycott was almost totally effective. It was decided to extend the boycott until the company met certain minimum demands and what were the demands? Courtesy, a first come first served system within the bounds of the segregated system and employment of black bus drivers on predominantly Negro lines—all these demands were rejected by the city officials and bus officials.

Addressing the mass meeting, King reviewed the long train of abuses, "our method," he said, "will be that of persuasion, not coercion." He went on to speak of the transforming power of love: "Love must be our regulating ideal. Love your enemies; bless them that curse you, pray for them that despitefully use you. If we fail to do this, our protest will end up as a meaningless drama on the stage of history, and its memory will be shrouded with the ugly garments of shame. In spite of the mistreatment that we have confronted we must not become bitter, and end up hating our white brothers. Let no man pull you so low as to make you hate him." Then building to a crescendo he said: "If you will protest courageously and yet with dignity and Christian love, when the history books are written in future generations the historians will have to pause and say, 'There lived a great people—a black people—who injected new meaning and dignity into the veins of civilization.' This is our challenge, and our overwhelming responsibility."

That's where it all began; that's where it all began. In August of 1963, eight years later, he would stand before 250,000 people who had participated in the great March on Washington—eight years of marches through the streets of the hardcore white supremacist cities, the years of police dogs, fire hoses, tear gas, repeated imprisonment, the years of student demonstrations.

The experience in Montgomery brought clarity to the thinking of M. L. King. It was out of that experience, as he would later attest, that he became more and more convinced of the power of nonviolence. Nonviolence became more than a method to which he gave intellectual assent; it became a commitment to a way of life. He had come to see that the Christian doctrine of love, operating through the Gandhian method of nonviolence was one of the most potent weapons available to an oppressed people in their struggle for freedom. Nonviolence would not accomplish miracles overnight, he knew. When the underprivileged demand freedom, the privileged react with bitterness and resistance, even when the demands are couched in nonviolent terms. But the nonviolent approach does something to the hearts and souls of those committed to it. It gives them self-respect. It calls up resources of strength and courage that they did not know they had. And finally, it so stirs the conscience of the opponent that reconciliation becomes a reality.

How did he hold on to those convictions? He knew few quiet days. Imprisoned twelve times, his home bombed twice, a day seldom passing when he and his family did not receive threats of death. Victim of a near fatal stabbing; battered by the storms of persecution. Tempted always to retreat to a more quiet, serene life, but every time something came to strengthen his determination to go on.

King was not satisfied to limit the practice of nonviolence to the struggle for racial justice in the U.S.A. He believed it was necessary to experiment with nonviolence in all areas of human conflict and particularly on an international scale. He had seen too much of hate, he said, to want to hate, himself: hate on the faces of too many sheriffs, too many white citizen's councilors, too many Klansmen. We must be able to stand up before our most bitter opponents and say: "We shall match your capacity to inflict suffering by our capacity to endure suffering. Do to us what you will and we will still love you."

It was on a hot August afternoon in 1963 in Washington that King spoke of his dream, a dream that every colored person in the world would be treated with respect, that justice would roll down like waters, as the prophet Amos once said, and righteousness like a mighty stream. That one day, war would come to an end, that swords would be beaten into plowshares and nations will study war no more. Many of his dreams were turned into nightmares; he became a victim of deferred dreams of blasted hopes, but in spite of that he still preserved his faith that the struggle for justice must go on, that injustice anywhere is a threat to justice everywhere.

My friend Jim Lawson, pastor of the Holman Methodist Church, said the other day at a prayer breakfast in honor of MLK, this day is not a gift to the Blacks. If the Blacks needed a holiday they would take it, just as Jews, Muslims and others take a holiday. But, he said, this day is important to the nation; the nation as a whole needs a MLK holiday as a human rights day. I have a dream that one day every valley shall be exalted, every hill and mountain shall be made low, the rough places will be made plains and the crooked places will be made straight, and the glory of the Lord shall be revealed, and all flesh shall see it together.

When we let freedom ring, when we let it ring from every village and every hamlet, from every state and every city, we will be able to speed up that day when all of God's children black and white, Jews and Gentiles, Protestant and Catholics will be able to join hands and sing in the words of that old Negro spiritual, "Free at last, Free at last, Thank God almighty, we are free at last."

COMMENTARY BY THE REVEREND JAMES M. LAWSON JR.

Rabbi Leonard Beerman and I shared a prophetic and biblical enthusiasm for the Montgomery, Alabama, bus boycott.[1] It was the first sociopolitical "equality and liberty" struggle in Western history that named itself a nonviolent campaign (nonviolence, a term coined by Mohandas Gandhi of India around 1906, to describe his initial experiments to resist the oppression facing Indian immigrants in then

Boer-British South Africa. He defined nonviolence as "love in action").[2] That campaign catapulted the very young African American Martin Luther King Jr. onto the world stage as the advocate and voice against "injustice anywhere" and for the wellness and beauty of all peoples.

Yet even in 1982, Rabbi Beerman was one of the very, very few people of influence in a congregational vocation or the academy or public life who could create and deliver such a carefully researched and empathetic message: how the people began; they selected a voice and with others executed the structures and logistics, and they effected the monumental rejection of Jim Crow law and custom and all the indignities associated with both. Dr. King articulated and lived out the simple yet awesome notion that ordinary people energized by the force of human/sacred love can defeat wrong and its tyranny. Beerman grasps Montgomery and King's meaning. The boycott was a terrific tactic for dismantling the injustices of the systemic injustice of the bus company and the city. The scholar Gene Sharp has since documented more than two hundred such tactics. But the rabbi of Los Angeles also insists that King practiced nonviolence as a way and theology and spirituality of life, to be applied and lived or acted upon.

Leonard Beeman was an intellect out of the spirit of God of the Jewish Bible, a mystic, thinker, and practitioner. Just a few days ago I met the immigration activists who walked from the Mexico-Arizona border to the detention and deportation center in downtown Los Angeles. A few of us represented a steady line from Montgomery to our continuing struggle for all residents of our country. After our rally and assembly there before that fortress-like structure of our national insanity, we walked around the edifice. I saw again the places where Rabbi Beerman and hundreds of us carried on a soul force campaign against injustice in El Salvador and Los Angeles. In those weeks and months of 1980 I do not know how many times Leonard was detained by federal marshals. But Leonard and Martin were signs of the "word made flesh."

6

First Encounter with George (Regas)

April 13, 2005

This brief fragment offers a recollection of one of Leonard Beerman's closest colleagues and friends, Rev. George Regas, who in 1967 became the rector of All Saints Church in Pasadena. Born to a Greek immigrant father and American mother who died when he was five, Regas served a number of Episcopalian congregations before assuming the leadership of All Saints in Pasadena, bringing to that congregation his unique blend of Southern-style oratory, theological sophistication, and a tireless commitment to progressive political activism. It was at a rally for peace to protest the Vietnam War held in MacArthur Park in downtown Los Angeles that the two first met. Out of that encounter, they developed a tight partnership on a wide array of causes, especially on behalf of nuclear disarmament under the rubric of the Interfaith Center to Reverse the Arms Race. They also remained very close friends until the end of Beerman's life.

It was in early January 1971 that we met.[1] I can't remember what kind of a day it was. But I do know that getting there was easy. Freeways were not crowded in those days. In less than a half hour after leaving the Leo Baeck Temple parking lot in Bel-Air, I was at Exposition Park.

Along the way I had begun to rehearse what I would say at the demonstration. The war was raging in Vietnam. President Johnson, swelling, outwardly at least, with optimism, assured us that more troops would quickly bring the enemy to heel. I was convinced that he was wrong and that the war was wrong. "A President has but one heart to give to his country," Senator William Fulbright had said. A President whose heart is at war in Vietnam, he concluded, does not have another to give to his promise of the Great Society, which would require a different war— against poverty, inequality, and racism.

At the park everything seemed to be ready for the event. There was a platform with a lectern and a microphone (and it worked). A crowd had begun to assemble. The program began when two young men, U.S. Navy officers dressed in their uniforms, solemnly wheeled a casket, draped in black, across the grass and placed it directly before us. No act of protest against the war could be so blatantly and unambiguously clear. I squirmed. It was too much for me. Yet I marveled at the power of their courage. Or was it simply madness?

An Episcopal priest was introduced and arose to speak. He was dressed in gray with a white priestly collar. His voice was deep and his words were strong and direct and they were lubricated with an accent right out of some part, some not too deep part, of the South. But what held me captive was not primarily what he was saying, but rather the rhythm of his speech, the way in which his words were linked to the movement of his body achieving a harmony that gave his talk increased power and significance.

7

Why the Prophets Are Important

May 20, 1983

In this Friday evening sermon, Beerman reveals the source of his admiration for the Hebrew prophets, on whom he frequently drew for inspiration throughout his career. Beerman juxtaposed the ethos and mission of the prophets to the ethos and mission of the Five Books of Moses. On his view, the Bible was devoted to the law and to instructing Jews how to observe it. The prophetic writings, by contrast, were dedicated to encouraging responsible moral behavior.

In a sense, Beerman was giving voice to a rather common tenet of Reform Judaism in its classical nineteenth-century form. That is, the essence of Judaism lay not in the laws and ritual prescriptions of the Talmud or Bible, but rather in the ethical dictates and demands of the Israelite prophets. At the same time, his reliance on the prophets drove his deep commitment to social justice, as it did for other notable Jewish thinkers over the course of the twentieth century whom he admired, including Martin Buber, Stephen S. Wise, Judah L. Magnes, and Abraham Joshua Heschel.

In traditional Judaism the five books that make up the Torah, Genesis, Exodus, Leviticus, Numbers and Deuteronomy, are considered to be especially holy. We take out the scroll of the Torah, which we keep in a very central place in the sanctuary. We read their sections in order, Shabbat after Shabbat, we read from Genesis to the very final verse of Deuteronomy year after year. But not so with the books of the prophets. We don't read through all of the prophetic books from beginning to end. For a long time prior to the past few months we have not been reading them at all at Leo Baeck Temple. But even in the traditional synagogues, custom is that only a small part, selected from the prophets, called the Haftarah is read from week to week. They are considered to be holy, but certainly not on the same level as Torah.

Liberal Jews have always considered the prophets much more important than that for our understanding of what Judaism was and continues to be. We have always found in the prophets' teaching something of our sense of Judaism as a changing, dynamic, growing religion. For liberal Jews the Torah surely provides the basis of Judaism and we certainly have not thought of Torah and the prophets as having completely different teaching, yet there are differences and the differences are as important as the similarities. For the most part the Torah instructs in matters of law, telling us what to do, regularly and for all time. While the prophets speak to a specific situation, frequently criticizing the way the community is behaving, reminding the people of what they should be doing for God.

Much of the law of the Torah deals with the sanctuary, the temple and the ritual that is going on there. The book of Exodus gives elaborate instructions for the construction of the ancient tabernacle. Leviticus is mostly about sacrifices of varying kinds. Large sections of Numbers and Deuteronomy are occupied with the priests and the Levites and their duties. These laws tell us how the ancient Israelites in Bible times believed they should serve God but they do not tell us very much directly about how we should live as Jews. There has been no temple in Jerusalem for about 2,000 years so the laws we read about in the Torah have not been carried out for all those many centuries.

When the prophets lived and taught, the temple was surely the center of the Jewish cult, but curiously enough the prophets do not spend much time talking about that. There are a couple of exceptions (Haggai and part of Ezekiel); instead the prophets were disturbed that the Jews of their time were not serving God in the correct way, were not building a better society. Amos, the first of the literary prophets, complains that they abuse the poor. Isaiah says that their rulers are not doing justice. Habbakuk criticizes the strong, the powerful for taking advantage of the weak. This all sounds very much like what is going on in our time, sounds very much as if it were talking at the things Jews ought to care about and try to help change. 2,500 years after the prophets Jews still believe that God cares how we treat one another and that how we treat one another, individually and collectively, should be an important integral part of our religious duty as Jews.

To God and the ways of God: "[It] hath been told thee what is good, and what God requires of you: to do justly, love mercy, walk humbly with thy god."

The Torah dealt largely with the Jews' duty to other Jews: the prophets' teaching is concerned with Jews and all people and thus has a contemporary relevance. The prophets address our condition of being Jews and yet at the same time being citizens of the larger society. The rituals of Judaism, the synagogue, holidays, and for those who choose the observance of dietary laws, all these are important but these observances have to go hand in hand with the practice of justice, the plurality of peace. The Torah focuses on details; the prophets focus on our goals. The Torah tells us what to do in all of its specifics; the prophets are more concerned about the purpose behind our religious duties. Isaiah and Amos tell us that it is useless to be observant if at the same time we deal unjustly with our neighbor. Jonah stressed God's willingness to forgive non-Jews, the great city of Nineveh.

But still more, the Torah teaches us what is always to be done, what is to go on continuously. While it is true that traditional Judaism has ways to help the law change with the passage of time, the main concern of Torah is with what one must observe always. In much that the Torah has taught us we are quite willing to have it continue—observing Shabbat, doing justice, but in some cases the modern age calls for radical change. The prophets suggest to us what the Jewish attitude should be.

The prophets were not wholly admirable men, they were not tolerant, they were in fact quite intolerant. They and we are quite different from one another. We might call it fanaticism, inspiration, a spirit of dedication, idealism, whatever it was it made the prophets recklessly uncompromising. They were not prudent men, at all. They asked, questioned, challenged, reexamined what passed for dogma, they were men of the critical spirit, they irritated, annoyed, disturbed, frightened their contemporaries by making them think. They were blasphemous, heretical, they questioned the sanctity of sacred place, where the covenant between Israel and God was eternal so it must be with us as liberal Jews, reform was once inspired by the spirit of inquiry.

COMMENTARY BY PROFESSOR JACK MILES

Like England and America, two great nations separated by a common language, Judaism and Christianity are separated by our common scripture. Christians honor Torah as scripture but not as Jews do. Jews honor the prophets as scripture but not as Christians do.

What this means is that a Christian is on shaky ground quoting the prophets to a Jew, but then a Jew doing the same thing to another Jew is on only slightly less shaky ground. T. S. Eliot was once asked if he believed that most editors were failed writers. "Yes," he replied, "I suppose so, but so are most writers." It's a bit like that between Christians and Jews quoting the prophets to each other about, to come to the sticking point, *Israel*. Most Christians fail in the attempt, and so do most Jews.

Beerman lives in my memory as a Jew who succeeded. Whatever his faults, he was touched with the fire of prophecy. I turned to him once for counsel about a critical essay I was trying to write about Israel. I never finished it. If I had, I would never *ever* have dared to go as far as he did in his astonishing last sermon, on Yom Kippur, when he said, "Another Yom Kippur, another 500 children of Gaza killed by the Israel Defense Forces." Beerman in that moment was like Nathan turning on the guilty King David with the electrifying cry *Attah ha'ish!* An ever kindly but sometimes terrifying voice. Remember him thus.

PART III

Faith, Doubt, and Duty

8

Handwritten Reflections on Doubt

Undated

This handwritten fragment offers insight into Beerman's philosophical and theological disposition. While noting the perils of doubt, he also believed in its liberating quality, its catalyzing role in forcing us to probe and question in order to achieve enhanced understanding. Doubt figured in an even more profound way in Beerman's world. He devoted the entirety of his career to the rabbinate, but he was an unmistakable agnostic for whom faith in God was a doubt-ridden proposition. While he did not loudly broadcast this view, he did see doubt, in this sense, as an essential precondition to integrity and probity.

To be a man is to ask why in every dimension in life. To question, to doubt is a sure sign of our freedom and our reason. It is the image of God within us—our doubt is an essential element in our capacity to be creative.

But doubt is an ambiguous blessing. It is a sign of freedom. It can also be a sign of our defensivism, our inability to give ourselves over to a decision, a commitment—our distrust of genuine passion. Through the luxury of our unexamined doubts we can evade the responsibility of taking a stand, all the while pretending to be open-minded. Doubt is our greatness but it can express our irresponsibility.

Some people are very free in their cultural doubt of traditional religious beliefs but quite unwilling to subject their capacity for objectivity to the same critical scrutiny.

The courage to doubt is the courage to risk one's own confidence in one's doubt.

Without doubt then can be no spiritual freedom, no integrity. With doubt there is the threat of utter meaninglessness. Whether doubt brings hope or hopelessness depends upon the individual's courage to accept doubt and its discipline.

COMMENTARY BY RABBI RACHEL TIMONER

It was doubt that enabled Abraham to create Judaism. It was doubt that brought Abraham to believe.

In this handwritten exploration of the "ambiguous blessing" of doubt, Leonard beautifully associates doubt with creativity and spiritual freedom. Doubt is how we know that we are alive. Doubt is one expression of the image of God that is within us. Doubt is the active use not only of reason, but also of intuition and conscience, in the relentless pursuit of truth. Doubt is necessary for our species' intellectual, moral, and spiritual development. It is the foundation of the scientific method and the prerequisite for all social movements and all true religion. Only when we interrogate facts, doctrines, and tenets of faith do we become free to consider new possibilities. This is how meaning is made. Religion without doubt is stifling. Religion with doubt can be thrilling. But doubt has become its own religion, preventing us from committing to justice, to God, and to life. What I love most about Leonard's brief reflection is his warning that when doubt becomes an abdication of passion, a shelter from conviction, a failure of responsibility, it becomes cowardice. In the name of open-mindedness, we fail to take a stand. In the name of all truths, we fail to speak any truth.

Leonard was like Abraham. He first allowed doubt to free him from the constraints of inherited beliefs and conventional wisdom. But then he stood for his convictions with passion. He had both the courage to doubt and the courage to believe.

9

Can We Excommunicate God?

April 30, 1965

The title of this sermon reflected Rabbi Beerman's willingness to ask provocative questions of his congregation—and of his own theology. He used the opportunity to express his support for a Reform rabbinic colleague, Sherwin Wine, who left his congregation in Windsor, Ontario, in 1963 to form a new temple in Birmingham, Michigan. At the heart of this initiative was the decision to excise the word "God" from the community's liturgy, a move that brought cascades of condemnation down on Rabbi Wine, including from prominent Reform colleagues. Wine would go on to establish the Society for Humanistic Judaism in 1969 as a reflection of his belief in the power of secular Jewish culture.

Beerman, for his part, affirmed that the guiding spirit of Reform Judaism was intellectual autonomy and the resistance to fixed dogma. He further noted that leading Protestant thinkers such as Paul Tillich, Dietrich Bonhoeffer, and the Englishman John Robinson bore a similar spirit by fearlessly inquiring into questions of God's existence. Intellectual integrity demanded this spirit of inquiry, Beerman suggested. So too, he argued, did the impulse to overturn oppressive racial and sexual hierarchies, as he made clear at the end of his sermon.

This evening has to do with controversy. If nothing else has tutored me, coming from Leo Baeck Temple would have served the purpose. I have become no stranger to controversy, and I have learned along with you the obvious truth: when argument enters a household, reason is usually the very first to be offended and to take its leave. This seems to be a universal principle. Now all of this happened while we were away from you. While we were walking the streets of Jerusalem, where life is tranquil and the only excitement is an occasional burst of gunfire a few hundred yards away at the Jordan border, there were some fearful noises being made in the American Jewish community over a controversial rabbi in Birmingham, Michigan. Two of our senior colleagues, Rabbi Solomon Freehof and Rabbi Jacob Weinstein, both of them distinguished leaders and teachers and deeply revered and respected by all of us, delivered themselves of denunciations of young Sherwin Wine and his congregation. Rabbi Freehof, in somewhat melodramatic fashion, is quoted as having said: "We must protect the Jewish community against this deception which will draw in innocent children and unsuspecting elders." Rabbi Weinstein contended that "there are certain inarticulate premises in every tradition . . . God is the major premise of Judaism. A synagogue without God is only a meeting place, and a rabbi who rejects the term because it is not precisely defined, becomes an ethical culture leader." "Excommunication," Rabbi Weinstein continued, "is not in the spirit of Reform Judaism. Rabbi Wine should not be defrocked, but he ought to have enough *derech eretz* (good manners) to consider himself unsuited for the rabbinate. In excommunicating the term God from the Prayer Book, he has separated himself—casting off the mantle woven by God-intoxicated men who for three thousand years have flung into the very teeth of adversity the battle cry 'I will live and declare the greatness of my God.'" Other rabbis and laymen joined in the denunciations in language much more intemperate, sanctimonious and self-righteous than that of Rabbis Freehof and Weinstein. And still others rose to the defense. Rabbi Daniel Friedman, Rabbi Weinstein's assistant, was one of them. There were several here in the Los Angeles area. In New Haven, my friend Rabbi [Robert] Goldburg had this to say: "Rabbi Wine and his temple may be among the few in America to take God seriously—so seriously that they deny his existence. Yet such a move means thought and study, conviction and courage. Our people all should be reminded that such qualities in this era of conformity and self-righteousness are hard to come by—rare and precious in any age."

And then from this pulpit Rabbi Ragins, dealing with this theme some weeks ago, strongly and cogently defended and explained the right of the rabbi and his congregation to hold fast to their position and to be included legitimately and honorably within the framework of Reform Judaism. We may not be ready to follow the path they have chosen, but the freedom of Reform Judaism, its abhorrence of fixed creed and dogma, leaves the conscience of the individual as the ultimate seat of authority about the content of his Judaism. This is a right not vested in any established tradition. We left such orthodoxies behind us when we chose to accept the daring and treacherous path of individual freedom. We have staked our honor on the mind of man in quest for a truth not fully realized rather than on the mind closed, fixed, determined, an obedient servant of that which has been received. We are not always pleased with the consequences of adhering to our affirmation of freedom but we are surely not ready to trade that displeasure for the horror of that tyranny over the mind, that obscurantism which would result from the abdication of the freedom for which we have so desperately struggled.

I suppose members and rabbis of congregations thought the land would have been less perturbed if Rabbi Wine had kept his opinions within the borrowed walls of his own temple. Surely Rabbi Wine is not the first rabbi to have doubts about the Jewish idea of God, nor am I. But his doubts have led him to an attempted kind of semantic purity. He and his congregation agreed that they must be openly honest about the confusion which the word God evoked in them, and rather than be confused, they preferred to eliminate the word altogether.

Their confusion about God and their elimination of God language should have come as no surprise to any educated and informed religionist. Our shock, our surprise, is, in a sense, a mark of the poverty and ineffectualness of theological discourse in our time. The theologians of our time must obviously operate in a very secluded and isolated realm. Having neither killed nor molested nor stolen anything worthwhile, having waged no cruel wars far from home, nor organized sit-ins or marches to dramatize their plight, and having been exiled to an occasional early Sunday morning or Sunday afternoon on television—the word has simply not gotten out—we have been passing through a time in which the old forms of belief show a structural fatigue or hardening of the arteries, and new forms of belief are struggling for some kind of definition. Churches and synagogues are apparently the last places on earth to become aware of this. They have only rarely been a place where people gather to think and feel seriously about God and man. Theologians at least try. For 200 years they have been arguing with one another endeavoring to relate the methods and results of science with regard to the world in which we live, to the inherited notions of God and man. The Michigan congregation has eliminated language about God from its prayer book. In so doing they have taken the theologian seriously.

Why all of this? We obviously cannot go into all of the reasons this evening. But first of all let us understand that we have been living through a time in which there are few intellectual frames of reference in which the idea of God is particularly advantageous. This was not always the case. The word God, the idea of God, had an honorable status in the intellectual schemes of the great philosophers of the past—Plato, Aristotle, Kant, Spinoza and others. No major philosophic system of today seems to find God particularly useful. This death of God, as the theologians call it, or this eclipse of God, has been a terrible burden for the theologians to endure. Christian thinkers in particular have been very troubled and sensitive to the demands they feel have been imposed upon them—to construct a relevant, intelligible contemporary theology. The Bishop of Woolwich, John Robinson, has almost succeeded in popularizing this theological discussion in his book, *Honest to God*. The Bishop is also concerned that the traditional concept of the deity has no meaning for modern man. Using popular language he says that the Bible speaks of a God "up there" and a three-decker universe consisting of the heavens above, the earth beneath, and the waters under the earth. That all of this was outmoded by contemporary cosmology; that the mental image of an old man in the sky has been gradually replaced, and instead of a God up there, we then accepted a God "out there." But that now even *this* image has lost its validity; hence the danger that man has and will discard entirely the belief in God. Drawing on the works of two significant Protestant theologians, Dietrich Bonhoeffer, a courageous German martyr who was hanged by the SS and whose *Letter and Papers from Prison* created a stir when they were first published in the early 1950s, and also on the works of Professor Paul Tillich, Bishop Robinson transposes God from the heights to the depths. It was Tillich who said, enigmatically for many: "The question of the existence of God can neither be asked nor answered. If asked, it is a question about that which, by its very nature is above existence, and therefore the answer, whether negative or affirmative, implicitly denies the nature of God. It is as atheistic," Tillich contends, "to affirm the existence of God as it is to deny it. God is being itself. God is not a being." So too with the Bishop. It is not the God up there or out there for him. He concurs with Tillich. He finds God as the very ground of all being—the ultimate reality—all language about God is in the realm of the symbolic.

As for Bonhoeffer, his work suggests that he was much more radical. The fragments of his thinking which have been made available and which have been having such a profound effect on theological thinking indicate that he too had misgivings about the traditional theistic intellectual apparatus. He said that the idea of God and the word God are dead. That the supernatural and characteristic theological use of the word God cause[s] troubles. He felt that the word God could be abandoned. He advocated a religionless Christianity even as he, like so many of us, cultivated the discipline of Bible study and prayer. He said that "the God who makes us live in this world without using Him as a working hypothesis is the God before whom we are ever standing." Daringly and subtly he wrote: "God is teaching us that we must live as men who can get along very well without him."

I am suggesting then that what has happened in Birmingham, Michigan, is but an expression of a larger theological quest as it has filtered into Judaism. That what it really involves is the confrontation of the contemporary religious thinker with the massive power of secularism. He knows that man is concerned with the here and the now, the tangible—that he pays only lip service to the transcendent. And he feels a compulsion, to be, in the words of the Bishop, honest to God and honest to himself.

This question of honesty, of an honesty, which knows no inhibition, is certainly a second aspect of the phenomenon we are discussing. In a totally different setting, but relevant to the problem before us, Robert Brustein, a critic of the *New Republic*, wrote of a radical change which is taking place in the American theater. Two insurgent movements figure prominently in this change. The one movement is the revolt of the Negro. The tremendous energies behind the Negro's drive for freedom have been poured into an enormous number of militant plays. For all the nobility of the cause itself, many of these plays have tended to be self-righteous and melodramatic.

The second insurgent movement is the sexual revolution; it too has accounted for a number of dramatic works. The plays dealing with sex seem preoccupied with the exploration of bizarre experiences. A great many of them, according to Mr. Brustein, are experimental, playful, exhibitionistic, pseudo-religious and even fake. But he believes that it is out of these faltering efforts that the important drama of the future will be created. What these plays reveal is a commitment to some kind of totalism, the totalism of absolute honesty, a complete and often terrible openness about all that one sees and feels and knows.

The current debate on theology is neither racial nor sexual, but it is occasionally dramatic and powerful. It too reveals some of the same elements: it can be playful, exhibitionistic, pessimistic, very personal. And there is a terrible sense of urgency about it, a compulsion to be honest, frank, to expose the nakedness of doubt and despair. And it too has about it a kind of militancy and shrillness. It is the honesty about that which men preserved for the private world of this reflection that has been so upsetting. By and large these notions have not yet touched the living reality of the churches and synagogues, but increasingly we are going to be forced to take a long and painful look at ourselves. Perhaps without militancy and shrillness we shall have to examine what it is that we really are. Surely it is no secret among us that only an insignificant numerical fragment of this congregation, and all liberal Jewish congregations, think about God in their daily lives. We are clumsy at prayer, if we pray at all. We certainly give no indication of believing that being a Jew is a part of a divinely established plan, that we are, as our own neo-Orthodox theologians keep insisting, a part of the covenant community, subject to a divine commandment. Very few of us have heard God speak to them, or listen to them.

What is it that we must learn from this? It is to acknowledge honestly, openly, humbly that to be here, is to be a part of a community of those who doubt the meaning of their being here, to be a part of a great fellowship of uncertainty. And though we may be afraid of this, be afraid of the consequences of our doubt, we need not be ashamed of it.

We are not alone. Our doubt is the bearer of our integrity and our dignity. It is the expression of our freedom. It is out of that doubt that we shall fashion our own perceptions of the beauty of our heritage. It is out of it that some of us will shape the meaning of our God so that if we be moved to say our God and God of our fathers—we shall know it is really ours, born of our own gust.

COMMENTARY BY PROFESSOR RABBI RACHEL ADLER

The Talmud loved *makhloket,* dissension. It was the engine that fueled Talmudic discourse. The rabbis interrogated each other's reasoning, assumptions, and conclusions, recording and respecting even minority opinions. But rabbinic discourse had ground rules. So does discourse about baseball. Debating baskets and penalty shots relocates you to a different conversation.

What kind of God-talk puts you outside Jewish discourse? Many thinkers push boundaries. Maimonides is a Neoplatonist; Isaac Luria describes a tree of divine emanations. For Shneur Zalman of Liadi there is no cosmos; there is nothing but God. For Mordecai Kaplan, God is a process comprising all cosmic forces friendly to human flourishing. All these views affirm something beyond the human that is holy. Each ties its belief to Jewish texts, tradition, and practices. Absent these commitments, the conversation is no longer Jewish. All moderns sometimes doubt or despair. But once you say, like Elisha ben Abouya, "There is no justice and there is no judge," there is nothing but despair.

What makes people risk themselves for others, for justice, is not doubt but certainty, and not despair but hope. Hope and faith led Jews like Rabbi Abraham Joshua Heschel to march with Dr. Martin Luther King and led Rabbi Beerman to the front lines of many principled struggles. Like the prophets he loved to quote, he had a powerful sense of what made God angry. Predictably, Rabbi Beerman and Rabbi Ragins uphold Wine's right to differ, but that doesn't make Wine's atheism an authentic Jewish theology or a motivation for Jewish ethics. Nor is it likely to reproduce in future generations a Judaism as lively and substantial as that at Leo Baeck Temple.

10

Duty of the Rabbi

Undated

This undated fragment captured a key credo of Leonard Beerman's rabbinate. It came not from his own pen, but from that of the towering American Orthodox rabbi and scholar Joseph B. Soloveitchik. Beerman reports that Soloveitchik recalled that his own grandfather defined the vocation of the rabbi as caring for the poor and exploited. The fact that the source was neither an ancient prophet nor a Reform rabbi but a modern Orthodox sage lent added credibility to this social justice imperative.

As for the duty of the Rabbi, I prefer the opinion of the grandfather of one of our country's foremost orthodox rabbis, Rabbi Joseph Soloveitchik, who relates that when his grandfather was asked to define the peculiar calling of the Rabbi, he answered that it was "to protest the neglect of the lonely and the abandoned; to protect the dignity of the poor; and to save the exploited from the exploiters."

COMMENTARY BY RABBI RICHARD LEVY

Rabbi Soloveitchik wrote "The Lonely Man of Faith"—and this was Leonard's faith: on one level, to eschew loneliness and seek out spokespeople for the poor and exploited, to denounce the exploited and to cry out for peace. For Leonard, loneliness and faith were two qualities permanently in tension in his life: he never expected to be "popular," yet he felt wounded by anyone who was moved by his words to disagree with him—he felt he had alienated his opponent. He opined that you can't be a successful rabbi unless at least one person walks out on a sermon of yours—and yet he claimed he was unsuccessful because there were still lonely and abandoned and poor and exploited people in the world. Did Leonard feel "called" to be a rabbi? He felt called to work against injustice, yet he knew that to work against it out of a Westside Los Angeles synagogue was a little ironic. In the 1960s, when "worker priests" would go out into the streets and the fields to witness with their congregants where they were, Leonard observed that when he would have lunch with congregants in their Bel-Air offices, he was being a worker priest too. And he was: he would speak with them about conditions in the world, and when he returned to Leo Baeck Temple he would contact his African American colleagues and his Episcopal colleagues and invite them to speak at the temple so that he could bring the world into Bel-Air, and from the inspiration of the beautiful sanctuary whose design he supervised, his flock could compare the differences between their lives and those of the oppressed, and contemplate seriously how they might bridge the gap.

11

From the Diary of a
Leo Baeck Temple Rabbi

February 5, 1971

Inspired and provoked by the exposé of a young rabbinic colleague, Beerman explains here to his congregation what his weekly schedule looked like. The account mixed the poignant and the quotidian, while also unearthing some idiosyncrasies of the rabbi's calendar. Through this report, Beerman offers an illuminating profile of the peaks and valleys in the daily life of an American rabbi.

One of our colleagues has his yarmelke, his tallis, and the back of his head festooned on the cover of the January 18 edition of *New York* magazine. The tallis is authentically ordinary but the yarmelke is psychedelic. The piece our colleague has written is called "The Diary of a Suburban Rabbi."

Rabbi Martin Siegel leads a Reform congregation in Lawrence, Long Island, and like every rabbi he is looked upon to solve a variety of problems: Jewish fear of black anti-Semitism, the alienation of young people from the principles of Judaism, and the need to make the principles of Judaism work in relation to the problems of the day. The diary tells us how Rabbi Siegel copes with these matters and also how he must cope with other matters, the more personal problems: his wife's breakdown, his own job security, his child. Ultimately the private and public problems fuse, and the diary, which covers nine months of the Rabbi's life, creates the picture of a whole man.

The picture is blurred and divided as is the rabbi. He sees himself as a symbol. His people know him only by his roles. To some he is a radical; to some the signature on the marriage certificate; to some the man who opposes the indulgences of the psychotic fear of anti-Semitism. People see him, he says, only as they need to see him. And he can't recognize himself in their eyes. He and his wife have to live as exhibits in the community. People are friendly, but they have no friends. For the rabbi is not a reality; he is an abstraction.

The result is a very embittered young man who feels neglected by his congregants—his wife hospitalized, ignored in her hospitalization, so he says, by the members of the congregation—and he himself confused and divided, no longer performing his functions as he should.

It is not a very pretty picture, and depending on your knowledge of such matters you can be moved, touched, or outraged by the rabbi or his congregants. The fact is that these are real live people he talks about; the president of the congregation is mentioned by name. A week after the article appeared in *New York* the synagogue was filled to capacity when the rabbi arrived for the Shabbos service; it was like a Yom Kippur or a review of *Portnoy's Complaint.*

The success of Rabbi Siegel prompted the sermon title for tonight: "From the Diary of a Leo Baeck Temple Rabbi." It seemed, ten days ago, when I gave the title to Sylvia Wexler to list in the Bulletin, that it would be an easy enough thing to do. Every rabbi has at least an interior diary that he is convinced would make good reading. The daily experiences of our work present us with a wide range of experience wherein we touch so many of the facets of life—there is, in short, enough stuff there to fill a thousand lectures and sermons. But what I failed to consider was that the stuff of a rabbi's life does not make for public disclosure, necessarily. In fact what distressed me about Rabbi Siegel's piece in *New York* was precisely that he was willing to spill out the private experience for all to read. If I am distressed with the behavior of my congregation; if I think they are unkind, crude in their tastes, inhuman in their consideration of me and my family, what is accomplished by bringing the matter to the attention of the hundreds of thousands of strangers?— well one thing is accomplished—money, fun, profit.

At any event, the experiences that fill my days and the fantasies that enrich my wakening and sleeping life are not exactly a fit subject for public disclosure, I learned, after I gave her [i.e., Sylvia Wexler] the title. That is the nature of the work itself—the confidences that are shared, and so forth, and they are not meant to be put on display—perhaps they should be saved for a work of fiction, or for the end of my days as a rabbi, whenever that will be.

But there can be at least a beginning tonight; it will be drawn from the experiences of many years, although it will be fitted into the days of a single week.

Monday—I dreaded this morning and felt some strange aches and pains, a slight dizziness; perhaps I had become the victim of a virus. Not enough to take refuge in, however—is that what I wanted, to take refuge in illness, or forgetfulness?? There was no such refuge. I had agreed to meet her in the waiting room at UCLA, where she would be receiving her cobalt therapy. Eight thirty, and I must be there, I had avoided her long enough. Isn't that what so often happens to people who are thought to have those hopeless diseases—they are avoided—avoided by me, avoided by their friends, avoided even by their doctors? Who is wise enough to know what to say under the circumstances, who is it that can move gracefully in such situations? For two years she had been fighting that cancer. I came to the hospital and there she was, smiling, talking to the people in that small room outside the room with the big awesome machine. Life and death are so filled with machinery, making it difficult to get through to the persons in us. "Well," she said, "we are going to try this new approach. The cancer has spread and we are hopeful that this will do it." Then I, trying to respond in some humor I saw in her language, said: "Who is the WE you are talking about—have you taken to using the plural of majesty—the royal we—and some phrase from Richard II came to my mind, 'we are amazed to wait thus long for the fearful bending of thy knee.'" "Oh," she said, "it is a we who are involved. I am alive today because of all of the people who have helped me through the various stages of this crisis. Where do you think I would be without the doctor who runs this department and the technicians who administer the equipment? It is not just me alone—it is we who are fighting this disease. It is nothing royal I am stating; it is not even modest; it is we."

The pains had disappeared when I made my way back to the temple. I had come to bring her some comfort and courage. And, as so often strangely happens, she had given it instead to me.

Tuesday—Money. Last night at the Board meeting was all about money, the money we didn't have—the almost 30,000 dollars we didn't have. Come April 1 there will not be enough money to pay salaries—to pay ME. We are so clumsy in this temple when it comes to money.

A man's character, the Talmud says, is revealed in these three ways: *B'kiso, bicoso, b'kaaso,* in his money pocket, in his cup, and in his anger. Like the rabbinic sages we too judge a man's character by his passion, or his anger, or, in words more familiar to our jargon, by his aggression or his hostility. And even as for his cup—the way a man handles his liquor—surely that too becomes a way of judging a man's character. We would observe a man at the end of two or three drinks and measure him by what alcohol has released in him. But when it comes to his pocket, his money pocket that is, the way he handles his money, makes his money, spends his money, what he buys, what he saves, what he keeps, what he gives—here we speak softly and act as though we are on some sacred ground—and perhaps we are. For money is a deity, a very visible deity. The pursuit of money is the common religion of all Americans, a quest which binds us together. It is not accidental that the coins of the realm bear the inscription IN GOD WE TRUST. That is our trust, our commitment, our ultimate concern, our God. There is no use pretending. We are all devoted adherents of the ritual, the pageantry, the dogma, of Money.

Around synagogues, suburban synagogues at least, we talk about budgets and building funds, and membership dues and the high cost of maintaining the whole enterprise—the whole disaster, but we do not talk about the meaning of money. And when we do talk about money, we always talk in delicate, silken tones, lest we offend. I remember that wonderful vibrant statement of Vinegar Joe Stillwell in

Indo China during World War II. General Joseph Stillwell, commenting on some ultra patriotic critics of his, said: "The higher a man climbs on a flag pole, the more of his ass he shows to the public." And it was Shaw who said that "the higher a man climbs on the economic ladder the more things he becomes ashamed of." The more affluent we become, personally and institutionally, the more we become ashamed of dealing with money, realistically, honestly. We do reveal the scale of our values, our character—the rabbis were right by the manner in which we use our money. A man will put his money where his soul is. He will pay for the things that matter most to him, arrange them in the order of his priorities. That's enough to say about money.

Wednesday—a young man came to see me about getting married to a non-Jewish girl. He had been in love before, three times, each time with a non-Jewish girl. Was that accidental? What is there about non-Jewish girls that makes them so attractive to him; or what is it about Jewish girls that might account for his not having found one to love?—well Jewish girls are more complicated, more demanding—or at least so it seemed to him. (And for him it was important that a girl not be demanding; in fact her function was to serve, to put him in first place—man must rule—*numero uno.*) Today I read a poem called "David Is Dying to Get Married."

> David is dying to get married.
> He is dying to share
> His heart, his insights, and the unspoiled island in the Caribbean
>   where he is the only American who goes there
> With someone feminine enough and intelligent enough and mature
> enough to understand
> That when he's hostile it's because he's feeling threatened,
> And when he's vicious it's because he feels unloved,
> And when he's paranoid, sadistic, depressed, or sexually inadequate
> It's simply because
> She has failed him. Yes
> David is dying to get married.
> He is dying to share
> His fish tank, his discounts, and the unspoiled restaurant in
>   Chinatown where he is the only Caucasian who eats there
> With someone secure enough and subtle enough and grateful enough
> to understand
> That when he's rigid it's because he has high standards,
> And when he's violent it's because he has no choice,
> And when he's manic, suicidal, or having trouble sleeping
> It's simply because
> She has failed him. Yes,

David is dying to get married.
To a woman like Lauren Bacall but a bit more submissive.
To a woman like Melina Mercouri but a bit more refined.
To a woman who understands that in order to share
His loves, his hates, his hopes, his fears, his low license plate,
His high tax bracket and his rent-controlled apartment with the
    terrace where he and his mother are the only people who live there
She better not fail him.

Thursday—Intermarriage again. A young couple came, very young, naïve—the girl did most of the talking. "Well, Rabbi, I feel it is very important to have religious unity in the home and that is why I wish to become a Jew. I come from a very religious home; my father is a deacon in our Methodist Church and I sang in the choir and taught Sunday school; religion is important to me and family unity is important and that's why I want to be a Jew." Turning to the young man, I said: "Why don't you achieve this unity by your becoming a Christian?" He sputtered out some answer. And to the young girl I said: "If religion, your religion is so important to you why become a Jew?" Her answer: "But, Rabbi, it's the Christian thing to do."

Friday—the Sabbath is coming, another service. How shall we ever resolve all of the questions and problems of that service? Will they, those Jews of ours, ever be able to pray? Will I be able to pray? What does it mean to pray? I cannot free myself completely from thinking of prayer as I did in my childhood. To pray is to ask for something—"oh God," the child in some grammar school prayed after taking an examination in geography—"oh God, please make San Diego the capital of California." Prayer cannot be that, at least not in any constant, significant way can it be that. Prayer must begin where one listens to a voice.

We cannot be sure what the voice is, but a voice nonetheless. And prayer must be a way of being reassured about our own uniqueness, and our equality with others.

Saturday—God rested on Saturday, but I, I like to play tennis. I would like a Shabbat in the park. The First Man was put into the Garden of Eden to dress it; we are here to look after the universe. We are here to help the universe achieve the goals it cannot realize by itself. The poet Auden says we are to think of ourselves as sculptors. No sculptor enforces his forms on nature. "The sculptor sees himself as laying bare, realizing in stone a form that is already there, potentially, or latently. We shall have a decent world when, and if we understood to treat everything as a sculptor, if we understood that to make a hideous lampshade is to torture helpless metals. When we make a nuclear weapon, we corrupt the morals of a host of innocent neutrons below the age of consent."

Sunday—religious school—I grow old, and I shall wear the bottoms of my trousers rolled[1]—Kominsky says he does not like being a policeman on Sunday morning—and part my hair from behind.[2] Some young people organized a project on ecology, caring about the environment. They are collecting newspapers and they in turn are collected from us. If we could convince the *Los Angeles Times* to cut the size of its Sunday edition in half, we would save more paper than all of the paper collected in a single week by the entire county of Los Angeles. But we will keep the environment cleaner, and spare nature somewhat through recycling and thus contribute to the Capitalist system. But what has this to do with Religious School or Judaism? Several telephone calls from parents, "I send my children to religious school to learn about being Jewish, not to collect newspapers." Is it Jewish to collect newspapers; is it Jewish to care about making a more human environment?

Monday again—A call from the Free Angela Davis Committee and the Committee for the Berrigan Brothers, and the Jewish Defense League, and UCLA all wanting to use our facilities so that someone can speak here. A disgruntled union calling, complaining about the labor practices of one of our members.

Another week has begun.

COMMENTARY BY RABBI KENNETH CHASEN

When I first read Rabbi Beerman's sermon, I was reminded of one of the Torah's most mysterious passages . . . Numbers 19, which details the rules pertaining to the red heifer, an animal that was used in an ancient purification process for anyone who had touched a dead body. The person in question was to be sprinkled with the ashes of a perfect, unblemished red heifer cow on the third and seventh days after contact. This was supposed to purify him . . . but it was also said to leave the priest who had sprinkled the ashes in an impure state. Now *he* required healing.

One of my mentors, the longtime chaplain at Cedars-Sinai Medical Center in Los Angeles, Rabbi Levi Meier, of blessed memory, once wrote of this passage: "The person who heals becomes wounded by the experience."

Clearly, this is what has happened to Rabbi Siegel, and he hungers for healing of his own. But Rabbi Beerman offers us a different lens through which to view the everyday struggles and sufferings that accompany his service as the Healer-in-Chief of Leo Baeck Temple. He sees himself bearing all the consequences that his care for others has produced. However, he experiences his wounds not as lesions that must be treated. Rather, they are the hard-won portals through which wisdom, whimsy, and vision have entered him. Yes, there are cracks upon his surface. Some run quite a bit deeper than the surface. Yet as Leonard Cohen noted, "There are cracks in everything. That's how the light gets in."

Now, it is upon me to lead Leo Baeck Temple with Rabbi Beerman's awareness of the great gifts that come with being a wounded healer. We all get to decide what to make of our wounds . . .

12

Rabbi Beerman's To-Do List

The date on this list is given as "Achshav Achshav Achshav" ("Now, Now, Now" in Hebrew), indicating the urgency Beerman felt for the causes enumerated, including his desire to buy Baskin-Robbins, presumably to satisfy his love of ice cream.

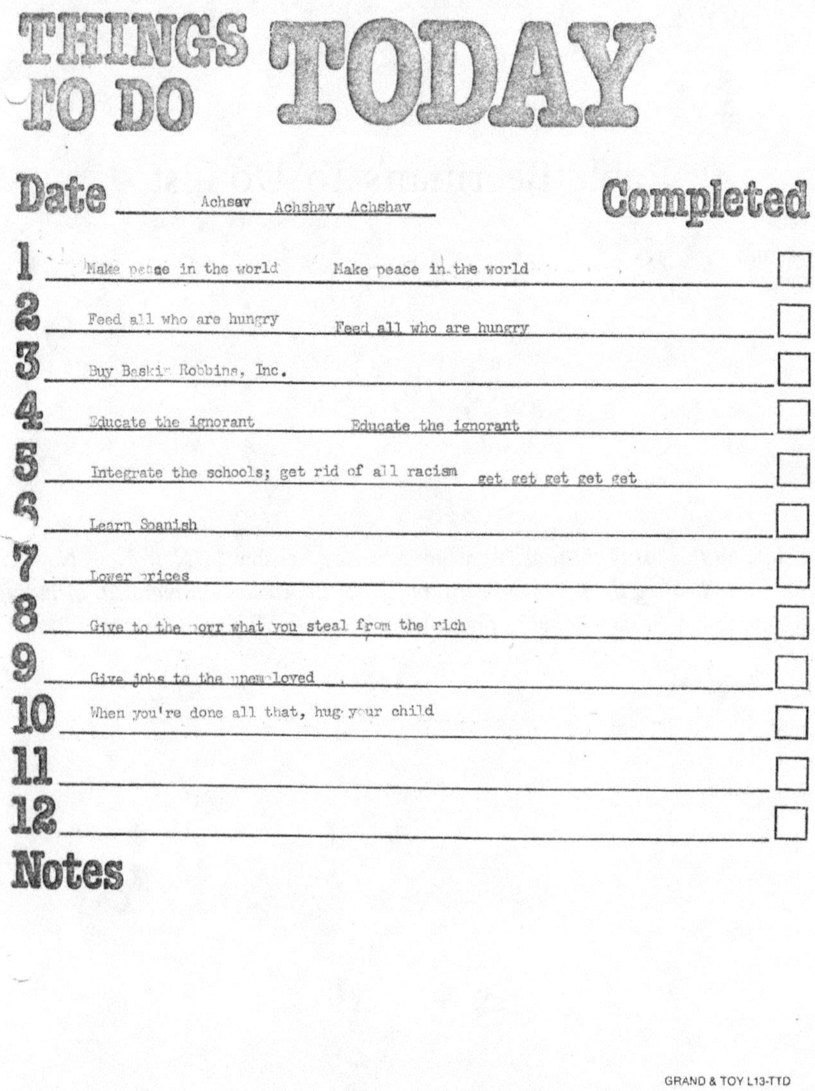

THINGS TO DO TODAY

Date ___ Achsav   Achshav   Achshav ___   **Completed**

1. ___ Make peace in the world   Make peace in the world ___ ☐
2. ___ Feed all who are hungry   Feed all who are hungry ___ ☐
3. ___ Buy Baskin Robbins, Inc. ___ ☐
4. ___ Educate the ignorant   Educate the ignorant ___ ☐
5. ___ Integrate the schools; get rid of all racism get get get get get ___ ☐
6. ___ Learn Spanish ___ ☐
7. ___ Lower prices ___ ☐
8. ___ Give to the poor what you steal from the rich ___ ☐
9. ___ Give jobs to the unemployed ___ ☐
10. ___ When you're done all that, hug your child ___ ☐
11. ___ ☐
12. ___ ☐

Notes

GRAND & TOY L13-TTD

FIGURE 14. Rabbi Beerman's To-Do list.

13

Yom Kippur Eve—Vocation of a Rabbi

September 17, 1972

*In this Kol Nidre sermon, Leonard Beerman reveals important facets of his personal-
ity and theology. With an erudition lightly worn, he laid out his vision of religion, as
well as the vocation of the rabbi. Beerman was mindful that not all of his congregants
applauded his bold political stands and statements; no doubt, they would have preferred a spiritual leader who hewed to the mainstream. But in this sermon, on the
day when the largest number of listeners was in attendance, he rejected this aspiration. It was impossible for religion to be disengaged from politics—and by extension,
for a rabbi not to be political. It was the rabbi's job to assure the "moral grandeur" of
Judaism by insisting that it raise rather than blunt the conscience of Jews.*

*As a prototype for this role, Beerman turned unsurprisingly to the Hebrew
prophets—and more specifically, to Isaiah, whose words are read on Yom Kippur
day. Like Beerman himself, Isaiah did not aim to please. He railed against his contemporaries who deluded themselves into thinking that rote performance of external
rituals (such as fasting) would led to repentance. The mandated act, the prophet
exclaimed, was "to unlock the fetters of wickedness, and untie the cords of the yoke; to
let the oppressed go free; to break off every yoke" (Isa. 58:6). Calling out injustice was
the prophet's—and the rabbi's—most important mission. In assuming this mantle,
Beerman here took aim at the moral numbing that Jews had undergone, losing their
sensitivity to the loss of life of others—and particularly to the millions of victims who
were injured or killed in the Vietnam War.*

Last year about this time I was given a cartoon depicting a bearded man marching
with a large placard on which were inscribed the words "Repent now; avoid the
Yom Kippur rush."

It was a great idea, but we all know it doesn't work. When it comes to repentance, we do not avoid the crowds, nor are we particularly as individualistic as we normally are. We prefer to take our repentance collectively. And so it has always been for us Jews.

It is the theme of repentance that sets this day apart from all others, and brings us together to observe it in a great show of strength. We Jews have always been small in number. We have never enjoyed political sophistication or power, with perhaps the exception of the Solomonic kingdom, 2,900 years ago. Nor has smallness of numbers, persecution, martyrdom, ancient or modern, transformed us into a morally superior people. We are and always have been incorrigibly human and fallible, prone to greed, sloth, and selfishness, and all the other vices both individually and collectively. But one of the greatest glories of our heritage is that it has not only never denied this, but in recognition of it has made this day of atonement—this Sabbath of Sabbaths, the day of repentance for the whole household of Israel—a day to seek repentance in all aspects of our lives where we negate by word or deed the ideals we claim to cherish. This is an annual reminder of the distance that separates our values and our conduct. It is a celebration of moral failure. It is therefore a call to conscience.

But a call to conscience implies that we have a conscience, that there are standards by which we measure our personal lives and our collective lives as well. We shrink from this responsibility. It implies, with Cassius, that the fault is not in our stars but in ourselves, that we are not the persons we pretend to be or wish to be.

Struggling with such questions is the professional task of the rabbi. Some of you would insist that that is what he is paid to do. Struggling with the question of conscience is the job of the rabbis, and their function on Yom Kippur is to serve as a guide to their congregation, to aid all of you through the process. To do this we try to make the vision contained in Judaism relevant to the world, as we perceive it. We cannot speak for you but only to you. We cannot even speak for *the* Jewish point of view. Out of the discipline of whatever learning and understanding of Judaism is ours as rabbis, we may say that this is *a* Jewish point of view that we bring before you. We try to speak with conviction and honesty. But to do so we must face the challenge of learning as we teach. And when we try to be serious about our task we know that what we say will not only comfort but also disturb. I have no burning desire to disturb you, upset you, but I am convinced that there are enough sedatives and tranquilizers traversing the bloodstreams of the members of this congregation alone, without adding to their number. There are enough clergy around to perform this role. As a model for this, one should go to the East Room of the White House on a Sunday morning, where each week two or three hundred invited guests, especially token priests and pastors . . . All of them solid, respectable, all of them giving their blessing to whatever it is that the President is doing.

Wherever it appears, in the White House, in churches or synagogues, this is not authentic religion. Wherever religion does no more than sedate and tranquilize, it becomes a drug, a snare, a delusion.

Some of you have been complaining that this pulpit and this temple are too political. A religion must be political. A religion divorced from politics is a religion divorced from life and from people. I am not talking here about partisan politics and supporting candidates in elections, which we never did, and shouldn't be doing. No, religion must be political because this world is political, for this world has to do with the decisions we make, the decisions that determine who shall live and who shall die, and how we live and how we die. A religion that does not help us, cajole us to confront the moral issues present in all of this, is another tranquilizer; it is at best a subordinate amusement. "It does not originate, it reacts." As C. Wright Mills once said, "It does not denounce, it adapts. It does not set forth new models of conduct, it imitates. It does not move the heart, it hardens it. It does not stir the conscience, it blunts the conscience."

A religion that blunts the conscience is deficient because it is rooted in selfishness. It is cowardly because it is afraid to define and expose what is morally atrocious. It is sterile because its passion is artificial. And further, those who want a Jewish religion which blunts the conscience would rob Judaism of what I believe is its moral grandeur, its heroic dignity, its power to exalt and condemn.

In light of these convictions what could a rabbi say to his congregation on the eve of the Day of Atonement? He might say that because of the serious expectations and demands of Yom Kippur, to confront our conscience, to seek repentance, to acknowledge our moral failure, the observance of Yom Kippur by this congregation is an appalling absurdity. From God's point of view it is an attempt to blackmail with a show of morality. The whole performance is intolerably pretentious. The smugness, the self-righteousness, the dogmatic refusal to admit your complicity in evil, the prayers, the fasting add up to sheer nothingness.

Lest you think I am being arrogant or blasphemous, what I have just said was a fairly accurate paraphrase of the words of the prophet Isaiah, which we will be hearing tomorrow morning. After a scathing denunciation of the day and its rituals Isaiah demanded freedom for all, and an end to poverty; he called for a radical change of both a social and personal nature. I can assure you that he displeased more than eighty percent of those who heard him, and had very few friends at the end of his sermon. That his words were preserved at all is a tribute to the passion for justice and truth that may weaken but never totally disappear from the Jewish people. Isaiah was himself something of an aristocrat, urbane, sophisticated, well-bred. He spoke in an era when there was a priesthood, a temple cult, animal sacrifices, and a nobility of considerable wealth, power, and privilege. He wasn't tactful; he didn't entertain. He stormed, warned, threatened, and promised hope only at the price of radical change. Hundreds of years later his book was included with that collection of books we call the Jewish Bible; and centuries after that the rabbis took out of his writings this passage and ordained that it be read on Yom Kippur. Surely it is a tribute to the Jewish people that on the holiest of days this denunciation of the rituals of the day can be read, is read from year to year. I stand in awe, in reverence, in gratitude before such a heritage of truth.

But rabbis are not prophets, nor are they sons of prophets. Even the suggestion of an analogy of roles is infected with arrogance. Yet surely something of that spirit lives in all of us who have inherited it, it lives on whenever we insist that we will not settle for what is, but only for what can be. Whenever we resist the forces that blunt the conscience we keep alive something of the glory of that Jewish spirit. Whenever we insist that religion cannot be divorced from life and from people, we breathe life into the Jewish spirit. Whenever we seek repentance we acknowledge a yearning to be finer, nobler and thus give more life to that spirit. In Judaism, Leo Baeck once taught us, the highest possible standard is imposed upon us. "The ethical command with its ceaseless Thou shalt, stands before us and demands our life. Our ethical consciousness is a consciousness of an unending task. If we can feel a reverence toward this task, then we can feel a reverence toward ourselves."

So we are challenged not to blunt the conscience, but to awaken it, not to pretentions of virtue, but to the acknowledgement of moral failure.

The rabbi who ventures to lead his congregation up this path is aware that he is engaged in a dangerous mission. For the rabbi is the bearer of a dark secret. He knows he is the servant of a religion which was not fashioned in a comfortable suburb, a religion which rarely developed any passion for the dilemmas of the privileged and the affluent. The calf worshippers of old who stood at the foot of Sinai sincerely believed that they were worshipping the God of Israel. A rabbi who serves a congregation as fashionable and respectable as this one, feels more like an Aaron, the brother of Moses, who took the gold, fashioned the calf, and gave the people what they wanted. The rabbi who serves the enlightened and privileged knows he is the bearer of a religion whose God pants after the disinherited, the underprivileged, the lonely, the abandoned, the forgotten, the pursued. Its God is the God of the hunted, not of the hunter, of the defeated, not of the victor.

It is a religion not of pious sentimentality, a faith, Heine once said, "not of muscular boys like the beautiful Greeks, but of men, powerful, indomitable men, who fought and suffered [not on the battlefield of war], but on the battlefield of human thought." It was a religion whose most cogent and undisguised invectives were directed against those Jews who might imitate the boorish refinement of the gentile, their manner, their foods, their dress, their affectations, their games. Do you remember the riotous caricature of that in *Portnoy*, when Philip Roth wrote: "Let *them* (if you know who I mean) gorge themselves on anything and everything that moves, no matter how odious and abject the animal, no matter how grotesque or *schmutzig* or dumb the creature in question happens to be . . . all they know, these imbecilic eaters of the execrable, is to swagger, to insult, to sneer, and sooner or later to hit. Oh, they also know how to go out into the woods with a gun, these geniuses, and kill innocent deer, deer who themselves nosh quietly on berries and grasses, and then go on their way, bothering no one . . . there isn't enough to eat in this world; they have to eat up the *deer* as well. They will eat *anything* anything they can get their big goy hands on! And the terrifying corollary, *they will do anything as well.*"

How does the teacher, the rabbi, or any knowledgeable Jew take this tradition and with it its literature of loneliness and pain, and the excruciating joy that is born out of being in the company of the insulted, the injured, and the defeated—how does one take all of this to guide his privileged congregation on the path that leads to the acknowledgement of moral failure, the awakening of conscience? How does the rabbi lead them through the well-manicured wilderness of their own lives, the lack of care, the lack of sensitivity to wives, husbands, children? How shall he lead them through the many valleys of neglect, a fellow Jew crying out for help in the Soviet Union, in Israel, in America itself? How shall he lead them through the enormous neighborhoods of poverty, racial injustice, urban decay—a neighborhood that grows and festers with each passing day? How shall he lead them past a million charred and mangled bodies of Vietnamese men, women, and children, twelve million more wounded or homeless, all victims of the soldiers and airmen and the bombs, and the bullets, and the napalm you and the rabbi have paid for? At this very moment, as we meet, even on this Sabbath of Sabbaths, our money kills . . . (the air grows colder on this path, very cold).

Men who kill, we have come to learn—Jews who kill, Arabs who kill, Americans and Vietnamese who kill, Germans who killed, all of them—we have come to learn, undergo a psychic numbing. No great psychological work, Dr. Robert Lifton says, is needed in order to avoid feeling the suffering of one's victim. Technologically distanced from those they kill, our young American pilots are preoccupied only with efficiency and performance. But this psychic numbing affects all of us. We have been brought to the point of exhaustion, an exhaustion of sensibility—it is boring and tiring to think about the war, more tiring than to wage it. The pilots who deliver the bombs on the Vietnamese at Quang Tri or Hanoi are as undisturbed as the postmen who deliver letters to our homes. The air war is a powerful but nonetheless boring symbol of the numbed violence that dominates our time.

How shall the rabbi lead his congregation through this freezing climate when numbing has set in, where Jewish hearts respond only to the terror that brings Jewish death? Are there still Jewish hearts that can beat with compassion for everything that lives, that can be passionately concerned for the defense of human life—Arab and Jew, American and Vietnamese—that can feel the terrible sorrow of being a part of the great fellowship of anguish? Who without condoning murder, or being passive before it, can still comprehend that we are all victims and executioners, those who kill, those who are killed, those who pay for the killing, and those who do it?

We all need to pray for forgiveness for one another, and nothing I know expresses that prayer better than these words of Daniel Berrigan:

> We pray the God of peace
> And of unity
> And of decency for all men,
> For the victims
> And the executioners,
> For those who stand in court as judged
> And as judging,
> For those who endure our jails,
> And our stockades
> And our trenches
> And our army depots
> And our ships,
> Hastening on the works of destruction.
> Let us pray for all those
> Who lie under bombs,
> And for those who dispatch them,
> And for those who make them;
> Let us pray for the innocent,
> For the villagers,
> And for the soldiers,
> And for those who go to kill
> And are killed
> Without ever knowing the alternatives
> That have awakened in us.
> Let us pray for those
> Who are powerful
> And for those who are powerless;

The path that leads to repentance is the path of yearning for the beautification of all existence. The path that leads to repentance is a winding way, overgrown with the thorns and thistles of hatred and suspicion, and it leads through a wilderness of doubt and despair. Only those whose faith in human decency is unlimited by fences of national, racial, ethnic, or religious differences, only they may dare to tread this path. But the reward will be equal to the effort, for the path leads to the very summit of our hopes. And when we have at last climbed to the top and by our own effort ascended the highest peak, then God will show us his vision of the future, for only then will we deserve to see it. On that day mankind will be cleansed from its sins and will sing a hymn of victory for the human spirit.

COMMENTARY BY RABBI SHARON BROUS

"The prophet's word," Heschel wrote, "is a scream in the night. While the world is at ease and asleep, the prophet feels the blast from Heaven . . ." What happens when a chasm grows between the rabbi and his congregation? When he lies awake at night, tormented by the blast from Heaven, the call of injustice from the street, but they would rather not be bothered? Who among us is willing to lead a flock out of the comfort of carefully manicured and rarified lives into the anguish? Who is willing to trouble the waters? Heschel learned from Jeremiah, Ezekiel, Amos, and Isaiah that the prophet's duty is to speak truth, *whether the people hear or refuse to hear.* But rather than take this call to heart, we read prophetic excoriations Shabbat morning in lilted tones, troubled only when the reader takes too long or stumbles over the musical notes. We, the descendants of prophets, have forgotten our calling. We have become convinced that our primary job is to not lose our job.

Leonard Beerman never forgot. He knew and lived that call of the prophet, long before it was fashionable. He did it because he knew that we needed it—not only his congregation, not only the Jewish people, but all who take religion seriously. "Wherever religion does no more than sedate and tranquilize," he wrote, "it becomes a drug, a snare, a delusion." His insistence that we fight not to blunt the conscience, but *to awaken it* rings out nearly half a century later. If only we would listen.

14

Fast between Rosh Hashanah and Yom Kippur to Protest Munich and Vietnam

September 1972

Beerman's call in 1972 for a fast between Rosh Hashanah and Yom Kippur (September 9–18) was the result of two events that weighed heavily on him: the ongoing U.S. military action in Vietnam, including the destructive American bombing campaign that he unrelentingly opposed; and the murderous attack on the Israeli Olympic team by Palestinian terrorists in Munich on September 5–6 of that year. The pairing of these two events reflected the integration of two facets of his personality and areas of concern: the universal and the Jewish. The mode of his protest, a fast, reflected his appreciation for the "Ten Days of Repentance" between Rosh Hashanah and Yom Kippur as a time of deep introspection and self-reflection.

The increasing complacency toward the violent and meaningless destruction of human life should be of particular concern to the Jewish community during the season of the Days of Awe. We feel that it is vital to express our intense anguish over the massacre in Munich and the massive bombing of Vietnam, to engage in serious self-scrutiny regarding our past efforts to oppose such violence, as a means of strengthening our affirmation of the sacredness of human life.

We shall therefore participate in a Fast for Life for 48 hours during the week between Rosh Hashanah and Yom Kippur. We invite our fellow Jews to join us in this liquid fast and to participate with us in daily services to be held at Leo Baeck Temple during the noon hour, Sunday, Monday, and Tuesday.

COMMENTARY BY PROFESSOR STEVEN J. ROSS

Leonard Beerman's sermons and calls to action were never meant to comfort. Rather, he wanted to create a profound sense of unease, the greater the unease the better. Complacent Jews were complicit Jews. Silence in the face of atrocities, whether committed against Jews or any human being, was simply unacceptable. For Leonard, a death was a death. He grieved as much for the five misguided Palestinians who murdered eleven Israeli Olympians at the Munich games as he did for their victims; and he grieved equally for the millions of South and North Vietnamese civilians killed by war.

A devout pacifist, Leonard Beerman hated war and the senseless destruction it brought. He cared little about laying blame; he cared only for the victims and the anguish experienced by their families and friends.

Like Moses Maimonides, Leonard did not ask congregants to be like the biblical Moses. He asked them to be the best of themselves. They could not undo the attacks at the Munich Olympics. Nor could they stop the relentless bombing of men, women, and children in Vietnam. But they could ask themselves what *they* could do to protest all forms of senseless violence.

In the fall of 1972, he challenged the members of Leo Baeck Temple to join him in a forty-eight-hour Fast for Life during the week between Rosh Hashanah and Yom Kippur. He wanted his congregation and friends to suffer a pain that would remind them of the pain experienced by the victims of senseless violence. This would not stop the death and destruction he so loathed, but it would be a start toward ending the complacency that allowed such vile acts to happen.

15

My Troubles with God;
God's Troubles with Me

February 9, 1979

This Friday evening sermon reveals Leonard Beerman's unusual candor as a rabbi. He openly confesses to finding little meaning in conventional ideas of God. He unfolds this idea through a series of autobiographical insights, beginning with the innocent prayers he offered as a young boy on behalf of his family through his more mature encounters with theological arguments and doubts. To an extent, the poles of this internal debate are marked off by Beerman's frequent attraction to the Dutch philosopher Spinoza, whose view of God as nature appealed to him, and the recurrent problem of theodicy. Throughout his life, Beerman could not leave behind him the question of how a just God could allow for such misery and barbarity in the world. He formulated this query in an age when thinkers had begun to develop the "death of God" theological tradition, associated in the Jewish tradition with Richard L. Rubinstein (with whom Beerman once had a tense exchange over Franklin Delano Roosevelt).

In sharing his own meditations with his congregants, Beerman engages a host of prominent thinkers from Marx to Leo Baeck. He ends up less of an atheist shorn of all belief than an agnostic for whom struggling with the idea of God is itself an essential vocation of the Jew. Like the biblical Jacob, whose adopted name of Israel means "to struggle with God," Beerman here displays honesty and integrity in attempting to make sense both of his theology and his profession.

The ancient rabbis tell us that Judaism stands on three pillars: on Torah (or study), on Prayer, and on the Practice of Good Deeds. Corresponding to these are the names of the synagogue: a house of study, a house of prayer, and a house of democratic assembly. But not only does Judaism stand on prayer, study, and good deeds, but also on God, Torah, and Israel.

Judaism stands on three pillars, but does your Judaism, rabbi, stand on all three? A person can stand on two legs, but can a Jew stand on good deeds and study, without prayer? Or can one be concerned with Torah, and the Jewish people, and not believe in God? Such are the problems of rabbis but I sense that they afflict many Jews. Most of us have problems with God. I have always had them, ever since I left my childhood behind me. Somewhere in my childhood (did this happen to you as well?) I learned that God had a human form, although he couldn't be seen; that he was all-powerful and all-good, and that he knew everything I did, and that He judged everyone by his acts; that He rewarded and He punished, that He was there . . .[1]

I am not a theologian, nor am I the son of a theologian, but just an ordinary congregational rabbi, as all of you know. Years ago–exactly ten years ago–when my friend Richard Levy was assistant rabbi here at Leo Baeck Temple, he described one of the frequent and important functions of the rabbi of this congregation, which was to serve as a tour guide. And, like all tour guides, after a time you developed a kind of pattern, explaining to the visitors who came to this congregation, how all the light switches of this Temple are on the opposite end of the room from the entrance and how the architects thoughtfully provided a diversion for dull sermons, by allowing wandering minds to count the holes over the ark. Richard used to say that the part of the tour he likes the most was the little sermon he developed for the three sets of doors directly facing the main entrance to the Temple; and if you are ever called upon to conduct a tour of our synagogue, here's a ready-made sermon for all of you to use. And this is how it goes:

The ancient rabbis tell us that Judaism stands on three pillars: on Torah (or study), on Prayer, and on the Practice of Good Deeds. Corresponding to these are the names of the synagogue: a house of study, a house of prayer, and a house of democratic assembly: Bet Midrash, Bet Tefila, Bet Kneset. You open our sanctuary door and there you introduce the tourist to the house of prayer. You open the social hall door and show them the house of meeting, or democratic assembly. And you open the library door and you show them the house of study. Then you go on to say that not only does Judaism stand on prayer, study, and good deeds; but also on God, Torah, and Israel. And then off the grateful tourists will go, leaving you behind to ruminate on what you've just told the visitor. Judaism stands on three things: but, does your Judaism, rabbi, stand on all three? A person can stand on two legs. Can a Jew stand on good deeds and study, without prayer? Or can't one be concerned with Torah, and the Jewish people, and not believe in God? Such are the problems of rabbinic tour guides. Perhaps they will not afflict you when your turn comes. But I sense that most of us have problems with God. I have always had them, ever since I left my childhood behind me. Somewhere in my childhood and perhaps this happened to you as well, somewhere I learned that God had a human form although he couldn't be seen; that he was all-powerful and all-good, and that he knew everything I did, and that he judged everyone by his acts; that he rewarded and he punished, that he was there in time of danger and sorrow; that there was a purpose behind everything that happened, even though I could not always understand it; and that he was a loving Father, or rather a Grandfather, sometimes with a white beard, distant and near, someone who answered when you prayed even though the answer was sometimes "No." And every night before I went to sleep I prayed the same prayer to this God, a prayer which my parents taught me. It calmed my fear of the night and of the darkness that sleep would always bring. I said it for so many years of my childhood that I remember it still. And this is the way it went.

> Before I sleep I close my eyes
> To Thee, oh God, my thoughts arise
>   I thank thee for the blessings all
>   Which come to us, thy children small.

And then, very quickly, I blessed all the members of my family, the most recently born, the last: God bless mommy–daddy–sissie–grandma–Jackie. And then, *Shema Yisrael, Adonai Elohenu, Adonai Ehad*—in the old Askenazic way—Hear, O Israel; the Lord our God, the Lord is one.

That was the prayer I prayed every night. And especially before tests in school—and tennis matches, when I was thirteen. I prayed when my sister lay bleeding from a rare blood disease, when I had typhoid fever after swimming in the filthy Shiawasee River that meandered through the small Michigan town of my grammar school days. But somehow, as I grew up, I began to have troubles with this God. I suppose it was because I couldn't understand why he let so many troubles come to the young and the helpless, why there was so much pain around, why there was so much disease and poverty . . . war and famine and cruelty. I learned along the way, some history and science. I read some philosophy. That did it. The old, simple, naïve theology of my childhood gave way before this learning. The God of my childhood was soon as outdated as my childhood.

In college I had to learn the proofs of Anselm and Aquinas, and how to demolish them. God became for me a matter for speculation and rejection, and then forgotten altogether. Oh, in my home we welcomed Shabbas and Pessah. I recited the *motzi* and *Bore Pree Hagoffen* every Shabbas. We avoided the forbidden foods. We ate the matzo and scorned the bread. I was bored, like most of the young people in my town, by Rosh Hashannah and Yom Kippur. But we were Jews, and I didn't think too much about it—until, in my senior year of college, when uncertain about the direction I must take, I left school, tramped around the country for some six months, found a job, and then, lonely, found my way to a shelf of Jewish books in the public library in a small town far from home, and began devouring with a strange, relentless pleasure, literature, history, philosophy, theology—all Jewish—and knew suddenly that I had found a possible direction for myself—to become a rabbi.

I returned to college for my final year, discussed the matter with my closest friend, who would go on to become a psychoanalyst. I remember his shocking declaration—"You can't become a rabbi—You don't believe in God." "By God, you're right," I said. "I must go and find one"—and with the passionate innocence that delayed adolescents wear, I poured over books in the college library until I found Spinoza, and his intellectual love of God—the God who was the underlying unity, that substratum, he called it, beneath and within all reality. And I took that for my very own and, carrying him in my intellectual baggage, went off to Cincinnati, as I took up my studies for the rabbinate. There I was taught the important principles of Reform Judaism. I learned that Judaism was a rational religion—that it encourages Jews to think for themselves and to accept only what was believable to them. I learned that Judaism addresses itself to the intellect and that its chief contribution to civilization was the concept of the one ethical monotheistic God. I learned also that Judaism was compatible with the best—the very best—of modern science and philosophy, and that the primary manifestation of devotion to this faith was an ethical life, which expresses itself in the responsibility for society and for the entire world. The crucial thing for us as students was the properly developed, reasoned idea. The crucial thing for us was to sophisticate our thinking. That was the highest expression of Judaism for us. We really didn't give much of a damn about some of the practical problems of the rabbinate. We really weren't interested in the rabbinate. We were, in my days, interested in cultivating our mind and our thought. And the school was divided into intellectual battlefields, but we were all agreed that somehow we were in the vanguard of change. We learned at college—at the Hebrew Union College—how not to take the Bible and the prayer book literally. We accepted the scientific implausibility of biblical stories of creation, of images of God, of miracles. The Bible, we learned, spoke the language and thought of its time; and we would speak in the language and thought of our time and thus be true Jews. The Bible was myth or legend, and some of it was history, and we were able to make the distinction, with the help of critical methodology, between myth and history. There was still, in that Bible, a reality worth preserving—a reality to be found there. Oh we'd choke sometimes in reading some of the passages of the prayer book in English. In Hebrew we were able to avoid their literal meaning and somehow deal with them and even respond to them. Some of us were attracted to the thinking of Mordecai Kaplan, the professor of Jewish Ethics at the Jewish Theological Seminary of America, who taught us, or at least tried to teach us, that we had to do away—he said—with the supernatural idea of God, and replace it with a naturalistic idea of God . . . that we had to think of God as the sum of the forces and conditions in the universe, and in human beings, which impel us to fulfill ourselves as human beings. We argued that the primary concern in Judaism is with the way of life—a way of life involving a sense of tradition and a determination to realize certain ideals in the concrete process of our existence—to move from the historic past with these ideals, by realizing them, into a Messianic future. From

Sinai we would move to justice for the orphan and the widow and the stranger and the abolition of war and the bringing of peace and harmony. The brotherhood of man is what we called it in those days before the era of feminism. We argued that Judaism is not an accumulation of beliefs. Christianity had imposed that way of thinking about religious faith on all of Western Civilization, but Jews, primarily, had never been concerned with belief. And we quoted always from the rabbis—When we appear before the throne of judgment we will not be asked, "Have you believed in God? Have you prayed?" No, we will be asked—"Have you dealt honorably and faithfully with your fellow man?" Our religion encouraged not only this, but also the search for truth. There were no dogmas, we were taught, in Judaism. Every generation of Jewish history had produced a new vision—a new understanding—of everything, including God. So it was with Abraham and Isaac and Jacob. Each of their visions of God and experiences of God was different. Did Jews believe that God existed? They had no word for existence. There was no effort made, we were taught, to define God—except always under the influence of the outside culture, particularly in medieval times—Jewish philosophers wrestled with the competition of the contemporary science of their generation.

Well, such was the stuff of our reasoning. And these notions carried us along. We made our peace with the psychoanalytic criticism of religion as illusion, insisting that that Freudian concept referred not to us but to orthodox religion. That indeed was an illusion, but not the kind of religion we were talking about. We agreed with Marx, most of us, that religion was the opiate of the masses—that religion had always functioned historically, to keep the dispossessed dispossessed, by diverting them from the truth about the cause of their condition. We insisted that that, too, referred to orthodox religion—traditional religion—Jewish and Christian—but not to us. Yet we were troubled that ours was the religion serving, very clearly, the upper middle class, graced with the good manners of that class—hardly demonstrating any seriousness about their Judaism—hardly showing any passion about the realization of the prophetic ethic, about undoing the evils of our society. Yes, we were able to believe that our religious faith permitted us, encouraged us, to be modern and Jewish at the same time. Yet we were always aware that the most vibrant activities of the general culture were not religious, but secular. We often—we rabbis—often made our best friends among the atheists and the agnostics—and felt closer to them than some of the believers.

I had grasped what I thought was the central theme of Jewish thinking—To believe in oneself—to believe in the inalienable right of Jews to legislate for themselves, to define for ourselves on the basis of informed thinking, the structure and the content of Judaism—to define for ourselves the content of our Jewish life. I searched for the ways of enhancing my humanity and the humanity of my congregants and in the process of stressing this human role, I neglected the role of God. I was a Humanist. I retained some abiding faith in humanity. I retained some abiding faith in the ultimate triumph of human beings. And I confess to you that I still do. For many people, that faith in humanity died when our people were killed at Auschwitz and Dachau and Bergen-Belsen, and the rest. That faith in humanity died in Vietnam—it died in the resistance to civil rights—it died in the exploitation of natural resources—it died in the continuing impoverishment of the poor. That faith died in the cynicism that has afflicted all of us in our culture, when we contemplated the banality of the evil perpetrated by our leaders. That faith died in the presence of the corruption which pervades even the highest of Western Civilizations. Those, as my colleague, Eugene Borowitz has said, those who put humanity in God's place found that they had frequently put a monster there. The God of triumphant modernism, he said, the God of faith in the omnipotence of education and culture and advancing scientific knowledge—that God fell for many when its arrogant ruthlessness was revealed. Many people filled this vacuum, and still do, by fleeing from society—by seeking refuge in the self, through the self. I did not join that flight, myself; but many people in this congregation did, and still do. Others fled into a new traditionalism—into orthodoxy. Others fled to a God who would tell them exactly what to do. And this became the ground in which all of the cults developed—those cults at least which demand absolute belief. It also became the ground which attracted so many again to Jewish orthodoxy. But most of the Jews we know would not choose to go that way. Oh, we would be attracted to some of the outer manifestations of tradition to yarmulkas and the like. We (as we did at Leo Baeck Temple) would invite over the Lubovitcher Hasidim to speak to us, and even into our homes. Some few in this congregation would envy the authenticity of some of these Orthodox Jews, but almost none of us were willing to accept their way of life—to accept the rigidity and the absolutism it demanded of us. In such a time as ours it becomes difficult to believe in anything. It certainly is difficult to believe in human reason. It certainly is difficult to believe in morality. It certainly is difficult to believe in people—and it certainly is difficult to believe in God.

All of the institutions we once believed in, we liberals—many of the people we believed in, betrayed us. What kind of a God would abide such a world? "If God is God," the poet MacLeish said, in his play "Job"—"He is not good. And if God is good, He is not God." Belief, steady belief has really not been possible for me. There were those whose faith was able to stand firm amidst all of these assaults. There were those who experienced only momentary failures of faith—only doubt. Borowitz reminds us that Leo Baeck, the great rabbi of Berlin, after whom our congregation was named, lived out the closing days of his life in Theresien, in a concentration camp.[2] He witnessed the destruction of European Jewry—yet he emerged from that camp without any apparent need to revise the thinking—the thought that he had developed in a number of written works in the happier times of his life. He was able to do that, in spite of the trauma which he experienced— but not so with me. I had difficulty in accepting a God of history—a God who intervenes in the affairs of nations—a God who was all-powerful. And now my effort to comprehend the meaning of human brutality, the senseless war, the cruel waste of human potentiality—all that convinced me that either such a God was a ruthless murderer, or there was no such a God at all. There is no God who ordains that millions of Jews must die; that blacks and Chicanos and other minority groups must live in isolation—that millions upon millions of men, women, and children must be forever doomed to live in hunger, beset by disease and poverty. And if there be such a God, I dedicate my life to fighting against him. Yet, I believe in the possibility of a reality greater than myself, beyond my understanding. There are many mysteries in my world—something finer than I can imagine. There is for me, many times, a presence beyond the human presence. It is a presence that is full of awe. I surely comprehend, or dimly apprehend, that there are inner forces at work in the world, itself . . . something creative—something that exalts. I have felt it on a hilltop, by the sea, in the face of a child, in the theater, on a canvas, in the presence of music. I have felt it when I sat beside the dying. I have felt it in a moment of prayer. I have felt it when the cantor sings. I believe it is possible to communicate with whatever this presence is, although I experience that presence never constantly—but only in fragments and in moments. I come to my life and my thought and my experience, not just as a single human being—not unattached. My individuality—my singularity as a human being, is a part of a people—a historic people—Jewish people. I come to my life with a cultivated consciousness of my people's past. And I come to my life with an awareness of my connection with all human beings—and my goal—which I believe to be the goal of Jews throughout the centuries—is essentially the same as it has always been to create for myself—to create for every person, a life that will somehow sanctify the ordinary part of my existence, to help create a society in which holiness, as was imagined by those who conjured up the metaphor of God's Kingdom of Earth, in which such holiness can be realized. I experience this all as a kind of command. Leo Baeck spoke of experiencing the mystery and the commandment. The mystery of life is the awareness of being in the presence of powers and forces beyond our understanding—that fill us with a sense of humility and awe and reverence. The commandment of life is the realization that we have been given a task to fulfill—that something has been asked of us—to fulfill ourselves as Jews and as human beings. I do not know the source of this command, although my ancestors gave many names to it—Yahweh—Elohim, Adonai, Shadai, and the English language was to endow it with the name God. I do not believe in the God of whom it may be asked—"Do you believe in God?" Such a God, of whom it may be asked, "Do you believe in God?" is a mere concept—an idea. It is as humanly significant to me as asking me if I believe in the Second Law of Thermodynamics. What difference will it make in my life if I believe in God as concept or don't believe in it? What difference will I make in my life if I say—"Yes, I believe in such a God." The experience of the nameless—of the presence—of the commanding presence of God, if you will—that will give reality to the meaning of the name, for it is in the experience that there is meaning. I believe in the possibility of an exalting presence. I believe in an ultimate presence within me, and all of you, and all of being. And I see all of that as being in the process of becoming something that has not yet been realized in my life—or in yours—or anyone else's.

The original name for God, according to our ancient teachers, was Yahweh—the nameless name—the forbidden name. We don't know exactly how to pronounce the name, even when we dare to pronounce it. We're not even sure what it means. Yet, by its form, it suggests a simple definition—He who causes to be. He who is somehow responsible for the process of becoming. And isn't that what all of us seek? To be a part of all of the processes that are at work in the universe of our personal lives and in the lives of those about us—everywhere? The process of becoming—the process of the realization of whatever it is we were meant to be.

I have many troubles with the word God. I prefer not to use it. It embarrasses me, because it crowds in upon me with its difficulties. I suppose God, if such there be, has troubles with the likes of me. We Jews have never been at peace with God. Even our ancestor from whom our people derives its name—our ancestor, Jacob, once wrestled with God. And his name was changed to Israel . . . which became the name of our people—the name of the State of Israel. Israel means He Who Strives With God. He Who Wrestles With God. Such has been the task of the Jews—some of the best and worst Jews over the centuries. Perhaps it remains our task as well. Until we have been able to bring into being a more human way of living, not just for ourselves, but for all humanity. Until we learn what it means to be a person—to be a Jew. Until we experience the task and the commandment and embrace it for our very own, and know that this day and all that we shall be privileged with has significance and beauty. We must continue to strive with God; and in so doing, we will realize ourselves as Jews, and as persons.

This is surely not the kind of faith and certainty that congregants expect to hear from their rabbis. And many of you will be disappointed and disenchanted. I've obviously left more questions unanswered than answered. But this is a subject and an experience that we shall take up again in the many days that lie ahead.

COMMENTARY BY DAVID RINTELS

God and Leonard—now that's my idea of a fair fight, between two heavyweights. It's like Jack Dempsey and Muhammad Ali—they were at their prime in different eras, but it's interesting to speculate about. God clearly had the advantage in experience and power. He was indomitable (if you disregard the story of Jacob wrestling with the angel), and His knowledge was encyclopedic, covering the whole world, though Leonard was no slouch in this area, either . . .

. . . but for humanity, kindness, warmth and humor, for the twinkle in his eye and his love of baseball, you have to give Leonard the decision on points. History will also record that Leonard was far nicer to the Palestinians, and for a longer time. He was also devoted without reservation to his entire family, and appreciated

To Rabbi Beerman—
You and the Dodgers
are both great.
Tom Lasorda

FIGURE 15. Tommy Lasorda, veteran Dodgers manager, signed photo.

that God was as well, although he did give God great credit for rebuking his own chosen people, the Israelites, when they cheered as the waters of the Red Sea swept over Pharaoh's men. Why are you celebrating?!, God demanded of them. My people are drowning.

When he was a child, Leonard spoke to God, every night. He called it praying. He got out of the habit when he grew older, but he never had a problem with people who did pray. He once said the only thing wrong with prayer was that people who prayed were usually hoping God would tell them that two and two do not equal four.

Now, for what Leonard really did and did not think about God . . .

Signed Photo from Tommy

Editor's note: Rabbi Beerman was a lover of baseball and a longtime season-ticket holder for Los Angeles Dodgers games. Above is a picture from veteran Dodgers manager Tommy Lasorda (1976–1996).

16

The Beginnings of an Outline for Jews to Consider

Undated

Beerman here offers up a series of guiding principles that define his vision of Judaism as it operates in his life. Medieval Jewish thinkers such as Maimonides (1135–1204) and Yosef Albo (ca. 1380–1444) formulated their own ikarim, or foundational principles, as a means of delineating the unique properties of Judaism and of distinguishing it from other traditions. Rabbi Beerman's list serves less as a magnet to fellow Jews, as in the case of his medieval precursors, and more as a credo of faith about the ideals and practices that animated him as a Jew. He never published the list, but kept it on the desk in his office as a reminder of the key values dear to him.

1. Judaism teaches me that each human being is created in the image of God; therefore each is entitled to respect, to dignity. I am to love my neighbor— how?—as myself. We are all of us creatures of dignity, not meant to abuse, use, manipulate one another—To be created in the image of God—that is a cardinal principle—Ben Azzai taught.

2. Judaism provides me with a framework of ideas about man, about God, about the good life, a library of human experience, of questions and answers about life and its meaning. It provides the framework; I must myself build, fill in the details, finish the work . . . and the work never ends.

3. Judaism gives me time for prayer, for serenity, for wisdom—those prayers and those silences have challenged me, irritated me, frightened me—as I respond to them.

4. Judaism gives me customs, traditions, they enrich my life, help me to hallow my days. I cannot eat without reciting a blessing.

5. Judaism gives me a reverence for learning—the search for truth—"thou shalt teach them diligently," a respect for the thoughtful man—perhaps that is what it means to be made in the image of God—to be endowed with reason, the ability to think—that is the way Maimonides saw it.

6. Judaism helps me to understand that I am not alone; I am a part of a people, an eternal people. My ancestors were slaves in Egypt, they stood at Sinai to receive those commandments—I was at Sinai too, I went forth out of Egypt or I am yearning to go forth. This IS Egypt. This place. This America. The process of liberation is an eternal one.

7. Judaism teaches me about the way, the way a Jew can live in order to be a man. It has taught me to abhor war, violence, to seek the way of peace. It has taught me not to be ashamed of gentleness, of compassion.

8. Judaism teaches me to be sensitive to injustice. To have been a slave, to have been an alien in every generation—is to know the heart of the stranger, to know what brings pain to another, and never to be at ease so long as a single person is denied his humanity.

9. I pass this world but once—whatever good I can do, do it now. I want to leave this place better for having lived in it. And this life is all and enough for me. Do it now!

10. Hillel's principle—what is hateful unto thee do not do unto thy fellowman. The negative and Jewish statement of the principle is crucial, as Ahad Ha-am once perceived. There is a principle of justice for all men to keep. I am not good to another so that he will in turn be good to me.

11. Being a Jew is being part of a Jewish people, being members of a special family. I have brothers and sisters in Israel for whom I care, from whom perhaps I can learn new ways of being a Jew.

COMMENTARY BY AZIZA HASAN

Rabbi Beerman lived a commitment to be good to others. To be gentle, caring, loving, and compassionate. I remember being dumbfounded the first time he delivered criticism to me directly. His voice was soft and yet painfully powerful when he told me that "organizations like *NewGround* come and go with the wind." The words struck me, but his delivery helped me hear his message. His words and example serve as a guide and a source of inspiration—living each of the articles of faith above. Articles that compel me as a Muslim woman to tap back into teachings in Islam. Most of all, what speaks to me of Rabbi Beerman's writing and example was his commitment to live in kindness and compassion—bringing to life Islamic text that calls on people to do what is better so that the enemy may become a dear friend (Quran 41:34). Firmly grounded in religious text, his words remind that I should not be ashamed of being a gentle and compassionate peacemaker.

Something I have struggled with is to be taken seriously in a world dominated by men, and yet my commitment to communicating in that way has helped others see my work and join my efforts to build bridges and strengthen my organization. These eleven points connect to my own foundation in Islam and my ability to live faithfully and care for the community around me.

PART IV

Social Justice

17

The Kindest Use a Knife

October 16, 1953

Beerman's sermon was delivered in the heart of the "red scare" in the 1950s when the United States Senate, under Joseph McCarthy, and the House of Representatives, under Harold Velde, alleged widespread Communist penetration of the government and cultural institutions of the United States. With blunt force, the young rabbi issued a searing indictment of "the pygmies of national shame" who falsely accused individuals of Communism without a trace of evidence of due process. In particular, he took grave offense at the fact that two heroes of his, both of whom were Reform rabbis, had been swept up without merit in the allegations of the House Committee on Un-American Activities (HUAC): Rabbi Stephen S. Wise, the most prominent and influential of midcentury Reform rabbis, and Rabbi Judah L. Magnes, the founding chancellor of the Hebrew University whom Beerman regarded as a uniquely coura-geous and prophetic voice in Palestine.

Beerman here perhaps angered those at Leo Baeck Temple who may have shared in the anti-Communist fear. But the stakes were too high for him to remain silent—nothing less than the "tragic deterioration of democratic values" in our country. It was a characteristic but bold act for the untenured rabbi, who was intent on living up to the prophetic ideals of Wise and Magnes, among others.

A day by itself can have no meaning. It is but a word which describes the rotation of our earth on its axis, while it makes its elliptical passage around the sun. A day comes and goes, whether it be bright or bleak, dismal or sunny. A day by itself has no purpose unless man puts purpose into it. It may mean one thing to the scientist, another to the artist or poet, something quite different to the military commander, to the aviator, or to the miner who works under the ground. But it is always people who give it cause and purpose, and whatever significance is in it is that which people seek to place there.

The Jewish people have sought to find in the day which began this evening at the setting of the sun, in the Sabbath, all the cherished values of life which have been passed on to them in the Torah, in the teaching of their most dedicated teachers and prophets. This day we call holy, sacred to Israel, and to the seeking of life's purpose by the children of Israel in each generation.

We have had our share of transgression and iniquities. We have never claimed a monopoly on human virtue among us. But we have proclaimed our choice of virtue and goodness as our mission among the nations. Since the days of the prophets, we have borne the message that our God desires neither sacrifice nor burnt offering, but the doing of justice, the showing of mercy, and the pursuit of righteousness. Not all Jews have lived in accordance with the ideals of our heritage. We have had our share of fools, knaves, and traitors. Yet in every generation there have sprung from the loins of Jacob men of courage and women of valor, who have championed every good cause among men, and who have fought and suffered, as Heine said, on every battlefield of human thought.

It seems as if the prophets of ancient Israel never died, for their spirit was resurrected not once, but a thousand times in the annals of the Jewish people. Generation following generation, the conscience of mankind was quickened and enriched by an Isaiah and then a Jesus, by a Maimonides, a Mendelssohn, and a Herzl, indirectly by a Freud and an Einstein and by a never-ending procession of men, whom all the world holds in deep respect and grateful reverence.

In our generation, not by any means the least of these, but a man whose name all of you know, and ... whose voice many here may remember, was a Rabbi who seemed especially reminiscent of the prophets of old—Stephen S. Wise. For all the world, Rabbi Wise spoke in the accents of a Jeremiah, with the passion of an Amos, and the eloquence of Micah: "What doth the Lord require of thee, but to do justice to love mercy and to walk humbly before thy God." While he worked and lived Stephen Wise made many enemies—the proud and the arrogant, men who placed the value of property and possession above human needs and brotherly concern. His critics were among his own people too, who called him actor, or a charlatan. The criticism of some was surely justified, but generally it betrayed the poverty of their own insights and their own corruption of spirit; it did not in any way diminish the stature of Wise. When the cause was just, he stood his ground like a lion, and roared his defiance of those who sought to ensnare him by either threats or promises.

In a day when labor struggled for recognition, this modern prophet joined them in their aspiration. At a time when freedom of the pulpit was a rare commodity among prosperous churches and synagogues, he turned his back upon the most prominent Jewish congregation in the land that he might speak without compromise and in accordance with the dictates of his conscience. In the struggle for the establishment of Israel as a free republic, his opponents taunted him by testing his patriotism. Fearlessly he answered them and said: "I have been an American for 150 years, but I have been a Jew for 3,000." While many of his fellow countrymen, and his coreligionists as well, would not recognize the danger of fascism, he roared his opposition and prophesied its future, storming even the citadels of the mighty. Always he labored for the end of man's exploitation over man, for the establishment of a more just and equitable social order than the one he knew. When the war ended he continued to work for mutual understanding, respect, and friendship between his own beloved America and the Soviet Union. However repugnant Communism was to him as an anti-religious philosophy; however much he disapproved of the theory and practices of Soviet Russia, he knew that another world war would not correct the evils there but would certainly bring new evils here. Moreover he understood the warning of the atomic scientists. And so he worked for peace. For many years before the war he endorsed the principles of Franklin D. Roosevelt because he believed that in spirit, they were most nearly in accord with the principles and precepts of Judaism. And then at the eventide of his life when he spoke in Cincinnati while I was attending the Hebrew Union College, as I remember him—he reiterated the task that was before us all, the rebuilding of the waste places and the necessity for establishing an enduring peace among men. This ever was Israel's mission, and now it took on greater significance than ever before. Editing the "Congress Weekly" which he founded, he warned in his editorials that fascism had not died with Hitler. He was not blind or indifferent to the challenge of Russia but he urged patience and understanding that men might explore all the avenues of peace as both a practical and moral necessity. He died on the 19th of April, 1949, and since that day, as it was said of Moses, there has not risen another like him.

Now in this year of 1953, in the month of September a committee of the Congress of the United States recalled the name of this man who personified for all the world the Rabbi and the modern Jew at his best [and] noblest. But the recollection of the name of Stephen Wise was not in a spirit of appreciation for the greatness and goodness of his character or for his many contributions to the welfare of our nation. The name of Rabbi Wise was conjured up for desecration by the House Committee on Un-American Activities under the chairmanship of Congressman Velde. The committee accepted and released the testimony of one of our new national heroes, the ex-communist, to the effect that Rabbi Stephen S. Wise was among those who "carried out the instructions of the Communist Party or collaborated with it."

The same monstrous accusation was brought against Rabbi Judah Magnes, now of blessed memory, who was formerly rabbi of Temple Emanuel of New York and for a quarter century thereafter President of the Hebrew University of Jerusalem, a saint-like creature whose brilliance and humility made him a model and an inspiration for thousands of young men, not the least of whom is Nelson Glueck, now president of the Hebrew Union College. I would not pass over the other courageous and liberal men of the Protestant clergy who were also slandered. But I think that our attention should be drawn not to them, but to their defamers, for it is they who are providing us with a crucial and critical test at this time in our history.

We should ask ourselves, it seems to me, the motive, the plan, and the purpose of Mr. Velde and his Committee. These questions are relevant because, after all, Mr. Velde is an American—not the agent of a foreign power, but like his many friends and allies in and out of Congress, a native American, the elected representative of the people of Illinois, sworn to uphold the Constitution of the United States against all enemies, foreign and domestic. Surely we, who are also his countrymen, must be puzzled and disturbed as we witness the desecration of two of our greatest religious leaders, men whose names most Jews have come to revere.

Yet for those of us who have paid attention to past events, who have heeded the storm warnings which have been threatening our liberties in recent years, this "shocking betrayal of elementary public responsibility and decency," as Dr. Maurice Eisendrath, the President of the UAHC [Union of American Hebrew Congregations] and spokesman for Reform Judaism, called it, was not a complete surprise. Nor is it, we predict with incautious certainty, the last revelation of its kind to emanate from the supposed guardians of our welfare. Indeed as time continues, unless the American people protest with more vigor than they have in the past, we may anticipate that while distracting our attention toward the menace in the East, the demagogues and the opportunists will pick our pockets of many liberties which we Americans of all religions and race have struggled and bled for in the past.

During recent years, the infamous destruction of democratic rights which is known to all the world by the name "McCarthyism" has lived by what it fed on—the ruined lives and reputations of numerous fellow citizens who have never been charged with a crime, tried by a jury, or found guilty of anything worse than invoking the First and Fifth Amendments of the Constitution. The victims of the contemporary reign of terror are more numerous than men realize; some have gone to jail on charges of contempt, some have been silent, but it is impossible to measure accurately the magnitude of the fear and intimidation of others. No wonder that Justice Douglas referred to the black silence of fear among us. But it remained for the world's outstanding scientist, professor Albert Einstein, a victim of Nazism, a refugee from its barbarism to sound the clearest warning of all. "If the intellectuals," he wrote, "cooperate with these committees, they will well deserve the slavery that is intended for them." A short sentence but a pungent one, by a wise and good man. In England, a Nobel Prize winner, Lord Bertrand Russell, spoke in a similar way. Lesser men than Einstein for such a challenge may well have been branded, fired from their positions, and condemned to economic hardships. The McCarthyites of course do not burn men, only books; they do not kill men, only reputations.

They remind me of the old adage about the man whose dog displeased him. "I will not destroy thee, Rover," he said, "for that is contrary to my principles /

but I will give thee a bad name." Whereupon he turned the dog out of this house and into the street crying, "Mad dog, mad dog." And so the neighbors came out alarmed and killed the poor animal instead.

To destroy a human reputation is as heinous a crime as actual murder. Whatever disease prompts a man to slay his fellow man in a moment of passion can be no worse than that of calculated character assassination—and this crime is one in which all of us as a community are guilty. For McCarthyism and everything related to it cannot operate in a vacuum. It can succeed only when the climate of public opinion is propitious, only when other men are willing to follow the leader and accept his protestations of patriotism at face value. Oftentimes too, people do know better, like many among us, but will resort to the totalitarian argument of the Communists and the Fascists, that the end justifies the means, and thus assuage the consciousness of their own guilt.

With such a tragic deterioration of democratic values as our country has witnessed during recent years, the current assault against the liberal clergy must be viewed only as a part of a larger program. For what possible motive could Mr. Velde have had in accepting and releasing the perjured testimony that desecrated the dead and injured the reputation of the living? The only answer that I can find to this question is the inescapable conclusion that native communism, by itself, never was nor is it now the real target. The word *communism* is used by men to include an ever broadening circle of people. These may be radicals, pacifists, or New Dealers, or people of critical minds, or finally anyone and everyone who will oppose the methods and the principle of some of our Congressional committees. We have always had our demagogues; we have always had cynical and ambitious politicians, and we have them now, and their ultimate aim is to achieve complete conformity, which will tolerate no criticism. They have already sown the seeds of perplexity and hatred and fear. The same perplexity, hatred, and fear which have formed the Communist herds and the Fascist gangs in the United States; and conformity of opinion and belief, the first demands of the mob everywhere, has been secured by methods which differ only in degree from the methods of Moscow and Berlin. When loyalty is put before freedom, and when loyalty is made to mean loyalty not to the right to be free, but to the demands of the majority, with economic and social destruction as the penalty for dissent, the drums of Moscow and Berlin are near enough to hear. When loyalty to the particular economic, social, political and military and diplomatic views of the inquisitors is put before loyalty to the rights of each individual to think and speak as he chooses, then we are marching into the frozen world of Nazi Germany and Communist Russia where everything coheres and conforms and the life of the individual mind and soul is of no more significance than the life of a single drop of frozen water in an ice floe. And since religion at its best and noblest is subversive to this tyranny, which masks itself as patriotism, it is logical and necessary that it be attacked too. Truly the demagogues have attempted to make our nation sick, for they are carriers of a virus more deadly even than the one they claim to cure. For these men and their servile collaborators are not the doctors of national healing, they are the disease. Today, because these men are in responsible positions, we are a sick people, but understanding and correction can make us well.

Put in the scale of balance on the one hand the memory of Stephen Wise and Judah Magnes, the principles of Franklin Roosevelt, and the wisdom of Albert Einstein, and weigh these giants of the earth with the pygmies of national shame—and choose between them. I lack the wisdom, the maturity, and the eloquence of a Rabbi Wise or a Rabbi Magnes, but I would rather stand with reverence in the shadow of these men than share the sunlight in which corrupt men now bask themselves.

As all men do, I hold opinions. My opinions may be right or they may be wrong. They may not always coincide with the majority. But because they are mine and because they are as honest as I can make them, I have the obligation to speak them. I have done so in the past and I hope to do so in the future. I speak now out of my belief in the vitality of the American people and out of my concern for the loss of personal freedom, my own, my colleagues' in the ministry of all faiths, teachers, writers, doctors, lawyers, and all of us whatever it may be. It is not that I believe that there has been a decline in our devotion to the ideas of freedom. Those who now attack our personal freedom are themselves obliged, as Archibald MacLeish has said, to use the vocabulary of freedom to justify their activities. It is not our belief in freedom that has changed, but our *Faith* in freedom has—our faith that freedom will really work, that it can, itself, by its own means, survive the attacks of gigantic enemies. For the faith in freedom rests necessarily upon faith in man, and faith in man is the heart and the substance of Judaism. And it is this concern which has prompted everything I have said here this evening.

I said at the beginning that a day by itself can have no meaning. But people can put meaning into a day, an hour, even a moment. In an instant a man can open his eyes, and look and see what was always there, but what he had never seen before. Let us then look at all that is past—at ourselves, our country, and the world in which we live. Let us look deep enough and hard enough, for then whatever blindness is in us will be vanished, and we will see better and farther than ever before. In so doing, we will give meaning and purpose and significance not to this day alone, but to days and days to come.

COMMENTARY BY RABBI JOHN L. ROSOVE

The prophets stood alone in the political world because their speaking moral truth compelled and repelled. This was so with Rabbi Leonard I. Beerman, whose moral eloquence drew many to him yet forced him to stand apart and frequently to suffer the pain of condemnation and aloneness.

The biblical prophets at first resisted God's call, but when they succumbed and did God's bidding from within the moral weight of the divine command, they were exposed, vulnerable, hunted, and often forced to flee from the king's wrath.

In our living-room armchairs and behind our computer screens it is so easy, without consequence, to excoriate, chastise, and speak truth to power—but in the real world, there are risks to be borne in speaking out, and there is suffering that accompanies such speech. Moral leaders must be prepared to be ostracized even if history ultimately retrieves them and lifts them up as our moral standard-bearers.

Such were the times of the McCarthy hearings in which Leonard wrote "The Kindest Use a Knife." There, Leonard defended Rabbi Stephen S. Wise, whose good name "was conjured up for desecration by the House Committee of Un-American Activities," which alleged that Rabbi Wise "carried out the instructions of the Communist Party or collaborated with it."

Leonard wrote of Congressman Velde, the chairman of the HUAC:

"Truly the demagogues have attempted to make our nation sick, for they are carriers of a virus more deadly even than the one they claim to cure. For these men and their servile collaborators are not the doctors of national healing, they are the disease. Today because these men are in responsible positions, we are a sick people, but understanding and correction can make us well."

Leonard understood that otherwise good people can succumb easily to hate and fear. They can remain silent, acquiesce, and betray their friends and people to their everlasting shame. Fear is indeed a loathsome motivator and an ultimate corrupter of the good.

Leonard's piece is an inspiration still, and it is as eloquent a moral clarion as any that has appeared in recent Jewish history.

18

Is There a Relationship between Judaism and Social Justice?

Temple Isaiah, April 14, 1954

Rabbi Beerman here joined a list of distinguished speakers (James Parkes, Samuel Dinin, and Max Nussbaum) in a speakers' series at Temple Isaiah in Los Angeles, whose rabbi, Albert Lewis, moved to LA from Hebrew Union College in the same year as Beerman. This speech was an early articulation of Beerman's belief that Judaism, as he understood it, was inextricably linked to social justice. He laid out three key points, beginning with the theological principle that God could never be fully seen or even comprehended by humans (following the great medieval philosopher Maimonides). Rather, humans seek to approach God by approximating divine attributes—chiefly, for Beerman, "justice, love, mercy." Second, he rearticulated the commonplace view that the essence of Judaism is not abstract principles (or creedal beliefs), but rather concrete experience rooted in the daily lives and moral choices of men and women. Finally, Rabbi Beerman offered up a juxtaposition between two worldviews, both of which were rooted in midcentury American culture. He expressed reverence for the "Judeo-Christian" ethic, a term that gained prominence in the 1930s and was elaborated in Will Herberg's 1955 Protestant-Catholic-Jew. This ethic bespoke, in his words, "love and compassion, tenderness and tolerance, sympathy and empathy." Beerman contrasted that ethic to the spirit of the mass best-seller of 1936, Dale Carnegie's How To Win Friends and Influence People. He believed that this book advanced a view of human behavior that was based on manipulation and exploitation, and thus the antithesis of religion, whose roots lay in an unrelenting commitment to social justice.

I am honored by the opportunity your rabbi has given me to participate in this lecture series. My only fear is that in doing so he may have rendered you an injustice.

I do not share the wisdom, the experience, or the years which the other lecturers—
Dr. Parkes, Dr. Dinin, Rabbi Nussbaum, and your own Rabbi Lewis, enjoy with
such abundance.

What I will present to you tonight will be immature thinking on a challenging
problem, and by good fortune I may be privileged to add to your insights. During
the question and discussion period I feel certain that you will add to mine.

My ideas on this evening's subject are held tentatively, not finally. As I have
altered and changed them thus far throughout my life, I have reason to expect and
to hope that this process will continue. My words then are to be understood as part
of this process of a groping and unclear perception.

The point of view I express is Jewish because my religious experience is Jewish.
But it is a Jewish point of view, not THE Jewish point of view. Judaism, I need not
remind you, offers a wide latitude of belief. No one can speak once and for all for
the Jewish point of view. The God of the prophets, for example, the God of the philosopher Maimonides, the God of the mystic Israel Baal Shem Tov, and even the
naturalistic God concept of Mordecai Kaplan are all Jewish concepts of God. And
yet they share something in common—and it is in their commonality that can be
found what I consider to be the chief source and basis for the relationship between
Judaism and Social Justice.

You will recall that in the second book of the Torah, the book of Exodus, Moses
begs God to let him see God's face, and God replies that no men can see His face
and live—but that (to quote) "I will make all my goodness pass before thee." Then
the narrative tells us, Moses stood in the cleft of the rock and a Voice cried out—
"The Lord, Lord God is merciful and gracious, long-suffering, abundant in loving-
kindness, forgiving iniquity, transgression and sin."

In other words, no man can know the reality of God's nature. That is to say, no
man can see God's face. What the prophets, theologians, and philosophers have
seen is only a shadow, an aspect of divinity, either by their personal religious experiences or by their powers of thought and reason. But God does manifest himself
to man by His ethical attributes. Man can encounter God through justice, love,
mercy; through the ethical attributes of God's nature, man partakes of Divinity.
Without understanding this, without appreciating this, man is removed from God
and from religion. To the extent that man does approach the ethical life in any and
all of the institutions that man has created to serve himself—the family, the nation,
society in general—to that extent, man approaches God.

The real test of religion is life itself. One of the clearest expressions of this idea
I have found in a sermon of Theodore Parker: "To know whom you worship, let
me see you in your shop, let me overhear you in your trade, let me know how you
rent your houses, how you get your money, how you kept it and how it is spent . . .
It is easy to repeat the words of David or of Jesus and to call it prayer. But the
sacramental test of your religion is not your Sunday idly spent, not the words of

David or of Jesus that you repeat; it is your weekday life, your marks and not your words. Tried by this natural test, the Americans are a heathen people, not religious, far from that . . . the national test of religion is the nation's justice—justice to other states abroad, the strong, the weak, and justice to all sorts of men at home. The law-book is the nation's creed, and newspapers chant the actual liturgy and service of the day. What avails it that the priest calls us Christian while the newspapers and the Congress prove us infidel?"

Judaism then has its roots, as well as its chief mode of expression, in the concrete experiences of people. Our ideas are not phrased in pious generalities but in clear and incisive phrases that laid bare the social ills of the community: "Woe unto them that join house to house, that lay field to field," thundered the prophet. Here religious experience is human experience. Religious problems are social problems. Religious values are the values of the common human life.

But I suppose most of this is self-evident. What we are seeking to determine in this series of lectures, as I understand it, is that satisfying blend of our Jewish heritage with American life today. Are the ideals of Judaism sensible and practical? Do they have any relevance for us? Or should they be regarded as something which belongs in religious school, the synagogue—something to be pulled out once a week or once a year on state occasions, like brotherhood week.

The reason we can ask such questions at all lies in the fact that as Americans, from the very beginning of our childhood, we are really taught TWO KINDS OF IDEALS. The one we may call for the purpose of our discussion, the Judeo-Christian ethic. It is the one verbalized in our schools and synagogues and churches. It is enshrined in the great documents of American history, in the writing of the prophets and the poets. It speaks essentially of cooperation among men. It speaks of love and compassion, tenderness and tolerance, sympathy and empathy. It is all based on the assumption that men are really brothers, capable of being friends, and that society is capable of improvement—and it says that these attributes of love and cooperation are truly human attributes.

But over and against this set of ideals are the ideals not so frequently spoken, but taught in more subtle ways, and seen operating in the world all about us, every day of our lives. And these ideals are ingrained in us as deeply as the others. They suggest the following—competition is the ferment of progress. Rugged individualism made us what we are. Nature decreed that life and business is a struggle and the fittest survive. Don't be a do-gooder; be a go-getter. What counts is not knowledge, but know-how. You can't change human nature.

Occasionally the ideals of this dog-eat-dog philosophy are honey-coated and dipped in chlorophyll or anti-enzymes. They go down the more sensitive pallets easier that way and are less offensive. A classic example of this type is the widely acclaimed book *How to Win Friends and Influence People*. The clue is in the title itself—not how to make friends or have friends—but how to *win* them. Friendship is not good in and of itself, the desired end is not a warm relationship between human beings—but the purpose is to influence people, and beyond this, to manipulate others into liking you. Stripped of the chlorophyll wording the real title might be *How to Make Contacts Which May Be Useful in Climbing the Ladder of Success.*

Now what is expected of us? Is it essential to do good, or to Make good? Which is it when the chips are down? Which is primary and which is secondary? Which will get shelved for which in time of crisis in everyday decisions? At a very early age the Biblical command about telling the truth comes into conflict with the laws of Emily Post. Do we not become civilized, gracious, and charming by our little lies; do we not win approval by learning the techniques of approval?

There is a lot of ranting and raving from the pulpits in the nation in particular that we are falling short of our ideals. People are individually falling short of their ideals. People are just following contradictory ideals, and a sign of our maturity will be our readiness to admit this fact.

The solutions to the problems which confront our society cannot be laced up in easy formulas. Our basic religious principles are not going to provide absolute rules of conduct that will automatically tell us what to do under all circumstances. Our basic ideas are the funded wisdom of human experience. They may not give us the answers but they can supply a method and an approach from which each of us after analyzing the particular problem can make a decision.

The question we have to answer for ourselves is, do we want our religious philosophy of life to serve as an active agent in our society? Do we want Judaism to cause us to act and to make decisions, to become personally involved and to make commitments? There are some of us who are content to have our religion be a way of speaking rather than a way of doing (a living).

COMMENTARY BY RABBI ZOË KLEIN

"The real test of religion is life itself," spoke Rabbi Leonard Beerman at Temple Isaiah in 1954. "Judaism then has its roots, as well as its chief mode of expression, in the concrete experiences of people."

I hear echoes in Rabbi Beerman's words of the nineteenth-century Rabbi Israel Salanter, who wrote: "The material needs of my neighbor become my spiritual needs."

These words were one of the favorite quotes of the Jewish philosopher Emmanuel Levinas, for whom the face of the other was as beautiful, terrifying, and unknowable as the face of God. To be in anyone's presence is to be on holy ground. The face is a revelation. Levinas wrote: "When in the presence of the Other I say 'Here I am!' This 'Here I am' is the place through which the Infinite enters into language."

When Rabbi Beerman taught "No man can see God's face. . . . But God does manifest himself to man by His ethical attributes," his words vibrated with twentieth-century theologian Martin Buber's philosophy: "When a person encounters another person in total immediacy, he or she may also experience a glimpse of God."

In other words, God is found between people. And social justice is the art of interactivity. If Judaism "has its roots in the experiences of people," as Rabbi Beerman shared, then Judaism is no less than the foundation and framing of Relationship.

Rabbi Beerman channels the voices of some of our most visionary sages, along with his own unique voice and fathomless wisdom, to issue a timeless challenge for us to bridge our religious ideals with our everyday actions. To be believing realists. One might imagine that religion has its roots in heaven, but for Rabbi Beerman, the roots of Judaism are in the concrete, and therefore are the tediously poured foundation of a just and Godly world.

19

The Problems of the City

A Jewish Dilemma

February 4, 1966

Beerman's speech on Jews and the city at an American Jewish Committee gathering in Los Angeles in 1966 in which Arthur Greenberg was to be installed as president captures well his unique position in the community. On one hand, he was friendly with Greenberg and knew many of those in attendance. On the other hand, he came not to assuage his audience with calming words, but rather to challenge them with prophetic fervor, delivering a jeremiad focused on the ills of the city. He was speaking in a time of increasing social and racial unrest in Los Angeles and across the country. The Watts riots had broken out less than a year before in August 1965. LA Mayor Sam Yorty was perceived by many to be increasingly insensitive to claims of racial inequities. President Johnson's stirring call in 1964 for a Great Society seemed ever more elusive.

Beerman used this occasion to articulate his vision of the vocation of the Jew. He began by expressing his own sense of alienation from the city—and, for that matter, from any place. Indeed, his place was not the here and now, but rather "the place that is coming into being." So too Jews, for all of their social and economic integration, carried within them a recollection of their forebears' marginality. This served as the inspiration for their hopes for a better future. Beerman concluded by summoning up the example of the circle surrounding the great sixteenth-century Jewish mystic in Safed, R. Isaac Luria (1534–1572). Luria built a new kabbalistic system around the recognition of the incompleteness of the world—and the moral imperative to engage in repairing it. Beerman, who was not normally given to mysticism, made frequent reference in his writings to the mystic Luria and his followers as sources of inspiration for effecting constructive change in the world.

I have a very special interest in being here, not only because Arthur Greenberg is about to be elected President of the American Jewish Committee, and not only because I am among so many friends and members of my congregation, but also because I share in so many concerns of this Committee: a desire to have a part in shaping the future of American Jewish life; to preserve the rich cultural and spiritual tradition which is our inheritance as Jews, even as we work toward the achievement of a more complete participation on our American democracy; to work toward the preservation of pluralism and voluntarism in the Jewish community, to seek that happy blending, never fully achieved, of the very best of our heritage as Jews and as Americans; to labor unceasingly to uphold the hands of our brethren who live in lands far removed from ours, in Israel and in other parts of the world, and to affirm their struggle for dignity and for freedom as our own; to labor with all of the weapons of learning and mind and persuasion toward the achievement of an America freed of the enslavements of bigotry, intolerance, and inequality, an America cleansed of those humiliations which so many millions of our fellow-citizens are daily forced to endure. (If I share these concerns with the members of the American Jewish Committee who are gathered here today, it is not that I give my blessing to all that troubles certain members of the AJC. As an example: With two-thirds of the world's population not being sure where their next meal is coming from, I have not been exercised over-much about the inability of a few Jews to be able to be members of certain exclusive eating clubs in the great cities of America.)

I feel singularly unqualified to be here discussing with you the subject assigned to me, "The Problems of the City: A Jewish Dilemma." After all, I am just an ordinary rabbi who desires nothing more than an ordinary chance to be precisely what I am: A rabbi, a member of that profession, according to a spate of recent articles, in search of a purpose and a meaning more relevant than the one currently assigned to us. I am not, nor have I ever been, an expert on the problems of the city. But push a button, and you can always get a rabbi to talk about anything and a Jewish dilemma. Sex and the Jewish dilemma, the death of God and the Jewish dilemma, Viet Nam and the Jewish problem, intermarriage and the Jewish problem, the elephant, as the story goes, and the Jewish problem. And so the button was pushed, and here I am to talk about "The Problems of the City: A Jewish Dilemma."

There is a second reason why I feel particularly unqualified to speak on this subject. It is because I have never been at home in the city. In fact, I have never been at home anywhere. I have never been at home anywhere that *is*. My home has forever been the place that is coming into being: Not the here, not the now, but the not yet. That has been my home, and that is what being a Jew means to me: The challenge of the not yet, the refusal always to accept that which is as being ultimate and final; the certainty that I cannot rest unless I am helping to bring into being something better than I am, something better than I know, a place better than I inhabit. "Get thee out of the land and go to the place I will show you" was the first command given to Abraham, and with it began the history of the ancient Hebrews, our forebears. To be a Jew has meant to leave the fixed, the comfortable, the familiar, and to reach toward that place which is not yet. Surely this sprawling, vulgar mess we call Los Angeles is nothing that any of us want to settle for. Gallantly, ceaselessly, we must all strive toward the creation of a place of greater dignity and integrity and responsibility than the one we now inhabit. And happily, there are willing hands to help us.

You have considered this morning the problems of the city. I trust you will agree that those problems are a local manifestation of a disease that poisons the bloodstream of the total society. All of the injustices and abuses of America drain into New York, Chicago, Los Angeles. The aged, the impoverished, the ill, the newly immigrated, the culturally disadvantaged, the castoffs of a ruthlessly competitive society, these are all huddled together in the great urban centers of America. In his address to Congress on January 26th, 1966, President Johnson listed in considerable detail the agenda of the American city: The problem of the poor and the Negro unable to be free from their ghettos, exploited in their quest for the necessities of life; the high human cost of these problems: Crime, delinquency, welfare loads, disease and health hazards. He spoke of the tragic waste and chaos that threaten their children, born into the stifling air of overcrowded places, destined for inadequate and segregated schools, a poor diet, streets of fear and sordid temptations; the problem of living without work or without a sense of dignity; the cities that grow like our own, without rational design, without a sense of their own integrity; the countryside being devoured before our very eyes; the flight to the suburbs of the more fortunate men and women who might have provided the leadership and the means for reversing the decline. These wounds of the city are there for all of us to see. If we stand here in this lovely room, set in this elegant segregated suburb, and we look out over the urban concentration camp you and I have helped to create, we ourselves can see the conflict between the central city and the suburbs, between those who have and those who are poor. We can see and feel the ethnic tensions that rend the fabric of our urban life. We can see and feel the frustration, the bitterness, and the despair. A city teeming with the constant threat of violence. But as Harvey Cox has pointed out in his book, *The Secular City,* the cleavages of the city correspond to the cleavages in the souls of men who live in the city. The way man has arranged the life of the city reflects the fears and the fantasies of his own inner life, and his own inner life is in turn molded by the very city that he devises. Where the sickness of segregation locks the Negroes and other minority groups into their ghettos, where we will not permit ourselves and our children to have normal contact with them, the racial stereotypes are not only perpetuated, they go unchallenged.

We have paid a terrible price, for all the greatness of America, we have paid a terrible human price for the kind of city we have perpetrated and perpetuated.

How shall we measure the frustration and loneliness and the despair and the bitterness and the loss of manhood and the sense of powerlessness and the nobodyness that we ourselves have had at least an unconscious hand in perpetuating? It is we, with all of our sophistication and education, we, who may be the most culturally disadvantaged people in all of the world; we, who may be the most deprived human beings we can possibly imagine. For many of our own young people are only able to find personal fulfillment in working with people who are supposedly the culturally disadvantaged, revealing their own impoverishment as human beings. We have lacked the moral courage, the ingenuity, the willingness to sacrifice, necessary to treat the burgeoning problems of our city as a burning responsibility. Perhaps the task is so far reaching as to discourage or frighten us. But far too many of our people have suffered from a special deprivation of their own, a deprivation of conscience, a shriveling incapacity to feel, a shrinking inability to understand that social and human responsibility may have to override the individual freedom to do with ourselves and our property what we will; the inability to understand that human responsibility must be primary.

And what is the Jewish dilemma in all of this? "What does it mean to a Jew in this society?" as Neil Sandberg and Rita Hoffman put in their communication to me. Are we to be concerned primarily with ourselves and our own special needs as a community, or do we have some obligation to this religiously and culturally pluralistic world of ours, some special obligation as Jews? Are we to be concerned primarily with ourselves and our problems? As Jews, we have been challenged, not only as inhabitants of the city along with the rest, but also as a community with a special structure of agencies and services. And problems born of the changing character of our city—the so-called invasion or the in-migration of the Negroes— are requiring Jewish agencies to ask questions about their role. We know that here in Los Angeles the Westside Jewish Center, with the cooperation of the American Jewish Committee and other community relations agencies, initiated a program to encourage integration and neighborhood stability in the area immediately bordering the Center where Negroes have been moving. But what of the social welfare agencies, the vocational and psychiatric services, the hospitals? We have automatically accepted the notion of the non-sectarian basis of hospital service. What of the other? Is the role of the vocational service, the family service, and the psychiatric service to deal solely with the problems of Jews, a purpose for which they were originally established? Or are they too to be available to the total community? These questions are being confronted by the professionals in the field. Other communities have had to face them sooner than ourselves because of the nature of their changing neighborhoods. And a variety of answers have been forthcoming, each of them reasonable, sensible, intelligible, and contradictory.

My own response is based on no profound analysis of the problem, but on a consideration of what the question means in the shadow of a more fundamental question, "What does it mean to be a Jew?" To be a Jew today, sociologically at least, no longer means to be a marginal man, an outsider. It means to be an insider, a status not completely achieved, to be sure, but more nearly so than ever before in our history. The other minority groups are the Jews of our time. The other minority groups are the marginal men of this year and the difficult years to come. To be among the privileged, we know, is to be a Jew. That is one way of looking at it.

But to be a Jew is something else again, inwardly at least. To be a Jew is to know the world's slow stain, and to know how that stain can touch every human being. To be a Jew is to be the bearer of a great hope, to believe with all your heart and all your soul and all your might that the world has not yet been redeemed, that man has not yet fulfilled the divine potential with which God has blessed us. This is what our tradition has always called the Messianic expectancy: The vibrant hope that leaves no place for contentment, complacency, for the rapturous acceptance of ourselves or our country or our city or the world as it is.

To be a Jew in this day, therefore, is to be willing to face the continuing risk of man's developing freedom. We must open ourselves and our energies to the task of the community. We must be among the healers of the city, and our healing must take the form of affirmative action. This we would do as Jews and as Americans: As Jews, motivated by a special obligation to the human, a special obligation to seek the fulfillment of the divine potential in all men. Urban planning, the war on poverty, merit employment, segregation, population pressures, exploitation, social disorder, racial tensions, education: These are all part of the unified problem as we understand it. And we must, both as members of this agency and all community agencies, know and study the problems of urban planning. As my colleague and friend Rabbi Richard G. Hirsch has said, we must be among those who stimulate the formation of citizens' groups. We must be among those who participate responsibly in these citizens' groups concerned with the rehabilitation and the reconstruction of human lives in our community. We must be among those who are willing to be engaged in the creation of a climate conducive to serious assault upon the problems of poverty, inequality, and segregation. We must be among those who are willing to work for equal opportunity, to support legislation and encourage the enforcement of existing legislation in the field of housing and employment. And we must be among those who are also willing to work for peace, because only in a world freed of the threat of war and Cold War can we invest an honest and significant amount of our capital energy into the enormous task of the rehabilitation about which we are talking. We cannot pretend that the war against poverty as it is presently being conducted is anything more than a series of skirmishes. And we cannot pretend that we are really being serious about the assault on the problem of the Negro and other minority groups, so long as the bulk of our financial capacity and energy is spent upon defense or the potential destruction of those whom we presume to call our enemies. Only in a situation of peace and in a world at peace can we authentically face the challenge of the creation of the kind of city we want to live in.

Lastly, we must have the courage to be honest with ourselves, and we must have the courage to dream. We must admit that some of us are really not eager to bring about an integrated society. We are honestly not ready to pay the price that an integrated society would demand of us. Already many of us are fleeing the public schools with our children. Many of those who live in our own comfortably segregated neighborhoods are surely not willing to make the sacrifice, inwardly, emotionally, of living in a truly integrated society. For the kind of integrated society that we are talking about will demand a sacrifice from us that many of us are not yet willing to give. With all of our pious protestations to the contrary, with all the remarkable efforts being made by this agency and others in the community and throughout the nation, I do not think that we are honestly ready to live in that kind of world that we have been talking about: To face the personal sacrifice of some of our own treasured, but not always significant, values. And we also bear a secret, you and I. We know that at that end point the deprived and the disadvantaged are now seeking to achieve, there stands a world that you and I inhabit, a world of unhappiness and discontent, where we really do not enjoy the blessings of freedom, where we drift without meaning and without direction, unsure of what we are and what tomorrow means, or what it is all about. And we know that this comfortable world of sham stands waiting for those who now so desperately want to live in it with you and me. We cannot take away from those disadvantaged their right to enjoy our unhappiness, the unhappiness that shrouds our struggle for personal meaning and fulfillment. That is their decision to make, but that is the terrible secret that we bear: The knowledge that we are caught in the midst of a way of life which brings both blessing and the terror of confusion.

In the sixteenth century in the city of Safed in the land of Israel, there lived a mystic brotherhood of Jews who were followers of a young teacher named Isaac Luria. This mystic brotherhood of men was composed of human beings of unusual piety. Among the moral precepts to which they pledged themselves, they were expected to make their hearts the abode of the Divine presence by banishing all profane thoughts and concentrating on holy things. They were not to speak evil to any creature; they were not to become angry at anyone or to curse. They were to speak only the truth, and they were to behave in a kindly spirit toward their fellow men, no matter who those fellow men might be. They were to confess their sins every night before they retired, and each night they were to sit upon the ground and to mourn the destruction of the Temple in Jerusalem and to weep over the sins that postponed the redemption of the world. No day was to pass without giving of *zedakah,* charity. This brotherhood of the school of Isaac Luria had as its chief aim the bringing of the Messiah by this series of spiritual exercises, and for them the Messiah was not to come just as a miracle of God's favor, as in Christianity. It would represent man's own unfolding achievement. The brotherhood believed that through spiritual discipline the sparks of holiness scattered in all things would be returned to their source in God. All created things, they believed, were made up of holy sparks.

They asked themselves how a good and perfect God could have produced this world of imperfection. If God is infinite, how could He have produced that which is finite? If God is everywhere, how could there be room for the world at all? Where could the world have fitted in if God fills all space? And according to one doctrine developed by these people, God withdrew from Himself into Himself, a shrinking Deity, in order to leave room for the world to emerge. And when God withdrew from Himself into Himself, He left an empty space into which the world of time and space and things could emerge. But it was not a complete withdrawal, since in principle nothing can exist without God; so a tiny, thin line of Divine light penetrated into the open space in order to sustain the creation. At first the light was too strong and shattered the vessel containing it. As a result of this breakage of the vessel containing the light, holy sparks, sparks of divinity, were left in all things in the universe. And the task of man was to live in a spirit of dedication, self-consecration, and humility, and thus reclaim these holy sparks and return them to their Source. When this work of restoration was completed, then and only then would the Messiah emerge into history.

Far removed as we are from the brotherhood of Rabbi Isaac Luria in Safed, sitting here in Beverly Hills surrounded by Mayor Yorty's Los Angeles, far removed as we are in thought and in time, could it not be that this human city of ours, this world of ours, still has need for us to be ourselves as Jews, still needs us to have the courage to stand apart from the coarse and the vulgar and the commonplace, still needs us to seek in our lives that which is holy in all things and in all people, still needs us to look upon our lives as a sacred responsibility to join ourselves not with the mechanisms of deceit and hate and destruction and division but with the life-giving, life-affirming forces of the universe, still needs us to aid in clearing all the waste places of ignorance, prejudice, and brutality, all that divides man against himself and against his own divine potential to be a man? Surely this dilemma of the Jew, one that we share with all thinking, feeling, compassionate human beings, is one that summons all of our courage and ingenuity and honesty. Let us not shrink from this challenge.

COMMENTARY BY PROFESSOR RABBI ARYEH COHEN

Rabbi Yehoshua ben Hananyah traveled to Rome and there he saw marble pillars draped in many lavish curtains so that they would not be damaged by the cold of the winter or the heat of the summer. Walking in the market he saw a poor person lying on a reed mat and covered by a reed mat (*Leviticus Rabba*, ed. Margaliot 27:1).

The very term: "beauty": do you
    hear that? Old man

unable to to even ask for anything anymore. The one without a written
   plea on piece of card-
board. The one just standing there by the door of the 7/11 so
drunk or stoned or hungover and *cold* he cannot even remember
      he is supposed
to ask—that is his role here in this hall of mirrors—ah friend—that man,
do you know him, the one I have to suppose you *will not walk past.*
(Jorie Graham, "Posterity," from *Overlord: Poems* 2006)

The moral gaze is aesthetic at its core, distinguishing between the beauty of people and the ugliness of their poverty. To maintain a moral gaze in the face of an amoral culture, which lauds artistic or architectural importance detached from the human pain and degradation in which it is mired, is an act of courage.

To be a Jew, in reality, to be a person, Leonard Beerman taught us, is to wake up in the morning, and while sitting with our coffee at the kitchen table, look outside and really see.

Everything follows from that.

20

UCLA Teach-In on Vietnam War

March 24, 1966

Beerman joined the eminent philosopher Herbert Marcuse, his friend Stanley Sheinbaum, and others at a teach-in on the Vietnam War at the UCLA campus in Westwood, as can be seen in the teach-in program that follows. As a confirmed pacifist, Beerman was deeply concerned about the war and the escalating loss of life that followed President Johnson's decision to increase air attacks on the North Vietnamese in 1965. In this talk, Beerman opened by situating the war in the twenty-year "adventure" into conflict that was the Cold War. The enmity issuing from the Cold War, he suggested, yielded no winners or losers, just more insensitivity to the desires and needs of the putative enemy.

Beerman held both sides in the Vietnam War responsible. The American aerial assault was, to his mind, "repugnant." But he also lamented the fact that North Vietnam, like the United States, held to "the arrogant certainty of its own utter rightness." The moral blindness from this certainty exacted a very heavy toll in human lives, as Beerman would continue to call out and mourn until the war's end.

"It was the best of times; it was the worst of times. It was the age of wisdom; it was the age of foolishness. It was the season of Light; it was the season of Darkness. It was the spring of hope; it was the winter of despair. We had everything before us. We had nothing before us. We were all going direct to Heaven; we were all going direct the other way . . ."

With these bitter words Charles Dickens opened his novel *A Tale of Two Cities*. The paradoxes to which he addressed himself persist in our time.

To live in the midst of such paradoxes is the particular challenge and burden of our generation.

VIETNAM TEACH-IN

presented by

THE UCLA VIETNAM DAY COMMITTEE

12 Noon - 12 Midnight

MARCH 25, 1966

Grand Ballroom

Student Union   UCLA Campus

FIGURE 16. UCLA Teach-In I (1966).

12 Noon-12:35   SI CASADY
Immediate past president, California Democratic Council;
owner and publisher of the El Cajon Valley News; winner
of the first annual editorial competition sponsored by the
So. Calif. ACLU in 1964.

12:35-1:00   STANLEY SHEINBAUM
Staff member, Center for the Study of Democratic Institutions, Santa Barbara; former consultant to the Government
of Vietnam; coordinator, Public Admin. and Economics, MSU
Vietnam project.

1:00-1:45   FELIX GREENE
Author of the book, China, and the producer of the docu-
mentary film, China; recent visitor to North Vietnam;
reporter, traveler, former commentator for CBC, BBC.

1:45-2:15   RUSSELL JOHNSON
Peace Education Secretary, New England region, American
Friends Service Committee; director, Quaker Conferences
in Southern Asia, 1961-65; recent visitor to South Vietnam
and Southeast Asia.

2:15-2:45   WILLIAM WORTHY
News analyst; reporter for Baltimore Afro-American;
visitor to Cuba, China, Southeast Asia, South Africa;
Ford and Nieman Foundation Fellow.

2:45-3:00   BERTRAND RUSSELL TAPE
A message recorded especially for this Teach-In.

3:00-3:30   BEN MARGOLIS
Los Angeles lawyer, specialist in labor and constitutional
law; member, International Law Committee, National Lawyers
Guild; co-author, Lawyers Brief on Vietnam.

**3:30-3:45   ENTERTAINMENT – JOSEPH BYRD AND THE
                     WORKERS**

3:45-4:00   LEONARD LEVY
National Vice-President, Amalgamated Clothing Workers
of America, AFL-CIO.

4:00-4:30   RABBI LEONARD BEERMAN
Temple Leo Baeck; special field of interest in ethical
implications of religion to areas of social concern.

4:30-5:00   FRANK GREENWOOD
Author of the play, If We Must Die.

FIGURE 17. UCLA Teach-In II (1966).

5:00-5:30 ARTHUR CARSTENS
Senior staff member, Institute of Industrial Relations,
UCLA; candidate for the Democratic nomination to Congress
from the 27th Congressional district.

**5:30-6:00 ENTERTAINMENT – NEW FOLKSAY SINGERS
AND LENNY HAROLD**

6:00-6:30 DON WHEELDIN
Immediate past president, Pasadena CORE; author; veteran
of World War II; on faculty of the New Left School.

6:30-7:00 MARSHALL WINDMILLER
Associate Prof. of International Relations, San Francisco
State; co-author of Communism in India; editor of The
Liberal Democrat; foreign affairs commentator on KPFK.

7:00-7:25 WILLIAM WINTER
News analyst; correspondent; publisher of William Winter
Comments.

7:25-7:35 REV. STEPHEN FRITCHMAN (Moderator)
Minister, First Unitarian Church of Los Angeles; leading
peace advocate; writer, lecturer on social and religious
problems and contemporary society.

7:35-8:00 HERBERT MARCUSE
Professor of Philosophy, UC San Diego; formerly, OSS and
State Dept., 1942-50; Senior Fellow, Russian Institute, Col-
umbia U.; Senior Fellow, Russian Research Center, Harvard.

8:00-8:45 MRS. FANNY LOU HAMER
Representative of the Mississippi Freedom Democratic Party;
appeared on nationwide TV and radio to defend civil rights.

8:45-9:00 ENTERTAINMENT – MIKE JANUSZ
International folk singer

9:00-9:30 MRS. DOROTHY HEALEY
Southern California chairman, Communist Party, USA;
former Deputy State Labor Commissioner, former International Vice-President, Cannery and Agricultural Workers
Union, CIO.

9:30-9:50 ISIDORE ZIFERSTEIN
Psychiatrist; Research Psychiatrist, Institute for
Psychiatric and Psychosomatic Research, Mt. Sinai Hos-
pital; lecturer and author on the psychology of war.

FIGURE 17. Continued

Forces of change beyond the control of even the best men are pushing aside the remaining ramparts of the old certainties, those truths, those values which once sheltered and comforted us. Peace is cracked in a hundred shivers. The air of the Cold War sweeps through the long winter night. In America we look outward and the world envies or despises or distrusts us, we look inward and are plagued by the rising tide of the poor, the urban hopeless, the massive and still unresolved protest of the Negroes.

We seem to be living at the end of one era and the beginning of another. And it can be emotionally wearing to be living at such a time, vaguely knowing that something is coming to an end, and something is being born.

For twenty years we have been living through a time euphemistically called a Cold War. For twenty years our government and its people have been acting on the assumption that communism is on the march for the conquest of the world, that it is the manifest destiny of the United States to save the world from suffering this fate. In the pursuit of this mirage, this myth, we have engaged in international adventurism. In the process our hands are covered with blood. We have become as brutalized as our enemies, as we have shown in Vietnam, torturing, killing, burning, combatants and non-combatants alike.

For twenty years we have sacrificed upon the altar of war and its preparation the greatest gifts of this nation, the gifts of mind and technique and sensitivity, and in so doing, we have demonstrated a total contempt for man.

This same era has given us a glimpse of what man's knowledge could have done for us. But we have made no serious effort to bring this golden age into being. Compassion has not been a full-time occupation for any of us. Our ingenuity, our resources, have literally been swallowed up by our consuming endeavor to stalk the enemy. Our laboratories, our universities, our research centers have found themselves dedicated to the same pursuits.

For twenty years the angel of death has hovered over our civilization, fending off any serious endeavor to re-cultivate the waste places or to make a serious assault upon the problems of human anguish. The efforts of the so-called Great Society are so feeble and shabby they can hardly be considered more than a token of what needs to be done.

The result of all this cannot adequately be measured, but you and I know it in the form of greater frustration and estrangement. The poor know it in the form of even greater poverty. For it is upon the poverty of [the] multitude that the unswerving, irresponsible, irrepressible, dedication to defense and war is built.

Such an age as ours may very well bring tourists to the moon but it will hardly make a contribution to the human spirit. For in such an age, the artists, the thoughtful man, the man of wisdom, the student, even the man of religion, is no longer able to see the healing role the responsible use of his talents would demand of him.

It is in the context of such a time that we have come, with all of our different and sometimes contradictory points of view, to consider the war in Vietnam.

And it frightens me to think that I do not have all the solutions to the conflict. It frightens me because I think I am, as Americans go, reasonably informed and intelligent and concerned. It frightens me to think what I think may never reach that cold heart where computers calculate the risk of continuing, enlarging, or ending the conflict.

And yet it frightens me even more to contemplate how I should be able to face the ugliness of my own silence in the presence of what I know to be criminal, the brutalization of our moral sensitivity, the indifference with which we learn of the daily body count.

I am not a military strategist. I was a terrible soldier. I cannot write a novel, or make a television set or send a rocket to the moon. But does that mean that I cannot make an intelligent judgment on whether a work of fiction or a television program is worthwhile, or whether the moon is not better off being just for lovers rather than for American or Russian tourists?

We are responsible for anything against which we do not protest. What we do here then is an expression of that responsibility. If we speak of the tragedy of Vietnam and the failure of governments to end that conflict, we think not only of Vietnam, but of a world torn by contending ideologies and ambitions. It is our task to articulate the human conscience in a world in which the conscience is shrunken, shriveled, petrified, rarely able to move beyond the narrow boundaries we have set for it.

Each of the contending ideologies is wrapped in the arrogant certainty of its own utter rightness. Our country asserts its determination to stop ruthless Communist aggression, to defend freedom for Vietnam and the world. North Vietnam, the National Liberation Front, the People's Republic of China proclaim their intention to throw back the ruthlessly aggressive American imperialists in defense of the right of the Vietnamese to govern themselves, and on behalf of all nations seeking national liberation.

We know what price has been paid for this relentless, passionate dogmatism. In Vietnam, war has become a way of life, conscripting the young, making widows, orphans. Freedom and justice are hollow words, a mockery. They mean torment. Both sides have been forced to commit atrocities to mock their claims of self-righteousness. Both have been drawn farther and farther into the maelstrom of destruction.

Surely we must know that war cannot serve the interests of man any longer. In this age, with these weapons, how can war do anything but destroy our hopes, our accomplishments, our pretensions of humanity? There is no moral justification for the horror that our planes, our massive firepower, our brutality have inflicted upon the people of Vietnam.

"All I ask," Albert Camus once told us, "is that in the midst of a murderous world we agree to reflect on murder and to make a choice. After that we can distinguish those who accept the consequence of being murderers themselves or the accomplices of murderers, and those who refuse to do so with all their force and being."

The United States has made such a choice, and we find it repugnant. We call upon our government to stop the air attacks as an affront to human decency and unworthy of a great people. We call upon our government to express a clear intention that it intends to end the war with a settlement that will include withdrawing its forces and dismantling its military basis. Such a pronouncement supported by immediate and meaningful actions to prove our good faith is necessary if either the regime in Saigon or the NLF or the N. Vietnamese will take seriously overtures to negotiate.

The people and government of North Vietnam and the NLF have chosen whether they will be murderers or accomplices of murderers, and we must be shocked and repelled. We must address to them this appeal to abandon the methods of torture, assassination, the terror. They too are an affront to the whole concept of human decency.

We ask of them that they declare their unqualified willingness to meet with representatives of the United States and the present government of S. Vietnam to negotiate peace based on the agreements of 1954.

It is difficult to imagine that a world such as ours, divided by suspicion and hatred, is capable of turning from war and toward the resolution of conflict by non-violent means. Yet this is the choice we must make. Whether or not we will compromise with murder.

We need those who have the muscle to care. And more than caring we need those who have the courage to be compassionate, who will preserve and cultivate an enduring vision of the good and the tender.[1]

COMMENTARY BY RABBI SANFORD RAGINS

Psychologist Carl Rogers taught that therapists must use words as scalpels—not to wound, but to heal. That aptly describes how Leonard Beerman, a therapist of the conscience, often worked, as in this powerful talk early in the war in Vietnam. A new term—"body count"—had just been added to the American vocabulary. Leonard immediately saw the horror and suffering lurking behind this ugly euphemism, and he resolved to use his words to awaken our consciences.

And what powerful words they were!

Incisive, even blunt: "Our hands are covered with blood."

Sharp: "Peace is cracked in a hundred shivers."

Eloquent: "It is our task to articulate the human conscience in a world in which the conscience is shrunken, shriveled, petrified, rarely able to move beyond the narrow boundaries we have set for it."

Challenging and tough, indeed penetrating: "We are responsible for anything against which we do not protest."

Leonard's passionately held core beliefs are also evident.

His pacifism: "Surely we must know that war cannot serve the interests of man [sic!] any longer."

21

Notes for Symposium on Black Power

January 6, 1967

Beerman's notes for this symposium on Black Power offer insight into the radical cast of his thought. He was writing in a time of growing unrest and consciousness-raising regarding race relations in the United States. Somewhat unusually for a rabbi sitting in upscale Bel-Air, he evinced considerable sympathy for the banner of Black Power, deeming it an essential rallying cry for the disaffected African American underclass. He evoked the words of Black Power leader Stokely Carmichael, who would earn the opprobrium of many in the Jewish community because of his strong anti-Zionist stance. Beerman asserted that, through his critique of integration, Carmichael was pushing toward a state of "psychological equality" in which black people would be empowered to lift themselves out of the state of poverty and deprivation in which white America continued to place them. Beerman affirmed that drive as an antidote to what he saw as the institutional racism of America.

The call for Black Power issued by the Student Nonviolent Coordinating Committee emerged on the Mississippi march led by James Meredith last July. But the concept of Black Power is not a recent phenomenon. It has grown out of the agitation and the activity of different people and organizations in many Negro communities over the years.

No organization has been able to speak to the growing militancy of young Negro people living in the urban ghetto. The significance of Black Power as a slogan is that black people are going to use the words they want to use. Black people are working to provide the Negro community with a position of strength or power from which to make its voice heard.

The double reality of Negro life in America is that Negroes are poor and they are black. All of the other problems afflicting the American Negro arise from this two-sided reality. The advocates of Black Power are attempting to win political power for impoverished Southern blacks. They are convinced that this is a country which does not function by morality, love, and non-violence, but by power. The purpose of political power and its achievement is that the community thus represented can make or participate in making the decisions which will govern their destinies, and thus bring about basic change in their day-to-day living. To achieve political power meant the struggle to achieve the right to vote in an atmosphere of racist terror, which ruled large sections of the deep South until recent years. Voter registration drives were begun. In Alabama, candidates for sheriff tax-assessors were placed on the ballot, and the symbol of their party was a panther, a bold, beautiful animal representing the strength and dignity of the black people, Stokely Carmichael says. Politically, Black Power means the coming together of black people to elect representatives and to force their representatives to speak to their needs.

And the reason for the drive to organize in the black community is the need for psychological equality. For the advocates of Black Power, the reality of America is that it is a nation that is racist from top to bottom.

How do the advocates of Black Power, Stokely Carmichael and the rest, see the United States? They see this country like an octopus of exploitation, "its tentacles stretching from Mississippi and Harlem to South America, the Middle East, Southern Africa, Vietnam." They see the United States as a great colonial power, and its colonies include the black ghettos within its borders, north and south. A totally different America must be born if the racism which sustains this pattern is to die.

White society, according to the advocates of Black Power, prefers to talk about integration. Integration means the man who makes it, it means that a man leaves his black brothers behind in the ghetto as fast "as his new sports car will take him," as Stokely Carmichael puts it. And integration speaks to the problem of blackness in a despicable way. It assumes, or rather it is based on a complete acceptance of the notion that in order to have a decent house or an education, blacks must move into a white neighborhood or send their children to a white school. This reinforces among both black and white the idea that white is automatically better, and black is automatically inferior. Integration, therefore, is a subterfuge, allowing the nation to focus on a few Southern children getting into white schools while ignoring the 94% who are left behind in unimproved, all-black schools.

What the advocates of Black Power are driving for is really a psychological equality. What they want to achieve is the revolutionary idea that black people are able to do things themselves. And the only way to bring this about, they believe, is through an aroused and continuing black consciousness. Black people must do things for themselves; they must get poverty money they will control and spend themselves, they must conduct tutorial programs themselves, so that black children can identify with black people.

America is racist from top to bottom, and this racism is not a problem of human relations, but of a pattern of exploitation maintained actively or silently by society as a whole. And the rebuilding of society is not primarily a task of the blacks; it is the responsibility of the whites.

COMMENTARY BY RABBI CHAIM SEIDLER-FELLER

Leonard was my mentor in social justice and in rabbinic dignity. It is an honor for me to comment on his "Notes for the Symposium on Black Power." Although I will take issue with him, I consider my reflections to be part of our ongoing conversation.

The primary problem with the call for Black Power was its overt appeal for separation and its concomitant identification of all white people as the enemy. The movement rhetoric was inflammatory, and the trappings of violence were evident from its inception. As a rule any call to power that is not contextualized in a constructive framework will quickly degenerate into militancy and will eventually self-destruct. And disenfranchisement never constitutes a license for nihilistic violence.

What's more, as a strategy, revolutionary zeal intended to overthrow the extant system was bound to fail. Social, political, and economic changes in American society were traditionally the result of evolutionary forces that worked to transform the system from within. Our deeply rooted commitment to justice as articulated in our foundational principles laid claim to *all* Americans. Martin Luther King's success was a function of the fact that his pursuit of rights for African Americans was framed as a campaign for a better America for everyone. Psychologically and societally my own commitment to civil rights is a product of my having internalized the moral imperatives of the Jewish tradition that compel me to act on behalf of the vulnerable and of my contractual responsibility (obligation?) as a citizen to America as a whole.

22

Letter to President Lyndon Johnson

April 13, 1967

Never content to remain silent in the face of injustice, Beerman penned a letter to President Lyndon B. Johnson in 1967, as he would on subsequent occasions. Here he implored the president to avoid using his recently submitted tax payment for the Vietnam War. Instead, he recommended to the president that he use tax revenues to pursue peace-loving activities.

Dear Mr. President:

Mrs. Beerman and I have just paid our income tax for the year 1966. That portion of our tax which helps to sustain the war in Vietnam has been paid involuntarily. We have no wish to support what we consider to be unjust. We should be happy to pay even a greater proportion of our income for works of healing and peace, but the acts of violence being perpetrated by our government violate our conscience. That portion of our tax that helps make these acts possible we pay under protest.

Our hearts reach out to you and to all who must face the terror of decision. We pray always that the courage of compassion and conciliation may come to those who guide and serve both our country and those who oppose it.

Sincerely,
Leonard I. Beerman

COMMENTARY BY JUDITH VIORST

The second half of the sixties was a time of accelerating political turmoil as objection to US involvement in Vietnam expressed itself in a widening range of private and public protests: massive demonstrations, teach-ins, the burning of draft cards,

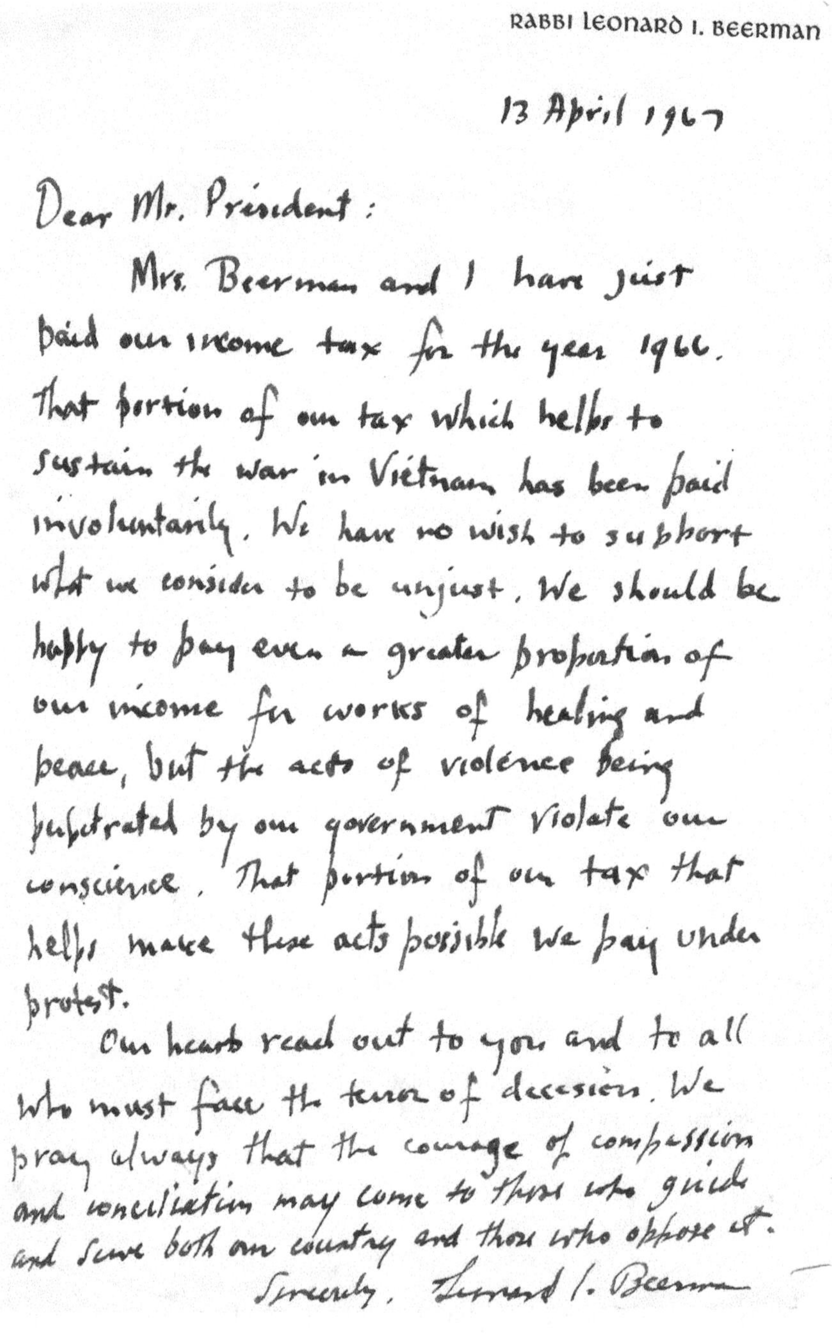

RABBI LEONARD I. BEERMAN

13 April 1967

Dear Mr. President:

Mrs. Beerman and I have just paid our income tax for the year 1966. That portion of our tax which helps to sustain the war in Vietnam has been paid involuntarily. We have no wish to support what we consider to be unjust. We should be happy to pay even a greater proportion of our income for works of healing and peace, but the acts of violence being perpetrated by our government violate our conscience. That portion of our tax that helps make these acts possible we pay under protest.

Our hearts reach out to you and to all who must face the terror of decision. We pray always that the courage of compassion and conciliation may come to those who guide and serve both our country and those who oppose it.

Sincerely, Leonard I. Beerman

FIGURE 18. Leonard Beerman's letter to President Johnson (1967).

the occupying of university buildings, pamphlets, and petitions and letters like Leonard's from women and men opposed to the use of their taxes to fund this war.

As a mother of young children living in Washington, DC, I joined Another Mother for Peace and Women Strike for Peace, spending many weekends marching my kids around the White House, chanting, "What do you want? Peace. When do you want it? Now." (On other weekends we picketed to the chant "What do you want? Freedom," while I explained to my sons that no, this wasn't a mistake—we were doing civil rights, not peace, today.)

The women I marched with back then made an effort to always be "properly" dressed, intending to make the point that even very middle-class, very "proper" Americans were passionately against this unjust war. Like Leonard and the decorous tone he strikes in his oppositional but law-abiding letter, we wished to set a tone of respectful rebellion.

By the early 1970s, however, even we proper ladies needed to up our game in protesting the war, joining a sit-in in the halls of Congress and going—briefly—to jail. And Leonard, in the years since his 1967 letter, vastly expanded the realm of rabbinical proprieties, showing us in a lifetime of courageous words and deeds what can and must be done in the face of injustice.

23

Rosh Hashanah Eve

September 30, 1970 (5731)

In this sermon on the eve of the Jewish New Year in 1970, Beerman reveals the full array of his homiletical talents. He begins by expressing delight at seeing old friends, members of Leo Baeck Temple, who appeared in the sanctuary once or twice a year, as was and is the custom of many American Jews. He then launches into an exposition of one of the most vexing of biblical stories, which is recounted on Rosh Hashanah: the 'Akedah, or binding of Isaac by his father.

The cautionary tale of the story is to warn against submission to irrational or destructive authority. Many in the modern world have replaced absolute faith in God with absolute faith in the State, which calls its citizens to express their loyalty by going to war. Returning to the theme of the Vietnam War, albeit in veiled fashion, Beerman takes stock of the destruction to human life caused by that war—and all war. The present-day challenge—and the opportunity afforded by Rosh Hashanah—is to break free from the modern "condition of servitude" and resist the impulse to barbarism, choosing instead justice and peace.

I come to this night always with a reverence and awe that befit an occasion which has so many mystifying powers. It is difficult to speak in the midst of such an accumulation of moods and expectations, the almost infinite variety of feelings which pulsate in this sanctuary tonight. It is not accidental that we are gripped by a feeling of elation as we return to the synagogue, that source from which our fathers in every age have drawn their will to survive as Jews. We have been drawn to this place by some seductive power whose magic is such that none of us can understand its sway over us.

To see the old faces and the new ones, to experience the vitality of numbers, is to be shaken by the possibility that there is something of value here after all, that our being here has worth, even a dignity and majesty. We are even more than just a little proud of ourselves, for we are, after all, a rather splendid looking array of people at least by the standards that most of us are still clinging to.

Perhaps nowhere else in the world does it feel so good to be Jewish, at least for those who have emancipated themselves from what they feel to be the rigorous demands of a more observant Judaism. It is easier to be a Jew in Israel, but Jewishness is taken for granted there; it becomes a natural, reflexive part of one's being. It is rarely experienced there the way it is here.

But perhaps it is better not to poke around at these feelings, and simply to revel in them; to be glad to be alive, to be here, to be near those we love in a time of elation—a touch of pride, a reverence, a breath of something called sanctity—all of this is permitted to bore through the castle wall of that rigid routine by which we ordinarily live our lives, do our work, scurry about making all those gestures of living.

Even this building begins to feel the difference; this orphan feels the warmth of care. No longer shivering in neglect, in the cold sounds of silence, it responds to the sounds of life.

How fortunate we are to have in the treasure house of our faith this precious holy day. Surely part of the subtlety of its power lies in its being a time of serious reflection, a time of self-examination and personal judgment. The New Year is certainly a time to be joyful, even to be proud of what we are and what we have accomplished. It is also a time to give some sober consideration to the manner in which we have fashioned our lives and the life of the society of which we are a part.

Our tradition treated Rosh Hashanah not only as a time of judgment and reflection, but also linked it with the date of the creation of the world. The New Year was a creative moment. An entire life could be restructured, transformed, begun anew, if only a man would awaken from the slumber of unexamined living.

All the mechanisms of this day are designed to do just that. Prayer and music are rich in imagery and suggestiveness. Even the crude and anachronistic sounds of the shofar come to shatter our composure, to awaken us, as Maimonides once said, from our slumber, to awaken us to what we really are, to what we really yearn to be. It awakens us to the still, small voice within us, the one that cries out: "Do I have any value? What are human beings for? Am I significant?" It is a voice that calls for an ethic of honesty and courage.

A rabbi who approaches this Rosh Hashanah 5731, and gives thought to what might be the proper subject of his sermon, is presented with an embarrassment of riches. For all mankind these are perilous times, and for the Jewish people in particular it seems so. The traumatic events in the Middle East call out for our consideration. The condition of the Jews of the Soviet Union, the future of the American Jew, and especially the future of our own Temple—(what is to become of us?)—that is certainly worthy of some thought and elucidation.

And what of the world—bristling with violence and instability—our own nation, poisoned and corrupted in its own fertility and growth, its universities at the ready, a mindless leadership, like so many bullies, flexing their muscles at the young? I can see some of the paths that might lead me into. There are so many matters to concern us here. I shall get to some of these places before the holy days are done, but by way of a circuitous route, by way of a Torah portion we read tomorrow.

Of all the elements that come to shake our composure at the Jewish New Year there is none that causes greater embarrassment than the story of the binding of Isaac, the 'Akedah, as it is called in Hebrew. We like to think that Jews are the bearers of an enlightened religious tradition, teaching some of the highest ideals ever known to man. How is it possible that our ancestors could have included such a horrible story in the sacred Torah, to be read on Rosh Hashanah yet, when all of us are here to listen? What kind of man is this terrible Abraham, the father of the Hebrew people, who would sacrifice his son? What kind of God is this who would demand such a thing? What could be more brutal, more ruthless? Here is the aged Abraham who had for so many years longed for a son and who had this longing fulfilled. Now he is commanded to offer his only son as a sacrifice, so that Abraham's faith, we are told, might be tested in the heroic exercise of it. But hadn't Abraham already proved his loyalty, his devotion, his faith? What kind of a god is it who is so relentlessly demanding of one of his most courageous, most dedicated servants? Oh, the Jewish tradition has a dozen ways of explaining away these difficulties. Sometimes the ancient commentators stress the heroism of Abraham. This was a test of faith but he stood the test. "Here am I," he said. He thus established a standard of character and integrity, which made him the first hero of his people. In every generation Israel would have such heroes—men who would respond, who would sacrifice what was most dear to them.

Or the most familiar interpretation: that the story of the 'Akedah, the attempted sacrifice of Isaac, is in reality an outcry against the practice of child sacrifice. Now we know that some of the neighboring cultures surrounding the land of Israel did indulge in child sacrifice. Israel rejected this practice. Why God should have chosen this devious method of teaching such a lesson is never told us by the commentators.

The most intriguing explanation of the 'Akedah was that of the late Professor Edmund Cahn, Professor of Law at Columbia, who attempted a juridical approach to the problem. He began with the question: What is the source of the evidence? Who has testified to the basic facts of the case? Who could be providing the account we have of this story? Only two possible witnesses: Abraham and Isaac. It seems plausible that Isaac rather than Abraham was the source of this story. He outlived his father. Besides everything we know about Abraham contradicts the story of the 'Akedah. Abraham was a man of superb dignity and valor who never silently would have accepted such a command. He had left his father's house, migrated to a strange land, believing he had a mission to perform. He laughed in his old age when he was told that God was going to provide him with a son from a wife who was almost ninety. We would have laughed too. Abraham was the man who inaugurated the greatest of all Jewish traditions when he stood outside the wicked city of Sodom and urged God to deal justly and compassionately with its inhabitants. He provided one of the great mountain peaks of Jewish history when he confronted God, demanding, "Shall not the judge of all the earth himself do justly?" How could such a dynamic hero have been the one to tell the story of the binding of Isaac?

What of Isaac, Professor Cahn continued. Could he have been the source? He survived Abraham. He had plenty of time to develop the story. What kind of a man was he? A shadow of a man, tolerably good, and yet had it not been for his father, Abraham, and for his son, Jacob, we might never had heard of Isaac. Isaac lacked insight. He was soft, submissive, ineffectual. It must have been he who would tell such a story.

But how did he come to tell it? Professor Cahn asked. It went very much like this: It was a family dinner in Isaac's old age, like some of our family dinners today. The wild, explosive Esau was quarreling with his brother, the dreamer, Jacob. The boys had become too big for their mother, Rebecca, to control, and she demands that Isaac do something. She nags at her husband and finally with her teeth clenched and her anger grinding within her, she screams at her husband: "For God's sake do something to stop Esau and Jacob." And Isaac does. He looks at his two sons and he knows in his heart that each of them is stronger than he and that neither of them will obey him. And so in a voice, which attempts to simulate the tones of his great father, he tells the 'Akedah story. He tells it to prove that when he was young his feeling of respect and obedience toward his father, was as absolute as his father's respect and obedience toward God. He tells it to show that his sons must obey without challenging, without the necessity of first being convinced. He tells it because when his father was alive he did not understand him, and now he does not understand his own sons. "Listen to me, as my father listened to God, as I listened to my father. Listen to me."

Rebecca sits there silently, stunned. The two sons sulk in their places. Jacob remembers the story and it is he who probably recorded it.

Of course this treatment of the story by Professor Cahn is a somewhat playful one. He knew just as we do that what the story of Abraham and Isaac reveals to us is the life-thwarting element, which can be found in the Jewish tradition, and in every religion man has ever fashioned. In all religions there is a strain which attempts to enslave man, which tries to force man to give up his freedom, his reason, his responsibility, which tries to make man an obedient and dependent child; it is a religion of submission where sin is disobedience, and virtue is the unquestioning acceptance of authority. In tribute or service to such authority a man is willing to perform the most irrational acts of faith, even as Abraham climbed the mountain dutifully to sacrifice his beloved son.

Well, what has all of this to do with us, here on the eve of Rosh Hashanah? You might suppose that I have come to tell this story just to show what horrible elements there are in our tradition, as though there were some need to overcome the overly sentimental, highly romantic notion that Jews have of their past. I could simply be here to say that what makes us important as a people is precisely that we are so very human, that even our sacred literature preserves for us those aspects of our past that show us and our heroes at their best and at their worst.

But that is not why I rehearse the *Akedah* here tonight in anticipation of tomorrow morning's Torah reading. What makes the Torah rich and enduring is not that it tells us interesting or even disturbing stories about Moses and Abraham and the prophets, and all the others. No, it is telling us something about man in his encounter with life; it is telling about the human experience; it is talking about us. In every generation of human history men have received a call to sacrifice their sons. In every generation, like so many Abrahams, men have responded to that call. Dutifully, in obedience to tribe, to clan, to king and country, to nation, to defend the fatherland, to rescue the Holy Grail from the infidels, to uproot the heretics, to defend our honor, our liberty, our credibility—in every generation the fathers have sent forth their Isaacs to be slain upon the altar of war.

As for us, we no longer believe in a commanding God. We find it difficult to understand an Abraham whose faith in God had such enormous power over him. But we merely substituted for God another power as great as God himself. Our god is no longer the God above gods Abraham served. Our god is our unswerving subservience to the nation and the way of life that has been created here, and in service to the State, the nation, its system of production, its law and order, its way of life, we and all of the fathers before us have been willing to destroy the life of our children.

Let it be remembered that the Torah does not permit Isaac to be killed. A voice speaks to Abraham on the mountain, calls out to him, "Abraham, Abraham, lay not thy hand upon the lad." And Isaac is spared.

One of the late Hasidic rabbis, Menachem Mendel, said that this story teaches us that only God has the right to command us to destroy another man, and that even if the smallest angel comes forth to counter such an order, we must obey the angel.

But ours is a history of the fathers who would not listen to that voice calling upon them not to slay their sons. We insist upon the way of death.

One of the great British poets of World War I, Wilfred Owen, shortly before he was killed in France in November 1910, wrote this poem, which he called "The Parable of the Old Men and the Young."

> So Abram rose, and clave the wood, and went
> And took the fire with him, and a knife.
> And as they sojourned both of them together,
> Isaac the first-born spake and said, My Father,
> Behold the preparations, fire and iron,

But where the lamb for this burnt-offering?
Then Abram bound the youth with belts and straps,
And builded parapets and trenches there,
And stretched forth the knife to slay his son.
When lo! an angel called him out of heaven,
Saying, Lay not thy hand upon the lad,
Neither do anything to him. Behold,
A ram, caught in the thicket by its horns;
Offer the Ram of Pride instead of him.
But the old man would not do so, but slew his son,—
And half the seed of Europe, one by one.

Is that not precisely what the fathers have done to their sons? How long will we continue to play the role in this brutal tragedy?

How do we kill the young? Not only by our dedication to the system of international violence, but primarily by way of perpetuating a way of life that ignores so many essentially human needs, a way of life that is single-minded in its dedication to organization and technical achievement, whose actions are not guided by what will make men healthier and happier. Behind the façade of freedom we think we have, we are enslaved, rigidly obedient to a society that mindlessly preempts human energies, exhausts human resources for non-human ends. It is a society, to use Hans Morgenthau's words, that grows monstrously for the sake of growth, that ravages natural and scenic resources, and where the work people do and the goods and services produced are not really judged by human needs.

Our way of life, the one that has made all of us its captive, the one into which we try to indoctrinate our children with all of the mechanisms employed by our society, does not permit any value to interfere with efficiency, organization, growth, progress—not beauty, not community, not even the supreme value of life itself, and the signs of death—the decay of cities, the destruction of the natural environment, racial conflict, poverty, are not the result of accidental misfortunes, or even poor judgment; they are the result of the way in which the social and economic policies of this society operate.

The militarization of American life, the war in Indochina, the orgy of wasteful production and distribution are all a part of a gigantic hoax that we are trying to perpetuate on our children. It is a huge joke that we are free. We are killing one another. We are killing our own capacity to be human. And a voice is calling out to us, the young, the blacks, the students, the violence itself, as ugly and brutal as it all is, is that not a cry for help—a voice calling upon us to put an end to the way of death and to affirm the way of life? Will we listen to that voice the way Abraham did and not slay our children upon the altar of a way of life which commands our total subservience? Do we still have the capacity to be free in our judgment of what is truly human in the life that has been given to us?

The task and the possibility of the human being is to move out of this condition of servitude to live at least as many moments as possible in freedom, in honesty, in responsibility.

That is what we must demand of one another, that is what the voice is calling us, begging us to do if we are to survive in this inhuman death-driven era in which we have been fated to live.

The Rosh Hashanah calls us to be free; the Rosh Hashanah calls us to be free from all the old enslavements; it calls us to the continuing possibility of our own transformation. This day a new world can come into being. A new person can come into being.

Once Socrates was describing the ideal society to his friend Glaucon. And Glaucon countered saying: "Socrates, I do not believe that there is such a City of God anywhere on earth." And Socrates answered, "Whether such a city exists in heaven or ever will exist on earth, the wise man will live after the manner of that city, having nothing to do with any other, and in so looking upon it, will set his own house in order."

Whether the City of God will ever exist in heaven or even here on earth the wise Jew is called upon to try to live after the manner of that ideal City and to begin by setting himself, his own household in order, that is what the New Year asks of us, and because we are asked, it must mean that we are capable of doing it.

COMMENTARY BY PROFESSOR
JONATHAN D. GREENBERG

Rabbi Leo Baeck called Judaism "the religion of moral optimism." The Hebrew prophets were "optimists" in their relentless expression of "scorn for the present, derision for the status quo"—and their fierce insistence that a broken world can be redeemed. Jewish prophets, ancient and contemporary, are "the great believers who hold fast to the future and lead step by step toward it. They are the consolers of the people, the humans within humanity [*die Menschen der Menschheit*]."

Erev Rosh Hashanah, 1970. Leo Baeck Temple, Los Angeles. I'm thirteen years old. Reading this text, years later, I hear Rabbi Beerman's voice. *What does it mean to be a Jew? A human being?* Leonard's voice revealed the path I traveled to answer these questions in my own life.

By "Leonard's voice" I mean the gentle, resonant *sound* of his voice, its human intimacy, and the feelings it conveyed: kindness, sadness and compassion, urgency, anger and power. I mean Leonard's voice as a writer, the elegance of his prose, the diversity and depth of his literary imagination. The way he opened our eyes and minds, moving us from complacency to disquiet.

Leonard's voice erased barriers between Hebraism and Hellenism. Between holy texts and secular poetry. Between peoples and nations. Even at Israel's triumph in the 1967 Six-Day War, Rabbi Beerman insisted that the heart-rending grief of Arab and Jewish mothers is the same.

In this Rosh Hashanah sermon, biblical struggles unfold in the present. The terrible shadow of the 'Akedah falls on us. We are Abraham, a gleaming knife in our hand, above Isaac, bound at the altar. Leonard called us to protest. Against the slaughter of innocents in Indochina; the threat of nuclear annihilation; the gross inequality of American society. He called us to recognize that all children, of all races and faiths, are our sons and daughters—and to act accordingly.

Like Isaiah, Micah, and Jeremiah—and Martin Luther King Jr.—Leonard called us to be socially *maladjusted;* to reject the unconscionable violence of national and global systems; to affirm the dignity, value, and life of every human being throughout the world.

Rabbi Beerman was a consoler of the people, a human within humanity. Fearlessly expressing scorn for the present, derision for the status quo, he showed us the path of peace, justice, and redemption.

24

How I Lost the Election in St. Louis

July 9, 1971

Beerman's report of his defeat in the election for the position of vice president (and thereafter president) of the Central Conference of American Rabbis (CCAR) highlights a certain ferment within Reform Judaism in 1971. His initial nomination for the vice presidency, followed by the unprecedented challenge to it, reflected a deep generational divide within the Reform rabbinate. Beerman, at fifty, represented the young guard, which was regarded with considerable trepidation by older rabbis. The issue at hand was not merely the question of who would be in charge of the movement. Reform rabbis were also divided at this time over whether they should be permitted to perform mixed marriages (the policy of the CCAR today is to discourage but not prohibit rabbis from doing so, though the movement did agree to regard those born to Jewish fathers as Jews in 1983).

Beerman also reports that colleagues were divided over matters of intense political concern in America of the time—for example, whether to oppose the military draft or to support bail for political activist and scholar Angela Davis. Moreover, he relates that at least one colleague opposed him for the vice presidency of the CCAR because of his views on Israel—an early indication of his critical stance, which would become a cornerstone of his political engagement, and a source of controversy within the Jewish community.

I have just returned from a most painful experience. Two weeks ago in St. Louis I suffered a defeat, and I didn't enjoy it at all. I came away from it licking my wounds, whimpering. I had my rabbinic nose rubbed in the dirt; I was clobbered in public. I played the role of victim in an event that made history. Oh, you won't ever read about it in the *Readers Digest,* or for that matter in the *Jewish Digest.*

It's the kind of history that is already forgotten, or will never be written. It isn't very important history. It concerns the 82nd Annual Conference of the Central Conference of American Rabbis. Within a period of less than 24 hours I was and was not the next Vice President of the CCAR. The nominating committee had selected me on Wednesday afternoon to the post, which according to conference tradition leads normally to the presidency two years later. Had the tradition of the CCAR been followed this time, I would have been perhaps the youngest president in the eighty-two-year history of the American reform rabbinate. But history was made in another way. In the closing hours of the convention after the majority of those attending had gone back home, for the first time in conference history a nomination was made from the floor opposing mine: and the new vice president, president to be, is not the fifty-year-old Leonard I. Beerman of Los Angeles, but the sixty-year-old Robert I. Kahn of Houston, a revered and distinguished colleague whom I fully expected would be the next president anyway.

Those of us who were in St. Louis will have trouble making sense out of what occurred there. It was a confusing time, and we are still too close to it to understand just exactly what happened, but there might be some value in talking about it. At least it serves a purpose for me. If I made a fool of myself in St. Louis there is no reason why you shouldn't know about it. Or for that matter if I had been a hero.

I think my troubles began when I was thirteen years old. To begin with, I was very slow in growing. The signs of maturity were delayed in coming. At eighteen I could still get into the movies as a twelve year old. Maybe that's why at fifty some of my colleagues counted me among the young rabbis of our rabbinic association. But something else happened at thirteen. I had straight black hair and I wanted wavy hair. I had rich and powerful fantasies about me with wavy hair. And sure enough in the summer of my thirteenth year I went swimming in the dirty old Shiawassee River that meandered through our little Michigan town, and I developed a good solid case of typhoid fever, in the process I lost my straight black hair, and wonder of wonders my fantasy became a reality; the new hair came in wavy and curly. And that's the way it remained, until twenty-five years later when baldness began to take over.

That's where my troubles began, when my hair was straight. Ever since then I have had a great reverence for fantasies. Fantasy enriches my life and quite often has made life tolerable to me. I use it especially at religious services and board meetings. If I don't like what's going on I create my own meeting out of my fantasies. It's exciting and pleasurable.

These last two years have been very difficult for me. I have been the secretary of our rabbinical association, the CCAR. I have been deprived. Secretaries *have* to listen, have to take notes. No place for fantasy. No private meetings. For two years I have had to bear that burden. I flew to St. Louis a couple of weeks ago knowing that this would be the last meeting at which I would serve as secretary. But that also meant no office in the CCAR. No trips to New York. No opportunities to see our daughter who attends College at 116th and Broadway. What would I do? The fantasy apparatus started working; starved, famished after two years of deprivation—bursting for expression. I couldn't be secretary again. They don't usually reelect men to offices. They like to pass the honors around. That left only the vice presidency. But I'm only fifty. It ordinarily goes to a man ten years later. Besides there's Robert Kahn of Houston; by all the laws of conference tradition—service to the conference, distinction, respect of colleagues—Kahn is our next president. Impossible for you; your turn might come, if you are lucky, in ten years, if it's to be at all. But not now. Forget it.

But the worm had entered the apple; the fantasy had entered my mind, and although I didn't really think about it until two days later—that's where the trouble began, back on the Shiawassee River.

Meanwhile the Conference went on its somewhat boring way. It voted down a resolution urging an end to the draft, which I had drafted myself. That was my first defeat. It avoided a statement which would directly support Angela Davis' right to bail; it postponed for a year a confrontation on the question of a self-imposed draft of chaplains for the military, and it postponed a consideration of a question Rabbi Kominsky was very much involved in, the question of mixed marriage. I myself was to give a formal response (at one of the low points of the meeting on Wednesday night) to a paper delivered by an Adlerian psychologist from Chicago, but that was still to come.

By Tuesday some of the youngest men of the Conference were ready to go home. One made plans to attend a rock festival in New Orleans, rather than stay in the heat of St. Louis. He discussed the idea with an older colleague who suggested he try to turn the Conference around—take a new direction; bring in a man who represents some of the diffused yearnings of the disenchanted, Leonard Beerman. The young Rabbi with hair and beard longer even than Kominsky, on little scraps of paper, circulated a petition, requesting the nominating committee to propose Beerman, and went about gathering signatures by the dozens.

Some signed out of conviction; others who never even heard of me. I made a half-hearted effort to stop it. I told the chairman of the nominating committee, I wasn't interested in the job, but two older colleagues and past presidents told me that was an arrogant, nonsensical thing to do. Arrogant to turn down a nomination before it was offered, nonsense to think I had any chance of being nominated in the first place.

Wednesday evening at dinner, while Martha and I were sitting making conversation with the psychologist who was about to deliver the paper that I was to give the response to, the chairman of the nominating committee came to me with the news—I was the unanimous choice of the nominating committee on the second ballot. The committee had felt it was time for a change, they wanted a candidate independent of existing power structures—some such talk—and like typhoid fever in the Shiawassee, and wavy hair emerging magically out of my fantasies it had really happened. I woke up in the middle of the night feeling proud of myself—already alive with new imaginings of what I might do for the young and the excluded, the forgotten men of the Conference.

Some eight hours later, two-thirds of the conference having gone home, a colleague took the floor, visibly shaken, pained at violating the established tradition of the Conference, and nominated from the floor Robert Kahn of Houston. More important than the sanctity of the nominating committee, which never in its history has had its choice challenged, was the sanctity of age. Age rose up to protect its prerogatives. How could the Conference trample over a man of age and respect and competence, no matter how worthy this Beerman might be?

Only one man rose to attack Beerman, someone who claimed to be liberal and of the left, but deeply disturbed by my position on Israel, something he had heard at Miami two years before, or thought he heard. Someone else got up to attack Kahn for his purported alliance with the military industrial complex. Kahn had served as chaplain for the American Legion. The young men who spoke, spoke for Beerman. The ballot was made secret. The atmosphere was very solemn, rabbinical, but tense. The vote was taken and Beerman went down, 77 to 55.

Several young men had raced out to pay their $35 registration fee, which many of them had not been able to afford, just so they could vote—but it was not enough.

What had happened? I am not sure. The young men had distributed the petition because they felt the Conference was ignoring them and their needs. Men under thirty felt they were not needed or trusted. Their feelings of impotence and frustration prodded them into this campaign to elect someone almost twice their age but whom they felt shared their aspirations. In the eyes of the elders of the Conference, although I was fifty, I was still identified with the young.

No question that the older men felt threatened, fearful of the radical change they somehow perceived in my election. But more than that there was a great unrest that permeated the entire Conference and the profession itself. Young men were concerned about being ignored and neglected—they perceived their Conference as moribund, not responsive to the changing needs of the time. Older men were very uneasy about their security.

One of the most distinguished colleagues, after seventeen years of service to a great congregation in the East, was summarily fired a few weeks ago. And that shook us all up, because he is a man of considerable distinction, and if congregations can treat rabbis of distinction and long service in what appears to us to be an arbitrary fashion, you can imagine how lesser men might have had their security severely shaken. Even the middle-aged men began to be threatened by the exaggerated attention being given to the young.

They found themselves suddenly passed over by a Conference, which had ignored them when they were young, and now they were already too old to be young.

The Conference was split over a dozen issues. Over mixed marriage, when an effort was made by the then President of our Conference to add more traditional teeth to the forty-two-year-old conference position declaring mixed marriages to be contrary to the tradition of Jewish religion and therefore to be discouraged by the American rabbinate. That's the way the words read forty-two years ago and still apply. Roland Gittelson, our outgoing president, in his opening address called upon the members of the Conference to declare officially that they would not officiate at such mixed marriages. That produced a strong division within the Conference.

There was a division of feelings about the new prayer book which is in the process of being developed, and which has been circulated throughout the Conference over the last couple of years and will probably reach the printer within the next two or three years—there too the response showed a broad diversity within the Reform movement.

What we see in our Conference is essentially what we see in our congregations. We are ministering to a divided group of Jews. An infinitely varied group of Jews. Somehow the existing structures are seeking a way to respond to the variety of needs and values and ideals which can be found within the individual structures, without trampling on the rights of any individual, with due regard for the need for change, with due reverence for tradition, trying to find a path that makes sense, that is intelligible, that will respond to the need for change and at the same time not trample on the feelings of the old or those who are content with the old. That is the difficulty that faces the Conference, even as it faces our individual congregations. The revolt of the young, and the willingness of the young, whoever the young may be, to try out the new, to probe and risk the new, of course appears always as a threat to the existing institutions and existing structures of power. Certainly that in part was true in St. Louis.

And as for me, I ignored that old Jewish lesson, "don't make waves," don't make trouble, and you will never get hurt. I for a moment was touched, puffed up with the spirit of ambition. I forgot the little boy who was swimming in the Shiawassee and I lived for a moment in the world of fantasy. I learned that it is possible to get hurt. It is possible to get your nose pushed in the dirt, and it is possible to have it done in the presence of all of your friends, your colleagues. I learned much more: That I have many friends, wonderful friends, particularly among the young men of the Conference, and among the old as well. I learned that the Conference will never be the same again, and in many different ways.

Who knows what the future will hold. Perhaps even these Reform rabbis, in their wonderful variety, will discover again, as my friend Richard Levy says, that Reform is something more than a struggle between the old and the new but rather a way in which, perhaps, we can turn this country of ours around. Perhaps we can find a relevant way to transform our lives as Jews and through the transformation of our own lives, the life of the society of which we are a part.

In the meantime I can go back now to my private meetings. As a booby prize they elected me to the Executive Board of the CCAR. So I'll get those trips to New York.

If I don't like the Executive Board meeting, I can conduct my own private meetings. I suppose there is some kind of poetic justice in that.

And so it was a hot seething week in St. Louis. A lot of feelings are ruffled, a lot of people were made happy. A lot of people came home wiser, more sober, more troubled, and maybe even a little more hopeful about the possibilities of the future.

COMMENTARY BY PROFESSOR WILLIAM CUTTER

I was one of those young rabbis who hoped that Leonard Beerman could revive the professional guild of Reform Rabbis, known as the CCAR. I was new to our shared work, but I already knew Rabbi Beerman to be a forthright speaker, a man of robust integrity, and one of those rare public figures with a sense of irony about himself. Soon after I joined Leo Baeck Temple to learn from him and to share in his quiet aura, I found that around the nation, other young rabbis were beginning to look to him for leadership. Without trying very hard (and we liked that, it seems), he was a man whose opinions had to be reckoned with. Among those opinions were certain beliefs about leadership, and a caution about univocal-homogenous support for Israel's new role as a power in the Middle East. Both aspects of his uniqueness inspired the original nomination, but probably helped to change the direction away from his nomination as our next president once the demographic balance shifted at the end of our conference.

I was not used to seeing Leonard display that much public ambition, and his generally gentle approach to things within the CCAR makes the document before us all the more intriguing—and perhaps more important historically. Leonard's words here bespeak a genuine disappointment with the outcome of a quirky situation, along with a concern that dissent of a certain kind may be respected but not viewed as appropriate for rabbinic leadership. A more conventional, and predictable, substitute was found in the elegant Robert Kahn. One could protest procedure, but not the integrity of the new choice.

Yes, many of us wanted someone more challenging, and our selection of Leonard reflected that aspiration. Perhaps we followed in the spirit shown at the Chicago political convention of 1968. And I, personally, regretted that I could not be in St. Louis for the challenge.

Many of us communicated for a long time after our rabbinic convention about our disappointment. None were more disappointed than Leonard Beerman, but none were more surprised than we, his loyal Hasidim, who were not used to thinking about Leonard's ambitions to turn his professional guild around. That aspiration is reflected in these surprising, humorous, and deeply human words.

25

Invocation for Religious Leaders
for McGovern

June 1, 1972

As a reflection of his own strong political proclivities, Rabbi Beerman delivered an invocation at a gathering of religious leaders to hear the Democratic candidate for president, Senator George McGovern. He held McGovern in high regard, as an intelligent and moral man—in many respects, the opposite of how he regarded President Richard M. Nixon. The invocation repeats, in large measure, the language of his presentation at the UCLA teach-in on Vietnam in 1966, with a slight change to take note of the passage of time—and the continuation of the Cold War.

"It was the best of times; it was the worst of times. It was the age of wisdom; it was the age of foolishness. It was the season of Light; it was the season of Darkness, it was the spring of hope; it was the winter of despair. We had everything before us. We had nothing before us. We were all going direct to Heaven; we were all going direct the other way . . ."

Those are the familiar words with which Charles Dickens opened his novel *A Tale of Two Cities*. The paradoxes to which he addressed himself unfortunately persist in our times, and to live in the midst of such paradoxes is the particular challenge and burden of our generation.

Forces of change beyond the control of even the best men are pushing aside the remaining ramparts of the old certainties, those truths that once sheltered and comforted us. Peace is cracked in a hundred shivers. The air of the Cold War has momentarily become warmer, but it still chills the night. In America we look outward and the world envies or despises or distrusts us. We look inward and we are plagued by the rising tide of the poor, the urban hopeless, the massive and still unresolved protest of Blacks, Chicanos, women and other oppressed groups.

It is emotionally wearing to be living at the end of one era and the beginning of another, vaguely knowing that something is coming to an end, and something is crouching toward Bethlehem waiting to be born.

For almost twenty-five years, we have been living through a time called a "Cold War." For twenty-five years, our government has been acting on the assumption that communism was on the march for the conquest of the world and that it was the manifest destiny of the United States to save the world from suffering this fate. In the pursuit of this mirage, this myth, we have engaged in the most fantastic kind of international adventurism. In the process, our hands have been covered with blood. We have become as brutalized as those we call our enemies, as we have seen how some of our best young men have been able to torture, kill, and burn combatants and non-combatants alike.

For twenty-five years, we have sacrificed upon the altar of war and its preparation the greatest gifts of this nation, the gifts of mind and technique and sensitivity, and in so doing we have demonstrated a total contempt for man. This same era has given us a glimpse of what man's knowledge could have done for us, but we have made no serious effort to bring this golden age into being. Compassion has not been a full-time occupation for any of us. Our ingenuity, our resources, have literally been swallowed up by our consuming endeavor to stalk the enemy. Our laboratories, our universities, our research centers have found themselves dedicated to the same fanatical pursuits.

For twenty-five years, the angel of death has hovered over our civilization, fending off any serious endeavor to re-cultivate the waste places or to make a serious assault upon the problems of anguish.

The result of all this cannot adequately be measured. You and I know it in the form of greater frustration and estrangement, a sense of impotence. The poor know it in the form of even greater poverty.

Such an age as ours may very well bring tourists to the moon but it will hardly make a contribution to the human spirit. For in such an age, the artist, the thoughtful man, the man of wisdom, the student, even the man of religion is no longer able to see the healing role the responsible use of his talents would demand of him . . .

COMMENTARY BY THE REVEREND J. EDWIN BACON

We were reeling in 1971—those of us in America's "peace and justice community." We had recently been struck by a season of assassinations—of President Kennedy, of Dr. King, and of Bobby Kennedy. And then there was the protracted immoral war in Vietnam, perverting the nation's leaders to justify the "fog of war." Our nation sacrificed on the altar of war innocent Vietnamese lives, American youth and technology, all the while draining limited resources from those who were poor and hungry to feed war's voracious appetite. When Leonard Beerman offered his invocation, a hopeful moment had arisen in George McGovern's clear and courageous voice, naming the immorality of the war in Vietnam and holding out a promise for a different national and global narrative.

That narrative was one of moral reckoning and self-critique about the sacrilege of what we were doing in the name of democracy. Leonard knew the paradox of the moment as he invoked the God of justice and peace in lyrical language and with a clear moral imperative, echoing not only the Torah and the Prophets, but also Dickens, Yeats, and Didion. Leonard never shied away from moral indictment and outrage, but always delivered them with words of love and hope.

Because of Leonard, we who heard his words and were inspired by his actions felt more deeply our discomfiting yet exhilarating mission: to join the resistance, to make a contribution to the human spirit, and to play our role in the never-ending enterprise of healing.

26

Survival in a Nuclear Age

February 17, 1984

The subject of Rabbi Beerman's Friday night sermon was a recurrent one: the threat of nuclear annihilation. He and George Regas, along with their close Muslim colleague Maher Hathout, had been devoted to the cause of nuclear disarmament for decades; together, they founded the Interfaith Center to Reverse the Arms Race, which was based at All Saints Church in Pasadena. The concern of disarmament advocates such as Beerman, Regas, and Hathout was heightened significantly by the election of Ronald Reagan as president in 1980. Reagan vowed to rebuild the US military and undertake an overhaul of the American nuclear arsenal. For Beerman, this was not merely a bad investment, but a choice of death over life. Summoning his characteristic prophetic wrath, he called attention to all of the suffering—poverty, illness, lack of education—that was prolonged by the billions of dollars sunk into the arms race. "Our ultimate commitment," he thundered in pointing to that race, "is not to what is humane, not to God, but to this super Moloch—in whose nuclear temple we have been prepared to sacrifice our children." He concluded by invoking the words of Holocaust survivor Samuel Pisar, which he quoted on other occasions, to the effect that true security resides not in weapons of destruction, but in caring for the well-being of people, and especially in educating the young.

Rabbi David Polish once wrote this: "There is a world out in space which is an exact duplicate of our own. It is populated with men and women like ourselves. They live in countries like our own. They conduct business and raise families. They live under various economies and governments, and are divided into different national, religious, and racial groups. They differ in only one respect. In each country, there is a pathological obsession with human welfare. As a result, over sixty percent of the national budgets are devoted to a compulsive and hysterical desire toward sheltering life from the normal ravages of human existence, which we accept more stoically. Billions of dollars are spent by governments on the conquest of disease. Over the years, nations have poured their resources into medical research and today no cancer, no vascular disease, no kidney ailments, no degenerative disease exist. Unheard of sums are spent by governments on housing. They have so tortured their fiscal policies that slums and blight are unheard of. They are so over-protective of their children that they overpay teachers, and training schools for teachers have to turn candidates away. The perverseness of these conditions reaches its greatest height in their legislation against all private charities on behalf of human welfare. The outlawing of private charity has, of course, stifled the philanthropic instincts of the people.

"There is only one exception to this restriction against private benevolence. Since the national budgets are so swollen with welfare appropriations, there is little left for national defense. It therefore becomes necessary for private citizens to raise money for armaments. Thousands of private organizations exist with this purpose alone. There are clubs to buy [guns]¹ through raffles. People stand with tin cups on street corners to collect coins for the purchase of hand grenades. Drives are conducted to acquire submarines. There are tag days for military aircraft. Charities sponsor dances to buy uniforms. The national government simply neglects the problems of defense, and lets the burden fall on private agencies. But the inadequacy of this system is apparent to all. People are grumbling that under such conditions, there can never be another war."

Like peddlers with packs on their backs, wherever Jews go, they carry an assortment of notions, ideals. Many of them are very old, and they have found their way into the very being of all that is held to be precious in this beloved country of ours and even in civilization itself. Some, like the belief in the possibilities of human compassion and peace, are battered and tired and worn. Others, since they come out of a people that has had such a long history, have to do with history itself, and history meditated upon can be very solemn and very haunting.

I do not like this idea (an idea about which Robert Sinai has so chillingly written), yet it haunts me more than I wish. It is this, history teaches, if nothing else, that every civilization has perished sooner or later. Human social systems with their human beings anxious, insecure, swollen with pride, driven by the will to power, corrupted by self-intoxication and self-deception, sooner or later sin against the laws of proportion and harmony and plunge into decay and self-destruction. Every civilization in human history has made such a fatal error.

Now our civilization may be in the process of making the same mistake. We have been so infused with the conceit that we could escape the remorseless fate that has overtaken all previous social systems, that we with our science and industry, our democracy, our ingenuity, could violate what appears to be an iron law of history. The arms race has doomed us to nuclear insanity. Technological processes have committed the United States and the USSR to collective mechanisms of destruction so gross that they defy our imaginations. Our nations have become vast armories, and we are now both engaged in enlarging our capacity to destroy one another. Pre-empting every other human purpose, the nuclear arms race in all of its arrogant compulsions imposes on a world of hungry, tormented people; imposes on a world where 700 million adults are illiterate, 500 million children do not go to school, 500 million suffer malnutrition; imposes on such a world more than 700 billion dollars worth of weaponry every year. For the sake of protecting their nations, the leaders of the United States and the Soviet Union have been brazenly prepared to sacrifice more than 100 million of their citizens on the first day of an all-out nuclear war.

So we are now in a position of asymmetrical nuclear parity: We, with our 9,500 strategic nuclear warheads; the Soviet Union with their 8,000; 50,000 in all types of nuclear weapons. And now, under the Reagan budget, a one and one-half trillion dollar expenditure over a five-year period has been approved, and the building of 17,000 additional nuclear weapons over the next ten years. A billion dollars a day, almost a million a minute.

You and I have permitted this to happen. We have permitted the so-called specialists in defense to set the priorities for our country and the world. We have permitted them to enmesh us all in the cycle of design, production, and obsolescence, enlarging their power, the power of the military industrial colossus over our lives.

And we pay a terrible price for that. President Eisenhower recognized that when he said years ago: "Every gun made, every warship launched, every rocket fired, signifies a theft from those who hunger and are not fed, those who are cold and not clothed."

Isn't it a perversion of everything that is morally precious in our religious tradition to permit the military to set the priorities for our country and the world? How can we pursue human goals, how can we reckon with the decay of our cities, how can we care for the poor and the hungry and the abandoned, how can we pretend to revere the dignity that is present in every human being, when our ultimate commitment is not to what is humane, not to God, but to this super Moloch—in whose nuclear temple we have been prepared to sacrifice our children?

This is the greatest threat to our life, to the life of the human race. This is the greatest social, political, economic, environmental, theological religious Jewish issue confronting us today. This is what we must set ourselves against, if we are truly Jews dedicated to the ideals of our tradition. This is why we must become a part of a developing religious voice in the land, the constituency of those who insist on reversing the nuclear arms race. How can we erect a religious commitment on a foundation of the believable threat to kill a hundred million of God's children?

Nothing is as hard to overcome as the will to be enslaved to our own moral inertia. Yet we know there is another power within us, the power of our own decency, our own critical intelligence, the power of the human spirit, a spiritual power present in every person—and it can be actualized. We shall have to actualize this power without pretending away our need for security, or that we do indeed live in a world brimming with anger and suspicion, inertia and adversaries.

There is a story members of the clergy like to tell. It concerns a minister or priest or rabbi who wanted to stage an object lesson for the members of the congregation, so the cleric places a lion and lamb in a cage just outside the entrance of his church. And they lived together in peace. And people came from miles around to see this remarkable phenomenon. Finally, the governor of the state, intrigued by this remarkable feat, sent a delegation to inquire how the minister pulled off the trick. "Oh, there's no trick at all," said the minister. "All you have to do is put in a fresh lamb from time to time."

In the real world, we know very well, lions and lambs do not live together peacefully. Even the prophet Isaiah, when he spoke of such a possibility, was referring to a time in the distant future, a messianic time. And that's where the rub is for us: How to face up to the truth of this real world of brutality, fear, mutual rivalry, the need for security, and still retain hope, still work for something different, work to reverse the arms race, work to retain our faith in human destiny, and still maintain a firm conviction that we can (to use Neruda's words) "approach a great common tenderness." We must not let this hope be crushed amidst the powers and principalities.

Let hope give us the courage to say "No" to all those mighty forces that would condemn us to the continuing despair of the waste and perversion of all that affirms the humane, the intelligent, and the tender that is within us.

In June of 1981, 6,000 Jews gathered in Jerusalem at a conference of survivors of the Holocaust, gathered to perpetuate the memory of the victims in a world whose memory is fading. They recalled their nightmares, remembering how their world was destroyed, and attempted to draw insights into how their children's world could be preserved. Speaking before members of Israel's Knesset, survivor of Auschwitz, world-renowned lawyer Samuel Pisar had this to say:

"We have a unique legacy to hand down to our fellowmen, Jews and non-Jews alike, especially to the young, because our message of blood and hope is not about the past but about the future . . . we must help save them from tragedy . . . We must impress upon them the true meaning of the dangers pushing mankind to a new Holocaust . . . For us, the Holocaust is not just a terrible memory that will never be erased, it is a constant warning. We feel in our bones the fear and the growing fury lurking in the roots of seething international disputes, which diplomats, economists, and politicians discuss with such dry indifference . . . For we saw at Auschwitz a model for destroying the human species. We are the ones who know that the unthinkable can happen . . . We have a duty to reaffirm, in this place and at this time, the primordial importance of the great values of Judaism in the continued quest for survival and peace.

"Here with the authority of the numbers engraved on our arms, we cry out the commandment of six million innocent souls, including one and a half million children: Never again! From where, if not from us, will come the warning that a new combination of technology and brutality can transform the planet into a crematorium? From where, if not from the bloodiest killing-ground of all time, will come the hope that co-existence between . . . enemies is possible. From where, if not from the slaughterhouses of World War II, will come the lesson that true security cannot lie much longer in defendable borders and powerful arms alone, but in a fundamental reassessment of the common perils and needs of adversaries who must drown their passions in a joint enterprise of economic, cultural and human development, and ultimately in the minds and schoolbooks of children?"

The earth is too small and life too short for anything to be more important than the quest for peace.

COMMENTARY BY THE REVEREND GEORGE F. REGAS

Leonard and I met in 1967 at a peace rally against the Vietnam War, and became the best of friends, a rabbi and an Episcopal priest, who traveled the world together in search of peace. Our different faith commitments drew us closer rather than separated us. I like to think that our friendship was a gift given to us so we could sustain each other in the hard, controversial work of peace in a hostile world.

The danger of unbelievable disaster in the escalating nuclear arms race was a threat that Leonard and I felt we must address. Leonard had incredible vision, and was always full of hope that we could create a more just and peaceful world. We wanted to call together leaders of the religious community of Los Angeles and ignite them with a moral passion for stopping the mad momentum of the arms race that was whirling us toward destruction.

In response, Leo Baeck Temple and All Saints Church jointly sponsored a major conference on reversing the arms race in October of 1979, which was attended by 1,000 people. From the success of this event, the Interfaith Center to Reverse the Arms Race was born. Over the ten years that we sustained it, the center grew significantly, involving many clergy and congregations in our mission, and included our first collaboration with the Muslim community. Our goal was to see the religious community become a powerful lobby for peace.

27

California People of Faith against the Death Penalty

Jewish Community Center, La Jolla, October 16, 2001
Episcopal Diocese, April 20, 2002

Rabbi Beerman remained to his last days an unrelenting opponent of capital punishment, a cause in which he joined the efforts of his friend the renowned actor Mike Farrell. The notion that the state would engage in what he called "premeditated and calculated murder" violated the core of his being. In articulating his opposition, Beerman drew deeply on Jewish legal norms. He noted that the Bible made reference to fifteen categories of capital offenses. But in good—and somewhat uncharacteristic rabbinic fashion—he pointed out that the Bible was not the last word in the matter. The rabbis of the Mishnah and Talmud, he observed, introduced a range of procedural rules intended to discourage, and even render impossible, the implementation of the death penalty. He quoted the medieval philosopher Maimonides' principle that a unanimous court judgment on capital punishment should be discounted because it rested on obvious bias. And he recognized that the State of Israel had formally forsworn capital punishment, with the singular exception of the execution of Nazi SS officer Adolf Eichmann in 1962. Beerman's revulsion at the practice led him to serve as a founding board member of Death Penalty Focus, a group established by Mike Farrell in 1988, at whose annual meetings the Los Angeles rabbi would regularly deliver a stirring benediction.

My friend, Mike Farrell, President of Death Penalty Focus, and one of the most impressive human beings I have ever met, once said: "It's only natural, on some level, to want to lash out at one who has inflicted pain on you. Like for like, I guess, is the root concept of ancient law. Blood for blood. If someone does ill to you, do it back to him in the belief that he will learn not to mess with you. That's the guts theory of deterrence. So I absolutely understand the desire to strike out. If someone were to rape, brutalize or kill one of my loved ones I'd probably want to tear him apart with my bare hands, I'm sure. The question is whether or not one actually does it. In a civilized society, retribution is usually taken out of our hands and made subject to the courts.

"The idea of a legal system, someone once told me, is to remove emotion from the equation and allow reason and fairness to be applied so that understanding and ultimately justice can result. While I would be the first to admit that the equation is often perverted today, I think the intention is a noble one; to move us to a higher place, to help us as a people in society move farther away from the caves and closer to the stars."

In the early 1900s, Upton Sinclair wrote a novel called *The Jungle*. His purpose in writing the book was to awaken people to the poverty and exploitation of those laboring in the stockyards of Chicago. It is said of his book that he aimed at the people's hearts, but instead hit their stomachs. Readers were revolted by his depiction of the slaughter of meat. So it was that the novel played an important role, not in improving the condition of the workers, but in the enactment of the first food and drug legislation of 1912.

Those of us who have been working for the abolition of capital punishment aimed at the hearts of our fellow Americans. We have tried to awaken their hearts to the realization that we are all bound together in a common humanity, that there is something inherently sacred in every human being, even in those who have committed the most bestial of crimes.

Then, we attempted to appeal to their reason, by challenging the idea of deterrence, by showing statistically that capital punishment does not deter. We have even tried to lure them by appealing to what sometimes appears to be the ultimate concern of all Americans, their pocketbooks. We were able to demonstrate that capital punishment is indeed more costly than life imprisonment without the possibility of parole.

But what may have at last loosened what appeared to be the fixed conviction of many Americans about the utter rightness of the death penalty is the appalling realization that in the last twenty-five years there were almost 650 executions, but that there were about 90 condemned persons who had convictions overturned by exonerating evidence. One out of seven. With the inescapable inference that some of the 650 executed were innocent. Conservatives in particular were taken with this revelation. For they realized that capital punishment, like the rest of the criminal justice system, is a government program. Always a reason to be skeptical.

All of this is merely prelude to my subject for today—A Jewish Perspective on Capital Punishment.

Let us begin at the beginning, with words of Torah: From the book of Exodus— "If men strive together . . . and any harm follow, then shalt thou give life for life, eye for eye, tooth for tooth, burning for burning, wound for wound, stripe for stripe."

And further on in the book of Leviticus: "Breach for breach, eye for eye, tooth for tooth. And he that hath maimed a man so shall it be done to him. And he that killeth a beast, shall make it good; and he that killeth a man shall be put to death. Ye shall have one manner of law as well for the stranger as for the home-born."

It is our Jewish heritage, which has given to the world the ancient law of retaliation—*lex taliones*. For *fifteen* different crimes the Bible prescribes capital punishment. Among the crimes punishable by death in the Torah—a rebellious son; trespass on sacred grounds; sorcery; bestiality; sacrifice to foreign gods; violating the Sabbath; adultery; incest; homosexuality; prostitution. And for thirty-six crimes, the whole body of Jewish legislation built upon the foundation of the Torah. But you must know that this is only the face of the Jewish law. For when Biblical law came to be translated into juridical practice, the ancient rabbis of the Talmud surrounded capital cases with so many restrictive prohibitions as [to] make it virtually impossible to enforce the death penalty. As early as the second century C.E., monetary damages had already replaced the literal words of the law, which inflicted upon the criminal the very injury he had caused. Although the ancient law, eye for eye, etc. seems barbaric, within its own historical context, it was not. It represented an advancement over the concept of limitless revenge. One eye, not two. One life, not that of an entire family, like the Hatfields and McCoys. Even so, it was a primitive form of justice. The ancient rabbis were uncomfortable with it, embarrassed by it. They insisted that in the case of bodily injury that the spirit of the Torah, not its literal word, should serve as a guide. They therefore substituted compensation in money, a principle of damages that we retain in our contemporary laws. But as for the crimes punishable by death, these were hedged in by a multitude of legal restrictions.

Jewish courts in Talmudic times differed from our modern custom. The first qualification applied to laws of evidence. According to the Bible, evidence is valid only if substantiated by two witnesses. Witnesses must have attained their majority, have never been accused of criminal offenses, cannot be related to the litigants, the judges, or to one another.

Another important qualification related to the acceptability of the confession of the accused. In a civil case if the defendant admits the charge, sentence is passed. But not so in a criminal case. The basic assumption is that a person does not belong to himself; just as one has no right to cause physical harm to another, so one has no right to inflict injury on himself. Therefore, the confession of a defendant has no legal validity. No man can be forced to incriminate himself; self-incrimination is unacceptable as evidence in court.

Nor is circumstantial evidence admissible. An extreme example is cited by the Talmud when it states that if witnesses see a man, sword in hand, pursuing someone, both entering a building, the pursuer emerges alone with a blood-stained weapon and the other is found dead inside, the pursuer cannot be convicted on the basis of this eye witness evidence. Witnesses can only attest to what they have actually seen with their own eyes.

Another important factor is clarification of the intentions of the defendant. A man cannot be sentenced to punishment unless he committed the deed with malice aforethought. How can you prove that? In most countries the law assumes premeditation on the basis of the actions of the criminal. Not so in ancient Jewish law. A person cannot be condemned to death unless witnesses attest not only to the crime but also to the fact that the defendant was warned (*hatra'ah*). That he was told before committing the crime that the act he was about to commit was punishable by death. It was necessary to verify that the defendant had taken note of it and accepted it by saying: "I know and I take it upon myself."

Unlike civil crimes, which were tried before a court of three, capital crimes were to be tried before a court of twenty-three qualified judges. Now in this court of twenty-three judges, a majority of one was sufficient to find for the accused, but a majority of three judges was necessary to declare the accused guilty. Even if the accused were found guilty, there were still regulations designed to protect against a miscarriage of justice. As he was being led to the place of execution, a herald would go forth calling out the name of the guilty one, proclaiming his crime, when and where it was committed, and the names of those upon the basis of whose testimony he had been condemned to death. The herald announced that anyone who possessed even a fragment of evidence favorable to the condemned man should hasten to produce it. Should anyone have produced such evidence, a stay of execution was granted. The final, and by our standards, certainly the most curious and enigmatic provision of the traditional law as interpreted by Maimonides (Mishna Torah IX, 1) was the requirement that if there were a unanimous decision by the court of twenty-three finding the accused guilty, the accused would not be executed, for a unanimous court was presumed to be a prejudiced court.

Need any more be said to clarify the implications of these legal strictures, many of them so obviously impractical? Others may interpret the tradition differently, but the Talmud itself was able to state that a court which executed one murderer in seven or even seventy years was a "murderous court." Rabbi Akiba and Rabbi Tarfon, living in the second century, are recorded as saying that had they sat as judges, no accused person would ever have been subjected to the death penalty.

So this opposition to the death penalty is what we must draw from Jewish tradition. And it must have been with this aspect of the spirit of Judaism in mind that the laws of the State of Israel specifically eliminated capital punishment. Israel made an exception in the Genocide Law it enacted in 1950, the law relating to the crimes of the Nazis and their collaborators. Under this law, crimes committed in the years 1933 to 1945, crimes against humanity and against the Jewish people, were liable to the death penalty. It was this exception, which permitted Adolf Eichmann to be tried, found guilty, and then executed in 1961 for "Crimes against the Jewish people" and "for causing the killing of millions of Jews." Despite onslaughts of terrorists in Israel, Eichmann is still the only person to be executed. I suppose if we executed only those who have killed defenseless millions, there would be far less debate about capital punishment.

It shouldn't surprise us that virtually every major Jewish organization has called for the abolition of the death penalty in America—The American Jewish Committee, the American Jewish Congress, the Central Conference of American Rabbis, the UAHC, etc.

Execution is not simply death. It is premeditated and calculated murder. For there to be an equivalency between the death penalty and murder, execution would, in the words of Albert Camus, have to "punish a criminal who had warned his victim of the date at which he would inflict death upon him, and who, from that moment onward, had confined him at his mercy for months." Such a monster is not encountered in private life.

We are responsible for how we punish. We can punish to educate, to improve, to seek, to redeem. We can punish to deter, to exact retribution, to protect. But to punish out of revenge, it seems to me, turns us into thugs.

COMMENTARY BY MIKE FARRELL

Leonard was a "resister." As he put it in another context, "To be most deeply human is to be among the resisters, to resist whatever demeans life." Keenly aware of the "terrible fragility" of our human condition, he believed we know intuitively "that there is in every human being the possibility of what is humane" and he saw that in "every moment we are given the opportunity to transform the human situation."

In this speech Leonard used his deep understanding of Jewish history, the Torah, and the Talmud to illustrate the fact that despite clear biblical assertions that death is the appropriate punishment for certain crimes, there is a deeply embedded human instinct that argues otherwise.

Positing here a "Jewish Perspective on Capital Punishment," he traces the torturous path of the ancient rabbis in which they "surrounded capital cases with so many restrictive prohibitions as [to] make it virtually impossible" to carry out. They were, he insists, "uncomfortable with it, embarrassed by it."

Tracing developments in legal and juridical thought through the centuries, Leonard here carefully demonstrates that the laws regulating the behavior of human beings, even as we labor to honor the demands and assertions of the ancients, must inevitably respond to the respect for life fundamental to human existence.

Given "the fragile brevity of life and love," he would argue, nothing in law or the requirement of order can overcome the fact that "we were all meant for a great common tenderness."

28

Piece on Human Condition Written for the Office of the Americas

University Synagogue, November 2, 2002

Rabbi Beerman was frequently called upon to offer invocations at the annual meet-ings of nonprofit organizations in the Los Angeles area; he did so on a regular basis for Death Penalty Focus and Human Rights Watch. This invocation for the LA-based Office of the Americas sought to peer into the human soul. It taught that human beings are, at once, solitary individuals alone in their creativity and desperately in search of belonging to something larger than themselves. Rather than privilege one over the other, Beerman conveyed with concise eloquence that human beings con-tinually navigate between these distinct states.

Who of us has not been thinking of this troubled time in which we have been fated to live? Where shall wisdom be found? You remember those words of Shakespeare: "What a piece of work is man. How noble in reason; how infinite in faculties; in form and moving, how express and admirable; in action how like an angel; in apprehension how like a god." Hamlet was of course mad, and looking at our world today, it is very clear, only a madman could say such a thing. When we think of what human beings have done to one another, how can we hold to a brighter vision of the human possibility?

There is no vision of human life worth having that does not include the two poles of human need and desire. All of us need a sense of our own, individual, private integrity; our own personality, something not meant to be breached, or assaulted, or violated by others. That is the basis of whatever dignity we possess. The right to be ourselves in solitude—that is what fires creation and discovery. And that is what is always under assault. For we are born into a world that precedes us, a world already made by other people and we must, if we are to become ourselves, turn that world into our own.

But we also need the other pole of human need and desire. We need to lose our sense of self, to be part of something larger than ourselves, sometimes in moments of great passion. And that is what is the basis of religion, and sex, and politics, and society. That is what it means to experience that exquisite sense of what one human being owes to another, can mean to another.

The right to be ourselves, a sense of an inviolable integrity, and the need to be part of something larger than ourselves. Is that not what we want for every human being? How shall we achieve this when these two poles of human need and desire are almost daily being threatened and mutilated? How shall we do that when we live on a precarious planet "where a small affluent elite perches fearfully on top of three continents of hungry peons" (to borrow Harvey Cox's penetrating words).

Something there is in us, a burning realization, which tells us that there is beauty, but there are the humiliated. And with the writer Albert Camus, we say: "Whatever difficulties the enterprise may present, I would like never to be unfaithful either to the one or the other." There is beauty and there, the humiliated. There is love, and there are the victims of injustice, and surely everyone associated with the OA would say, I would like never to be unfaithful to the one or the other, whatever difficulties the enterprise may represent.

We pray for all those who work for a world of reason and compassion, may courage be given to those who work to abate life's miseries and heal its wounds, who are comrades in the only battle worth waging, the battle to create a more humane world.

COMMENTARY BY STEPHEN ROHDE

With the memories of 9/11 a year earlier—"this troubled time"—on his mind, Leonard addressed the annual gathering of the Office of the Americas, founded in 1983 to pursue international justice and peace and oppose "the long-standing international culture of militarism," on whose Advisory Board he had served for decades.

Here, as throughout his life, Leonard confronted "what human beings have done to one another," expressing his commitment to the twin goals of upholding "individual, private integrity" while being "part of something larger than ourselves."

Leonard knew and taught the Jewish tradition of placing life above all else. It was his compassionate opposition to the death penalty, which brutally denies the dignity of each human being, which had first brought us together in the struggle to abolish capital punishment. Here he bemoans how the "inviolable integrity" of the individual is "almost daily being threatened and mutilated."

In Leonard's words, one can hear the third-century Mishnah text: "Therefore, humans were created singly, to teach you that whoever destroys a single soul,

Scripture accounts it as if he had destroyed a full world; and whoever saves one soul, Scripture accounts it as if she had saved a full world."

In the end, Leonard urges his audience, "whatever difficulties the enterprise may represent," to build "a world of reason and compassion," offering courage to "those who work to abate life's miseries and heal its wounds" in "the battle to create a more humane world." Leonard was describing his entire life's work.

29

A Vision for a Bewildering Time

Commencement Address at
Washington & Jefferson College

May 18, 2007

On the occasion of receiving an honorary doctorate from Washington & Jefferson College in Washington, PA, Beerman faced the challenging task of delivering the commencement address. He drew on a mix of religious and literary sources to lay out a familiar set of dichotomies: between darkness and light, a culture of materialism and a state of poverty, and greed and love. His message to the Washington & Jefferson undergraduates was not to rest content dwelling in these opposing tendencies, but to seek out the interconnectedness of life. It was especially in great works of art that one could most readily grasp this interconnectedness. A sense of connection, in turn, lends us a measure of "ardor and courage" in engaging with the world.

I am so grateful to Dr. Tori Haring-Smith for giving me the opportunity to be with you today. With this invitation she has allowed me to return to a geography I have not visited for at least eighty years. I was a boy of six when l accompanied my father, a traveling salesman, as he made his [way] through the small towns of this area.

And thinking of my father reminds me of one of the valuable principles I learned from him when I was very young, one so easily forgotten on occasions like this one. For I still remember when he took a baseball bat and placed it in my hands, showed me how to swing it and then, very solemnly declared, "Now son, you must remember to keep your eye on the ball." Ever since, often failing, I have tried to make those immortal words my guide, and I offer them to you. This means that our task is to consider always what is taking place, to focus, center on that, lend ourselves to it, lean into it, permit ourselves to become servant to it.

So what is the ball here that I must strive to keep my eye on today? Is it not really something very clear and simple? Is it not that some wonderfully impressive young men and women are about to take their place in the great processional of those who throughout the ages have wished to advance the cause of human learning? And at such a moment, custom dictates that an older one step forward to address them. And the message to be delivered, no matter what its apparent form or content, the message is always the same. The old one faces the young and says: Blessed is the God who has kept us alive and sustained us and brought us to this joyful time. For we look at you and we feel the swarming of youth and hope and voices, and the generations to come, the thing others will see. We want you to be armed with hope, and to be awake to the consciousness of the good, the beauty, the tenderness, the passion, the gaiety, the rhythm, the music of life. We want you to be awake to all that is sweet and noble.

As for us, the world we have helped to fashion for you is a dark place, and we older ones often fumble in it. We confess to you, paraphrasing the words of James Agee, that our desire and our faith delude us into wrong visions and attributions; that the best of our knowledge is but the shade and shape of a dream, and full of pretense. Nevertheless, we have faith in you, and we pray that your eyes and your hearts be honest and lovely and a little clearer than ours. We embrace you with our love and our prayers, and we welcome you into the company of those to whom no acceptable answer has yet been given. We welcome you to the company of those who wish to sing God's song in the land.

The voice trails away. It is enough to say that. Let the ceremony continue. Let the commencement come. It is enough, is it not?

Ah, but you know as well as I that that doesn't always work for members of the clergy of any persuasion (did you imagine that a rabbi would be any different?) and at my age the eye is not so sharp to see the ball, the heart melts just a little with gratitude and nostalgia—a most incendiary mixture. And I see those windows here, windows that connect us to the real world, to remind us that outside is that crazy, mixed-up complicated brutal world we shall have to live and work in. And there, lurking just beyond those windows, waiting for us, are some haunting questions: "How shall we sing God's song in such a strange land?" How shall we know the good and the tenderness, when we live on a precarious planet where a small affluent elite perches fearfully on the top of three continents of hungry people? How shall we know beauty, when there are so many humiliated? How shall we experience the rhythm, the music of life?

You and I, as Lewis Lapham has written, are or will be members of the possessing classes, those who are able to recline at their ease among computers and cellular phones. On the other side of the walls, in the desolate slums, in the third and fifth worlds, the mass of poor, the terminally impoverished, tear at one another for bones. Most of us here agree, I am certain, on the moral unacceptability of the persistent and growing "savage inequality" in income, in education, in opportunity, here and throughout the world, whether caused by discrimination or economic policy. But there may be some among us, and certainly many out there, who accept this world as it is, as if it were given to Moses on Mt. Sinai or were the ultimate expression of the inexorable process of evolution. What's mine is mine. I haven't stolen it. It is a privilege I have earned or deserved. In this view, as Peter Marin said, we are in our proper place; others are in theirs. We may even bemoan their fate or even try to do something to change it, but in essence it has nothing to do with us. Nothing to feel guilty about. The self, fulfilling the self, even the quest for self-esteem, even the yearning for certain kinds of spirituality, here replaces everything else. The other just disappears. Disappears in the morning coffee. Disappears in the business news, where you might learn of some cautions about the booming economy and of the wisdom and the courage and the efficiency of the leadership of this or that corporation, trimming its costs by the elimination of thousands of employees.

"You can't eat an orange and throw the peel away. A man is not a piece of fruit," Willie Loman cries out, in *Death of a Salesman*.

"He's not the finest character that ever lived," his wife Linda says to their sons. "But he's a human being and a terrible thing is happening to him. So attention must be paid."

A spirit is characterized not only by what it does, but no less by what it permits, what it forgives, what it beholds in silence.

We know that we have been inhabiting an age brimming with cruelty and violence and mendacity, where human beings, even the best of them, act in what could kindly be called morally ambiguous ways, and often in the name of the highest ideals and noblest visions. We have been stunned and staggered by the violence. Who of us has not felt fear and uncertainty, who of us has not had feelings of shock, sorrow, loss, anger, and a heightened sense of our own vulnerability?

Did something go wrong at the very beginning?

The poet Joseph Pintauro thought so, and described it this way:

> Something went wrong
> In the garden.
> Eve said to {Cain} her first
> Born son, "get over
> Here or I'll break
> every bone
> in your body.
> And Adam said, "do what your mother tells you."
> And the boy said, "someday."

So here we are, you and I. We have been taught from the most ancient times, long before the insights of Sigmund Freud, or the modern adaptations and departures from his thought, that God created us human beings with a cluster of contradictory drives and hungers—the impulses of greed and envy, and mutual hatred. The ability to tear the world apart. The power to invent war and tyranny.

But we have also been endowed with another set of impulses. The ones that draw us toward one another in connection, in community, in love. "The ones that helped us discover liberty, equality, fraternity, and though they remain unrealized, we have labored our way toward them" (Peter Marin, *Freedom and Its Discontents*). We are not expected to be saints, to achieve the unattainable. The greatest of our Biblical heroes, in the Hebrew Bible, what Christians call the Old Testament, every one of them, was flawed, and the best of us as well. Are we forever condemned to be the prisoner of the balance of power as it presently exists between the two warring impulses within us? The one future beautiful fragile and humble truth that can bring us all to a better way of being is in guarding and cultivating the awareness that whatever value we have has come to us because of the accomplishment of others, the living and the dead. The other is always there, always present in our lives. We can hear it in our voices—does it make you suspicious that you speak a language that was invented by dead people?—you can see it in the color of your eyes. Other is always there, even when you are alone, a book on the shelf, a table, a bed, a chair reminds you that other is always there. It's the hands of others, always the hands of others that make our lives possible. The hands of others lift us from the womb, nurture us when we are most weak and vulnerable. The hands of others weave the clothes, build our homes, the hands of others bring pleasure to our bodies in moments of passion, and ultimately for us all, it will be the hands [of] others that lower [us] into the grave.

We, and all human beings, need a sense of our own individual, private integrity, something not meant to be breached, or assaulted, or violated by others. That is the basis of whatever dignity we possess. The right to be ourselves in solitude—that is what fires creation and discovery. And that is what is always under assault. For we are born into a world we have not made, a world fashioned by other people, and we must, if we are to become ourselves, turn that world into our own.

But we also need the other pole of human need and desire. We need to lose our sense of self, to be part of something larger than ourselves, sometimes in moments of great passion, and that is what is the basis of religion and sex and politics and society, that is what it means to experience that exquisite sense of what one human being owes to another, what one human being can mean to another.

Do we not wish to see and to feel the interconnectedness between all things and to be an instrument of that interconnectedness? Is that not the divine part of ourselves?

I shall always remember what the poet Ann Lauterbach once wrote, some of which I paraphrase: When choices are displayed in the service of the possibility of meaning, in the making of objects of art (for example) we call the results, beautiful. That is, we stand before a painting of Van Gogh or Claude Monet, or we read a poem of Robert Pinsky or Amichai, or we listen to the music of Bach or Beethoven or Mahler, and we say, this is beautiful. "But what we are really announcing is our pleasure and gratitude in the choices the artist has made. We recognize something in how one stroke of the brush brushes up against another stroke of the brush; how one note moves toward and away from the next in an astounding sequence; how one word attaches itself to another and to another and to another until something that has to do with all the words separately, gathers into a connection which allows us, which invites us, [which incites us] to experience the meaning of meaning."[1]

Is that not what we are seeking to do and to teach: To see and to feel the union, the connectedness, the beauty of it all—in the marvel of human conscience, in the structure of our bodies and our imaginations and our passions, in all the disparate parts of our lives, in the ties of humanity itself that link us to one another?

This is a vision that can bring ardor and courage to visions of the world, a reaffirmation of our sometimes fragile belief that this world, for all of its cynicism and its suffering, for all of its barbarism and stupidity and anguish, is also a place where change is possible, where love and human will can be transforming. In this endeavor there is no guarantee of victory, but there is a choice: one either collaborates with the enemy—with whatever is, whatever is miserable, or inhumane, with whatever is unjust, with whatever demeans the life of any human being, even those we call our enemies—or one joins the resistance, and insists on being among those who strive to diminish the store of insult and agony in the world, insisting on being among those who dare to believe that every woman, man, child is a disclosure of the divine.

And this comes to you with a wish, a yearning, a prayer, one I discovered in the Library of Congress while prowling around on the Internet, a fragment of a poem in Walt Whitman's own hand: "uncage in my heart a thousand new strengths, and unknown ardors, and terrible ecstasies."

That indeed is what I wish for you.

Blessed are the parents who bore these young people and together with wives and husbands and friends and significant others cajoled, threatened, nudged, [and] lovingly encouraged them to reach this day.

Blessed are the teachers for the enormous power of their faith in the worth of what they do, which makes it possible for them to do so much when the reward is often so ambiguous. Blessed are they for their exquisite patience, for their stubbornness, and for the persistence of their belief in ideas.

Blessed are the students for their laughter, for not giving up, for their courage in overcoming all resistances to learning. Bless them even more with the wisdom to reexamine everything they have learned.

Yes, we have faith in you, and we pray that your eyes and your hearts be honest and lovely and a little clearer than ours. We embrace you and welcome you into the company of those who wish to sing God's song in the land.

COMMENTARY BY PROFESSOR DAVID ELLENSON

As I write these words reflecting upon this address that Leonard delivered to the graduates of Washington & Jefferson College, the 2016 American presidential campaign is raging. I have little doubt that if he were alive, Leonard would be a supporter of Senator Bernie Sanders. The calls by the Vermont senator for a redress to the plague of societal inequality that mars our nation echo the sentiments and commitments Leonard expressed throughout his lifetime as well as in this speech. The contemporary context only highlights how prescient and prophetic Leonard was when he uttered these words. By reminding the students that he and they were members of the "possessing classes," Leonard challenged them to think about how they would respond to their privileged position. As Leonard stated, who we are as persons is characterized by what we permit, what we forgive, what we behold in silence. Inaction evokes human responsibility as much as the deeds we perform.

Even as Leonard congratulated his listeners on their achievements, he called upon the audience to remember the grandeur that can mark the human spirit. He emphasized that the miracle of human existence is the miracle of the moral in the human being. The aesthetics of his rhetoric and the sweep of sources he cited to make this point remind us just how literate and inspiring as well as challenging Leonard always was. His ability to be all these things simultaneously was a rare and precious gift, and it makes me realize all the more how much our world is impoverished by the loss of his physical presence. However, his voice continues to cry out in this speech, reminding us that it is we who must mold community and shape the world. It is a message as vital today as when he delivered it in 2007.

30

Letter to President George W. Bush

April 11, 2008

Forty-one years earlier, Rabbi Beerman addressed a letter to President Lyndon Johnson, requesting that his and Martha Beerman's taxes not be directed toward the war effort in Vietnam. Here in 2008, he requested that his and Joan Beerman's taxes not be directed toward the war effort in Iraq, but rather toward "works of healing and peace." His language is much the same in the two letters, although there is new language in the 2008 missive calling for the return of "our brave soldiers to their homes and families." This represents a key attitudinal shift in American society after Vietnam whereby US soldiers went from being perceived by many in negative terms—as complicit in the war effort—to a new appreciation for the difficult plight in which they were placed and for the scars that war inflicted on them.

President George W. Bush
The White House
Washington, D.C.
April 11, 2008

Dear Mr. President:

My wife Joan and I have just paid our income tax for the year 2007. That portion of our tax which helps to sustain the war in Iraq has been paid involuntarily. We have no wish to support what we consider to be unjust. We should be happy to pay even a greater proportion of our income for works of healing and peace, but the acts of violence being perpetrated by our government violate our conscience. That portion of our tax that helps make these acts possible we pay under protest.

We pray that you may have the courage and the wisdom to bring this war to a swift end, and return our brave soldiers to their homes and families.

Sincerely,

Leonard I. Beerman

COMMENTARY BY NORMAN LEAR

This letter to President George W. Bush is a perfect example of who Leonard Beerman was, as a man, and as a citizen. *He was willing to put his money and morals on the line—and speak truth to power.* Whatever the issue, the cause, the question, you never had to doubt where Leonard stood—he made his opinion known. Leonard was that man not because he saw it as a duty, but because being responsible was second nature to him.

Leonard Beerman was sweet-tempered and mild-mannered. One could call him reticent, unassuming—even shy perhaps—but underneath that there was a layer of wise conviction that placed him, from my point of view, in the Man of Steel category. Leonard's wisdom came with enormous courage and conviction. Who else, speaking on the Fourth of July at the All Saints Episcopal Church in Pasadena, would remind America that its "wanton use of power had abused others, killed, wounded or driven them into exile . . . and was now abusing so many of its own citizens . . . having organized all of the dominant workings of a society to move in total subservience to an economy that enriches the very few."

In another sermon, speaking of the Jewish people whom he had devoted his life to lead, he honored their generosity, endurance, and accomplishments, but then had the guts and temerity to refer to the now and then "chasm between their ideals and their deeds . . . in such contentious matters as Israel's treatment of the Palestinians and the continuing moral outrage of its occupation of the West Bank." That behavior, said the good rabbi, "threatened the ethical core of Israel's being."

In 1980, fearful of the mix of politics and religion emanating from televangelist Pat Robertson's 700 Club, Jerry Falwell's Moral Majority, and the like, I wanted to do something about it, and I needed advice. Of course I sought out Leonard Beerman and learned that, with his good friend George Regas, he had already been mounting a mainline church effort to counter the Religious Right. "Stick to your last," Leonard advised me, and encouraged me to go after them with the tricks of *my* trade. People for the American Way grew out of a sixty-second public service announcement that followed my acceptance of Leonard's advice.

Wisdom, with courage and conviction, was freely dispensed by Leonard Beerman on a daily basis. I'm grateful that much of it is still available in his published sermons.

31

Human Rights Watch

Beverly Hilton Hotel, November 17, 2009

Below is one of the many invocations that Rabbi Beerman offered (along with George Regas) at the annual dinner of Human Rights Watch, an organization on whose board he sat and for which he served as a kind of rabbi-in-residence. In this set of remarks from 2009, Beerman identifies a persistent danger that he often mentioned in his speeches: silence in the face of injustice. As a foil to his point, he summoned forth the words of Rabbi Leo Baeck, the great German-Jewish leader after whom Beerman's congregation was named, who once remarked that "a spirit is characterized (by what) it beholds in silence." Not content with this sensibility, Beerman referred to two contemporary events about which one could not remain silent: the ongoing US military engagements in Iraq and Afghanistan, and Israel's rocket attacks on and invasion of the Gaza Strip in late 2008/early 2009. In both instances, Beerman believed that the loss of civilian life did not—and never could—justify military action. Consequently, vocal opposition, not silence, was called for. In the case of Israel's Gaza conflict, he was well aware that his willingness to be critical would generate anger from some in the Jewish community, including from members of his own liberal congregation.

If I were to fashion an appropriate epigraph or motto for this evening in which we celebrate the work of Human Rights Watch, and the extraordinary valor of Elena Milashina and Daniel Bekele, I could think of nothing more appropriate than the words of Rabbi Leo Baeck, the leading rabbi of Germany when Hitler came to power, a concentration camp survivor: "A spirit," Baeck wrote, "is characterized not only by what it does, but no less by what it permits, what it forgives, what it beholds in silence."

Permits, forgives, beholds in silence.

What do we behold in silence? One must be very careful with one's silences, for silences rise to heaven as well.

In being here tonight we express our appreciation for those who have had the courage to refuse to be silent wherever human rights are trampled upon; and, to the great discomfort of some, have refused to be silent about certain sensitive, controversial issues, like the behavior of the military forces of our own country; or, although it consists of a small proportion of the focus of our work, about what really happened last January to the people of southern Israel and Gaza, and the manner in which the men, women, and children were killed there.

In Israel, there was a great poet, Daliah Ravikovich, who died just a few years ago, considered to be the outstanding woman poet of the Hebrew language. One of her best known poems is entitled "Hovering at a Low Altitude." In this poem, there is a female narrator who presents herself in a very satirical way as witness to the rape and murder of an Arab shepherd child. The narrator watches from the safe distance of a low altitude and does nothing. As she watches she says, "I'm not here." She sees the little girl, yet she says over and over, "I'm not here." The image of hovering in this poem (the Hebrew word is *rechifa*) contains a double meaning, connecting the language of army bulletins—"Low flying helicopters in hovering formations over the Gaza strip"—with Tel Aviv slang, where *l'rachef* means "to be cool, by staying detached from the political situation." The image of low altitude hovering over an atrocity is an emblem of the situation of the ordinary citizen knowing, but choosing not to see certain terrible acts being perpetrated. It is primarily a parable of the moral untenability of detached observation.

What is it we choose to affirm in being here tonight? Not for us detached observation. Not for us to behold in silence. No. We *are* here. And wherever Human Rights Watch is, a voice goes forth to cry out, "We are here!"

COMMENTARY BY JANE OLSON

We began a tradition at Human Rights Watch (HRW) galas in Los Angeles during the early 1990s of having Rabbi Leonard Beerman and Dr. George Regas open dinner programs with invocations that included a blessing in Hebrew, in the Jewish tradition, and in English, in the Christian tradition, a tradition not followed in New York or other city HRW dinners. The two set a solemn and loving tone for the evening, and our guests expressed gratitude.

The invocation became an eagerly anticipated opening, and after a few years we asked Rabbi Beerman to present a more substantive message that acknowledged both the historic roots and contemporary nature of human rights abuse.

Leonard's messages were deep, literary, and poetic. A thousand noisy and hungry attendees would become absolutely still, riveted on Leonard's words. Every year I received many requests for copies of his text.

A memorable invocation delivered by Rabbi Beerman on November 17, 2009, demonstrated his own courageous stance against human rights abuse. He used the occasion to focus on recent violence in Israel, expressing his disappointment in military forces, whose recent retaliation in Gaza killed many innocent men, women, and children.

Leonard challenged actions of his beloved Israel, standing up to many conservative Jews who rejected and condemned any criticism as anti-Semitic. By so doing, he defended the research and reporting on Israel by Human Rights Watch, which held Israel to universal standards of civilian protection and rule of law, with no exceptionalism.

Leonard also challenged us all as individuals, using a poem entitled "Hovering at a Low Altitude." The narrator, witness to horrendous abuse of a child, stood silently by as a "detached observer."

An ordinary citizen, Leonard said, by choosing not to see certain terrible acts being perpetrated, but to behold in silence, violates basic moral standards of humanity.

"Not for us, detached observation," he declared. "We are here!"

We could always count on Rabbi Leonard Beerman to *be here,* as our moral compass and North Star. Even in his passing, his inspirational and passionate words and his uncommonly brave and moral life continue to guide all who are fortunate enough to hold his memory dear.

32
___

A Sermon for All Saints

July 3, 2011

As rabbi-in-residence, Leonard Beerman was a frequent guest and preacher at All Saints Church in Pasadena. And as an "eternal dissident," he understood well and often practiced the principle of speaking truth to power.

His sermon on the eve of the Fourth of July at All Saints was an exercise in prophetic application. He retreated to the Hebrew Bible to recall the case of the foreign prophet Balaam who, surprisingly, refused to curse the Israelites, recognizing in them a set of special qualities. Among those qualities was "a certain restlessness in its spirit" that fueled, according to Beerman, a willingness to challenge convention and struggle for justice.

That quality still animates Jews today, he declared, expressing what was surely a personal credo. He himself sought to exemplify the quality by discussing the meaning of Independence Day—and the United States of America. He did so by grappling with the figure of Thomas Jefferson, who, of the Founding Fathers, delivered some of the most soaring language about the equality of men. Yet, Beerman noted, Jefferson intended men, not women—and white men, decidedly not black men. In this sense, he extracted from Jefferson's oratory not only inspiration but also aspiration, the desire to improve upon ourselves, to transcend the deficiencies and inequities in our present lives. Therein lay, according to him, the challenge and promise of America.

Standing here near my dear friend George Regas is a vivid reminder for me that the gift of our forty-four years of friendship is one that has kept on giving. It has not only brought the four of us—George and Mary, Leonard and Joan—into a loving connection—but also this gift, the privilege of being here so often with this extraordinary congregation, to have been able to feel the embrace of your welcome, and the constant affirmation of the conviction that though we come out of different faiths, we are united in the same quest, draw inspiration from the same roots—we belong to one another.

On more than one occasion, I have heard George describe himself as a country preacher. Yes, quite a country preacher, coming out of this humble dwelling, surrounded as it is by all that farmland. But it is here, in this pulpit, that he was able to move so many with his sermons, sermons which displayed the remarkable ability to sneak up on you with those soft and warm quotations from the New Testament, and then suddenly strike with prophetic passion the great issues of justice and peace and love which have always been at the heart of his ministry.

Today, with my friend Ed Bacon on sabbatical, if I were giving a sermon based on a biblical text for this fourth of July weekend, I would be turning to what might seem to you and me to be a most unlikely place, a section of the book of Numbers in the Hebrew Bible (24–25) that centuries before July 4, 1776, was assigned for reading this coming week in all the synagogues of the world. It's that enigmatic one that contains the story of the talking ass. Animals are supposed to be semantically blocked, so if an ass talked it was a miracle. So we used to think, until the modern age and our encounter with some of the candidates for political office.

But let's try to imagine the situation here. The Israelites, led by Moses, are now entering the last stage of their journey to the Promised Land. Beset at every turn by obstacles, rebellious, straining even to return to the security of the slavery they had left behind in Egypt, they have nonetheless advanced toward the ultimate goal. They are a fierce, unpredictable, frequently obnoxious people, and yet they are about to undertake the conquest of what is to become their national home.

The Moabites who live on the eastern border of the Jordan are fearful, filled with dread at the onrush of the Israelites. Their king, Balak, is afraid with them, and he reaches out for help; he sends a delegation to a heathen sorcerer, a strange figure who lives near the Euphrates river, and he invites this diviner, Balaam is his name, to come to Moab and stem the tide of these dreadful hordes of invading Israelites by bringing a curse upon them: "Come now, curse me this people, for they are too mighty for me. Perhaps I shall prevail that we may smite them and drive them out of the land, for I know that he whom you bless is blessed, and he whom you curse is cursed."

This Balaam is a baffling creature; he's a prophet of sorts who could use his powers for evil. It wasn't that he lacked cleverness or wisdom; it was character that he lacked. He was capable of the most penetrating observations, but he was for hire—a prophet for hire; he was a man who could be lured by the promise of honor and riches, not unlike people we have come to know about, men and women who can stifle their moral impulses out of their desire to be close to the ruling power, or to be a ruling power. The Hebrew prophets, Amos, Micah, Isaiah, Jeremiah, were men of stern, dogmatic integrity; fear, or the desire for honor, could not corrupt them. They therefore became aliens, solitary, suffering, tragic men; such was the demand of truth upon their lives. But Balaam was ready to hire himself out, but strangely in his case, the true prophet emerges out of the false, overcomes the false, for Balaam cannot perform the service for which the king is ready to pay him. He cannot bring the curse. Instead, he looks out at the oncoming Israelites and utters the words with which pious Jews have begun their morning prayers throughout the centuries. He looks out and says, "How goodly are thy tents O Jacob, thy tabernacles, O Israel."

Balaam saw something about the true nature of this people. It was a people of Jacob. It had descended from the patriarch. It had an ethnic identity. It had undergone certain experiences in its history. It was a people like other peoples, full of imperfections (like Jacob himself). It could rebel; it could be ungrateful, unbelieving, doubting, fearful. It could reject, it could even abandon its God on behalf of others. It could degenerate. Balaam must have seen that, that here was a people like others, living within all of the circumstances which had made it a people.

But then Balaam saw something else. That this people was invested with a unique quality, that it possessed a radiance that accompanied it wherever it went. For this was not only the people of Jacob, this was the people of Israel. Israel was the name given to Jacob after he had wrestled with someone in that dark night of his soul: "Jacob will no longer be your name, but Israel." Israel, which means one who has wrestled with God. That was to be the distinctive quality of this people—a certain restlessness in its spirit. For very early in its history there entered a ferment that would give it no rest. In the midst of the pagan world, so magnificent in its grandeur, this people questioned what was universally accepted by those who lorded power over them. When all about them the great nations of the world worshiped many gods, this people refused, for it had come to believe (in the words of Martin Buber) that just as there was the One who had set the sun and the moon in the heavens above, so there was a Lord of being and becoming who had set a commandment of justice and truth above the heads of the human race, and that the great duty of this people was the realization of truth and justice in the fullness of everyday life. So the whole of Jewish history becomes a record of wrestling and struggle against all those forces, within the people, and without, that would divert our people from the truth of its being, from the fundamental principle of its civilization, which called upon the Jewish people to be bearers of a great moral aspiration.

That struggle goes on today. We Jews can acknowledge the wonder of our endurance and celebrate our remarkable accomplishments, our love of learning, and even our capacity for generosity, sensitivity, and humaneness, and even the rise of the State of Israel out of the ashes of the destruction of European Jewry, yet so many of my people are haunted by the chasm between our ideals and our deeds, not only in our personal lives, but also in such contentious matters as Israel's treatment of the Palestinians, the continuing moral outrage of its occupation of the West Bank, and the blockade of Gaza. Yet I would insist that the real threat to us is not the danger of the lingering anti-Semitism, or the hostility of Israel's neighbors, and the religious fanatics, dedicated to its destruction. No, what is threatened today is the ethical core of our being.

The ethical core of our being. The chasm between our ideals and our deeds. What does that suggest to you? The disjunction of ideals and deeds—that is the great historic embarrassment of all religions, yours, mine, Christianity, Islam, Judaism, and all the rest, is it not? And what of America itself?

Tomorrow is the day our country declared its independence from England. The long-standing resentment against British occupation had turned into war. 235 years ago, yesterday, the Continental Congress adopted the declaration, and issued it on July 4. After it had been written on parchment it was brought back to Congress and on August 2 it was signed. But the news had actually reached New York on July 9, and there it was read to cheering crowds who, marching down Broadway to the lowest tip of Manhattan, became a mob, and they tore down the gilded statue of George III on his colossal horse. They hacked off his head and severed his nose and mounted what remained of his head on a spike outside a tavern. I can just imagine . . .

It was these treasonous, raucous, riotous rebels, in the battles that followed, who helped to bring forth a new nation dedicated to the proposition that all men were created equal. Created equal, endowed by their Creator with certain unalienable rights, Life, Liberty, the Pursuit of Happiness—those were all the words of Thomas Jefferson; who can hear them and not be moved by them?

Fifty years later and ten days before his death, Jefferson wrote that the declaration would be "the signal arousing men to burst the chains and to secure the blessings of self government. All eyes are opening to the rights of man . . . The mass of mankind has not been born with saddles on their backs for the favored few booted and spurred, ready to ride them legitimately."

All men are created equal, Jefferson had written, all men, not yet women. Created equal, all white men, not yet black. You cannot read any of his beautiful soaring words without some ironic discomfort, without looking down into the chasm between his words and his deeds, that even today's children come to learn. He decried the slave trade and yet bought and sold slaves. The God who gave us life gave us liberty—yes, but he tracked down and punished slaves who, claiming this liberty, had run away. He was convinced that slavery was wrong, immoral, and yet he wrote a slave code for the state of Virginia. He opposed any effort to limit the expansion of slavery. And he was able to discuss slave breeding as though he were talking of dogs and horses, as Benjamin Schwartz has written (*LA Times,* July 3, 1994).

If you have ever visited the home Jefferson built in Monticello you will see a marvelous revelation of the man himself. It is an incredibly beautiful place displaying the many-faceted talents of our country's first genius. In Charlottesville at the University of Virginia, which he designed and where George spoke recently, and on that hill in Monticello there is a note of balance; everything he designed has this balance: the curtains in his bedroom, the self-winding clock in the foyer. The very style of his life was Olympian, everything properly proportioned. Jefferson lived on this hill, and from it he could see all the contradictory forces of life. He, like all of us, was composed of contradictions. Monticello, for all of its beauty, like the Egyptian pyramids, rested on the back of slave labor.

So Jefferson has left us with an assignment: To live up to his ideals, not his prejudices. Abiding by those ideals, he prophesied, "The American people would go on, puzzled and prospering beyond example in the history of man."

He, and the other founders, left us with a dream, and we have indeed been possessed by that dream, but they have also left us still yearning for an America, in the words of Martin Luther King, that would "live out the true meaning of its creed."

July 4 is a time to summon up the honesty that would be worthy of so great an accomplishment as bringing an America into being, remembering that ours is a nation that has not fulfilled its promises, that it is not the chosen instrument of God. We might even acknowledge how tarnished our greatness has become. If ever there was a time for the celebration of humility, it is now. With the wanton use of our power we have abused others, killed, wounded, or driven them into exile, in Iraq, Afghanistan, and now in Libya. Not to mention our own dead and wounded, many beyond repair. And now our power has been abusing us, sucking away at our financial resources, abusing so many of our citizens, leaving them in want and despair. And how decadent it is to have organized all of the dominant workings of a society to move in total subservience to an economy that enriches the very few, but leaves so many deprived of a decent job at living wages, health care for all, a quality education, protection from hunger, a secure retirement, too many deprived, even, of hope for a better way of life for themselves and their children.

Look, I know that those who come to All Saints are not a congregation of utterly naïve faith-based idealists. You and I are aware that democracy has always been a dangerous business. To use the words of Lewis Lapham, "it allies itself with change, which engenders movement, which induces friction, which implies unhappiness, which assumes conflict not only as the normal but also as the necessary condition of its existence. The idea collapses unless countervailing stresses oppose one another with competing weight—unless enough people stand willing to sustain the argument between the governing and the governed, between city and town, capital and labor, men and women, matter and mind" (*Harpers,* April 2011).

So, let us here highly resolve that we wish to [be] among those who stand willing to sustain the argument.

"Let America be America again. Let it be the dream it used to be," the African American poet Langston Hughes wrote in 1938, as the country had not yet fully emerged from the Great Depression.

It may have been in that very year that Thomas Wolfe, a highly acclaimed American novelist of the time, wrote these words for the final chapter of what would be his final book, *You Can't Go Home Again:*

I believe that we are lost here in America, but I believe we shall be found. And this belief . . . is for me—and I think for all of us—not only our own hope, but America's everlasting, living dream. I think the life which we have fashioned in America, and which has fashioned us—the forms we made, the cells that grew—was self-destructive in its nature . . . I think these forms are dying and must die, just as I know that America and the people in it, are deathless, undiscovered, and must live.

I think the true discovery of America is before us . . . the true fulfillment of our spirit, our people, of our mighty and immortal land, is yet to come. I think the true discovery of our own democracy is still before us. And I think that all these things are certain as the morning, as inevitable as noon.

COMMENTARY BY MEL LEVINE

America enthusiastically celebrates the birthday of our Declaration of Independence every 4th of July. But we don't ask: How are we doing as a nation? On the eve of America's 235th birthday, Rabbi Leonard Beerman added an accounting to the celebration. Why not? Surely this is the essence of Leonard: shining a spotlight on our failures to achieve justice but with his resolute optimism that we do better, urging us to strive, as he put it in this sermon, to live up to our ideals, not our prejudices.

Leonard's sermon at All Saints on July 3, 2011, was titled "What America Can and Should Be." He began by describing his longtime close friend George Regas, legendary pastor of All Saints, as possessing "the remarkable ability to sneak up on you with those soft and warm quotations from the New Testament, and then suddenly strike with prophetic passion the great issues of justice and peace and love which have always been at the heart of his ministry." These words could just as easily have described Leonard, but with an Old Testament template.

Referring to "the chasm between our ideals and our deeds," Leonard extolled Jefferson for the Declaration of Independence, but chastised him for his moral failings regarding slavery. And this duality in Jefferson, he continued, also existed in the biblical people of Israel: "a people like other peoples, full of imperfections," but that possessed "a radiance that accompanied it wherever it went."

America's birthday is a time for consummate honesty, he declared, recognizing that "ours is a nation that has not fulfilled its promises, that it is not the chosen instrument of God. . . . If there ever was a time for the celebration of humility, it is now." But, as he always believed, if we have the courage to see what is true, we can summon the power to remedy even terrible wrongs. He echoed Thomas Wolfe, who said: "I think the true discovery of our own democracy is still before us."

PART V

Israel/Palestine

33

Time in Israel, Parts I and II

November 1967

In the wake of his third trip to Israel in 1967 (after earlier visits in 1947 and 1964), Beerman penned some of his thoughts about the Six-Day War, which took place between June 5 and 10. In them, Beerman reflected on, among other subjects, the idea of a Jewish state, his connection to it, and his general view of nationalism. Below are two products of that reflection, not fully completed in either case, in which Beerman bares his soul about his Israel.

In the first, he reveals his typical capacity for grasping complexity in any given historical moment. He observes the fierce sense of pride and unity that the Six-Day War induced in Israelis—and, for that matter, in many Jews around the world. He also calls attention to the unrelenting hostility of the Arab world toward Israel and its existence. At the same time, he identifies himself here and later as a congenital skeptic, one who is good at identifying problems. Even in the midst of the post–Six-Day War euphoria experienced by many Jews, he asks probing and prescient questions: What is the nature of a Jewish state? Can it be fully democratic and equal for its Arab citizens? In this regard, he anticipates a pitched debate that broke out in Israel in the 1990s over whether the country should aspire to be a Jewish state, a state of the Jews, or a state of all of its citizens.

In the second set of reflections, Beerman enters into a more introspective state, meditating on his own connection to Israel. He declares himself to be a deep lover of Israel. He even demonstrates dexterity at rebutting claims from the Arab world that the State of Israel has no right to exist. But he also makes clear that he finds nationalism, including Zionism, to be chauvinistic and exclusionary. He resists the impulse to yoke or reduce the entirety of his Judaism to support for the Jewish state. And he gives voice here to his discomfort with the triumphalist sensibility that took hold in Israel and the Diaspora after the Six-Day War. Along the way, Beerman recalls his encounters with Judah L. Magnes, under whose influence he came to Jerusalem in 1947, and with the Israeli author Aharon Megged, with whom in an Arab café in the Old City of Jerusalem in 1967 he shared concerns over Israel's new militarism.

TIME IN ISRAEL, PART I

There are many Jewish travellers to Israel these days. They come for a host of old reasons but they come now specifically to see what Israel [has] wrought since those fateful days in May and June of this year.

It was once a tiny land, at best no larger than the state of Rhode Island. Now its dimensions along with its people's pride have been broadened. In the central region its belly is puffed out with the territory of the west bank of the Jordan. In the north its head is now bigger with the acquisition of the forbidding Golan Heights of Syria looking down upon the now tranquil Galilee. Its feet reaching westward to the Suez Canal planted firmly upon the desert of Sinai. It is now, for those who have known it intimately in these past twenty years, a huge land for so small a people. The mantle of authority over these newer borders is new and even tentative, at least in whispered conversation.

The traveler who comes [from] America, France, or England enters a strange atmosphere when he comes to Israel. At home in England, France, or America there rages conflict intellectual, political over any of a dozen issues. Last June, I met a French businessman in Beverly Hills and asked him how he felt about his government's policy in the Israel-Arab Conflict. His answer, very simple: It is not my government. It is de Gaulle. The English rage over the implications of the devaluation or the manner in which thousands of cattle are being destroyed to contend with hoof-and-mouth disease. Here at home the conscience of the nation is troubled and divided over a war in Vietnam that no one wants. There are many who love America dearly and who think it would be horrible for us if we were to win this terrible war. Coming from all these places where we are troubled about what our nations do and do not do, we are in Israel confronted with a ringing national unity. Its citizens still swell with the pride and vitality won with the swift victory of the six days of June. Its people is alive with enthusiasm which even though much paler than that of three or four months ago is still there to be experienced.

All those lingering fears and uncertainties about themselves were dispelled in those days. They were uncertain about the young, about the capacity of the young to meet the challenge of crisis. They were worried about what they called the disco-tech generation—that fear was dispelled when their young rose up in a manner even better, some said, than the old. They were even more troubled by the lurking suspicion that these newer immigrants to the land, those who had come since 1948 from Africa and Asia, those whose cultural traditions appeared to be so feeble, whose dignity so shabby, whose manners so primitive, whose emotions so fragile, that these might crumble before the onslaught of the Arab armies and terrible noise of their weapons. But that did not happen, the *edot hamizrach,* the congregations of the East, the Afro Asian Jews who now constitute a majority of Israel's Jewish population demonstrated their courage and their resourcefulness. It is one of the victories of the war that they emerged with a new sense of dignity.

One encounters this fierce and often uncritical unity at least in so far as Israel's relationship with the world is concerned and an intense preoccupation with the nation itself, which is strange for us who lack this sense of identity with our country and its destiny. American Jews who visit quickly take on this intense preoccupation with self and revel in it; it brings a sense of order, purpose, [and] meaning ...'

I am by nature not the best kind of a person to visit any country. I am a problem-oriented person. My wife is not. She considers herself a citizen of Jerusalem and is probably convinced that whatever is good for the Jews of Jerusalem is good for her, come war, come napalm, come what may. I, on the other hand, am interested in the more abstract problems of justice and even of human destiny. I measure my own achievements against what I consider to be high and lofty goals, which I haven't reached. I measure nations in much the same way; what they are must be evaluated in terms of what they can become. As a consequence I am not at home anywhere in the world because I am not satisfied with anything the world is presently making available to me.

Israelis are very realistic and pragmatic people. They want to live in security and peace. It is as simple as that. They fought a war to insure that security. They will hold on to the territories they now occupy until they can be assured of an agreement that will confirm their right to exist in peace and security. The Arab states continue now their belligerency. They continue to spew forth their venom. They continue to look upon Israel as the violator of Arab soil. Now that Israel has proved her vitality, her refusal to give up the ghost, the Arabs instead of reexamining their premises only rage the more. Israel knows this and it is using the implements of force and diplomacy and simple stubbornness to meet the situation.

My primary concern in visiting the country was to learn what I could about [the] future nature of the relationship between Israel and the Arabs within and without the country. I was concerned with Israel's existence but also with a number of gnawing problems that touched, it seemed to me, upon [some of] the fundamental moral nature of the nation's existence. My colleague Rabbi Jack Cohen, the Hillel director in the Hebrew University in Jerusalem, had raised some of the questions. They are disturbing questions and they are perhaps not of much interest to many people: Should a state any longer be erected along lines [of] ethnic, religious, or racial preference? How can we speak of the quality of citizens where one group has more equality than others? How can we say that Israel is a Jewish state but that Arabs have full equality as citizens? What does it mean for an Arab to be equal in a state that is called Jewish? In what sense should Israel be a Jewish state? How far should the power of the majority rule? When symbols of the Jewish state are taken from Jewish religious and national sources, what is an Arab supposed to feel? Once peace is established, won't Israel find itself a small unit in the midst of a large essential[ly] Islamic Arab civilization?

First, it seems the Arabs have to be convinced that the state of Israel has the power to survive. Second that Jews have come home to an area occupied in their absence by another people who have earned the right to live there. Recognizing those rights and establishing humane relations with Arabs must be a primary moral concern for Jews. How to enable the Arabs to feel a part of Israel and participants in its emerging culture is the major challenge.

I said [some] Jews [are] not interested in this problem. 1. Some are not concerned about Arab comfortability. Arabs do not exist. They are relaxed in [their] own majority status; they have lost empathy with [a] minority. 2. Make it uncomfortable, so they will leave. 3. Israel must discriminate in favor of Jews, to care for needs of Jewish people. The real issue is whether Israel sees its future in this region and with these peoples in solidarity with their fate.

TIME IN ISRAEL, PART II

I wonder sometimes what all of those people in this congregation and others who feel that religion and politics shouldn't mix feel about the discussions of Israel which have taken place since the closing weeks of last May. Surely strife between nations is political. As such the concerns of Israel and her Arab neighbors would for those who contend that the political and the religious are separate realms have no place whatsoever in a synagogue. The absurdity of defining Judaism so narrowly and parochially becomes apparent to all of us when we consider the academic question of Israel. The conflict should render once and for all the problem [of] whether we are merely a religion. Strife between nations is a political question; but political questions have a relevance for religious faith and for its values.

It is no secret to you that over the years I have not been among the rabbis who have devoted a major portion of my concerns to Israel. It was not that I (. . .).[2] I was bothered by what I felt were the uncritical celebrations of Israel at every public meeting. I was offended by the politicians who used Israel to curry Jewish favor. Moreover, I felt there was something basically unwholesome in deriving one's sense of inner worth as a Jew from accomplishments made by someone else. We had become significant as Jews because of the courage of the Israelis—this theme was exploited in many Jewish communal endeavors and in much fiction— not the least of which was the novel *Exodus*. It was not that I loved Israel less, I do not believe, but rather in a different way. We were members of the same family, American Jews and Israelis; we had an obligation to one another that being a part of a *mishpacha*[3] should produce. We shared a common history, a common agony and glory, and a common destiny as Jews. But we each had a right to our own integrity. I am proud of my brothers' achievement, but this achievement alone does not make me significant or great. What I am as a Jew must be drawn from the resources within me. We are related; we rejoice in each other's accomplishment; we are disappointed in each other's failure; but neither of us can survive on a borrowed glory.

It need not be said my interest and concern for Israel have deep roots. They are born of my more than bowing acquaintance with Jewish history and of the love for the land of Israel that comes inevitably to those of us who have achieved some intimacy with our heritage. They grew as a result of visits to Israel. Our first trip was in 1947 when Martha and I and the world were much younger, and we lived there for six or seven months at the time when the new state was coming into being. And then again three years ago, another six months of living in Jerusalem. And now a recent and hasty encounter again. I have come to know that Israel is a remarkable achievement, but not a Utopia. It is a human state, subject to the same standards of moral judgment which must be brought upon all states. Moreover, I confess I have no particular reverence for nations, Jewish or otherwise. It is people, living, breathing, dreaming, and even lusting people I care about. I care about the Jewish people in a very private and special way, because they are my people; we are part of the same branch of the human family. The political entity of the state of Israel has not been particularly moving to me simply because it is the creation of Jews. I have accepted it as political necessity, as a means of guaranteeing the right of Jews to live peacefully and productively in the land together with the prior inhabitants of the land, the Arab people. Had it been possible to secure the right to live peacefully and productively to develop Jewish cultural life and to redeem the land without a Jewish political entity called a state, I should not have been troubled at all. I was one of that tiny group that in 1947 supported the idea of a bi-national state along with men whom I then and still now revere, Judah Magnes and Martin Buber. They were very unpopular men when they proposed that solution to the Palestine problem, as it used to be called. They were almost totally rejected by the overwhelming sentiment of the Jewish people in the land of Israel. Bi-nationalism as a solution had a certain moral dignity but like so many of my ideas it lacked any political realism. The people of the Yishuv, the Jewish settlement of Palestine, the nations of the world, the Zionist movement had decided on the establishment of a Jewish state. And so it came to be.

I feel today a deep love for Israel, even a deep yearning for Israel, and yet I do not share the intense national feelings which others have for it. I am a person without any feelings of national identity, American or otherwise. Perhaps that is why I have never called myself a Zionist, and I have some hesitation in being an American.

I said I loved Israel. I should probably be happier living there at this juncture in history than anywhere else I have come to know. But love is not blind. To love does not mean or should not mean that we pretend away the imperfections we find in the one we love. Such has always been my love for Israel. A love mixed with a wholesome ability to be critical.

Our first day in Jerusalem a few weeks ago we walked to the Old City, which we had not seen for twenty years when the city first became a divided one. It was mid-November and clouds came up suddenly out of the west, and as we explored the winding, twisting narrow streets of old Jerusalem behind the walls rain began to fall. It wasn't just rain, it was an enormous cloudburst and before we knew [it] a flood was sweeping powerfully through those narrow streets. We retreated into an Arab cafe. Another couple was there before us. It turned out to be one of Israel's outstanding literary figures, Aharon Meged, a novelist, playwright, and editor. Somehow the conversation turned to the question of my reaction to what had happened since the Six-Day War. I said that I consider war to be always a tragedy. That I derived no sense of pride from military accomplishment. I wanted desperately for Israel to survive but I was perturbed at the spirit of triumphalism. The Jew as military hero or as expert in the use of air power, tanks, and napalm was very difficult for me to accept. I don't know what prompted me to be so free with my feelings, but I was taken aback when Megged said: That is exactly what I have just written about in [an] article, which is published in America this very month. I returned to find Megged's piece on my desk; it was entitled "Israel's new image." The new image he says is that of a heroic people, mighty in war, pursuing its enemies, destroying its foes with lightning speed. One more day and we would have stood at Cairo. Or those endless obscene jokes. We were no longer the boy David facing the giant Goliath. It is a liberating image, which did away with the need to feel compassion and guilt or pity. The old Jewish sentimentality with its moral complexities was disdained.

But Megged says that new image will not endure because the Jewish national character has been shaped in another way through its history. Certain character traits were formed in our history that were to serve as models and ideals for Jewish culture. Abraham the lover of peace and justice who pleaded against the destruction of Sodom, Isaac the shepherd and digger of wells, Jacob the dweller in tents—these myths were formed when Israel dwelled in the land of Canaan. This was our self-image and it differed radically from the tales of heroism and passion, which were incorporated in the images of Gilgamesh and Odysseus, and Siegfried, the men of arms who shaped the historical course of other cultures. It was Moses, not Joshua, whom we revered. It was David the boy and the man not as conqueror, it was Solomon the wise king and not Solomon the glorious potentate; it was the prophets, not the Kings. Even in Israel itself [among] the generations who grew up there without knowing the Diaspora existence this image was perpetuated. The literature [of] Israel has by and large identified with the fate of the vanquished, the refugee, the prisoner, the displaced. There was no place for hatred and revenge.

Megged goes on to say that the land of Israel is indivisible not as a consequence of military conquest but because such it has always been in the Jewish consciousness.

The land of Israel's indivisible geographic and spiritual wholeness are enhanced by one another. This is what it has always been, he insists, in the national consciousness of Jews. That is why Jews are in Israel today, because of that national consciousness attached inexorably to the land—there is a historical and mythical bond with the land and its skies. That is what I feel when I am there too.

The difficulty has always been that the land also belongs to the Arabs who have lived there for generations; it is also a part of their individual and national consciousness. And they are entitled to be themselves. They cannot be displaced or oppressed. They must be dealt with as equals, not in the language of orders and decrees, but in the manner of a dialogue between two nations whom history and fate have destined to inhabit one country.

How shall that come to pass? That is the central conflict which confronts the future of Israel. Where spirit and geography are joined nationalism is born. National aspirations are by necessity mutually exclusive. Must they be mutually aggressive?

The Arabs have steadfastly refused to recognize either the viability or the authenticity of Israel's right to exist as a nation. The record of their aggression is well known to all of us. It is good to know what the Arab case is, since by reason of it Israel's existence has been threatened for twenty years. There are three arguments employed by the Arabs: 1. The artificiality of the Jewish state; 2. That it burdens the Arabs with the consequences of Hitler's persecution of the Jews; and 3. That Israel is the bridgehead of imperialism in the Middle East, a European enclave serving to suppress Arab nationalism.

The Six-Day War should have brought home with thundering truth the reality of the state of Israel. The reality of states is not proved by intellectual discussion, but by the way they stand up to the test of extreme necessity. The response of Israel's people to the recent war should have proven once and for all that Israel is not [an] artificial creation, a conglomeration of refugees. There were some Israelis who had serious doubts about this too, suspicious of the *edot hamizrach,* of the discotheque generation of the young. Their united response to impending catastrophe put the lie to all of these suspicions.

As for burdening the Arabs with the consequences of Hitler's persecution of the Jews. Jews have not been a problem. The influx of Jewish immigration is not only the result of what happened to Jews in Europe but also what has happened to them in Arab lands. Fully half of Israel's population came as refugees from Arab countries. But the basic question behind this argument is whether Palestine is an Arab or Jewish country. This is a point of collision between conflicting national myths. Where national myths collide history provides examples [of] how such collisions are solved. The first by exterminating the opponent. This the Turks did with the Armenians. Or a second method would [be] through a recurrent probing with force, the hereditary enemy—the Germans and French, the Poles and Russians—there was bloodletting for centuries but eventually there were no significant changes of frontiers. Third is through an accommodation between conflicting dreams—finding a way to live together. Such accommodations have historically come about after long struggles—the nations of the Soviet Union or Yugoslavia, the English and the Scots, the Swiss.

The rise of super powers in our world today has really transformed the meaning of national independence. The very possibility of war today is dependent on the readiness of the super powers to provide conflicting forces with weapons. Arabs and Jews in trying to assert themselves by confrontation become increasingly dependent for their very existence upon the great powers. Against their will they become instruments in the struggle between these powers.

Arabs claim that Israel is a bridgehead of imperialism, Western imperialism. There is some truth in that statement. Israel has introduced Western technology, Western ways of living. There is probably nothing in Israel quite as Western as an oil corporation the presence of which has not disturbed most of the Arab leadership.

COMMENTARY BY DANIEL SOKATCH

In November of 1967, just months after the Six-Day War, Rabbi Leonard Beerman returned home from a trip to Israel to preach about what he had seen there. Today, his words and his worries seem almost prophetic. One wonders how they were received forty-nine years ago, as the aftershocks of the war transformed Israel's sense of itself, and the American Jewish community's sense of Israel. It must have been jarring for Leonard's congregants to hear him, so soon after near catastrophe and then the cathartic triumph of the war, not only question the "spirit of triumphalism" that so disturbed him but also begin to dig down into the deeper questions of what the war might mean for the future moral fiber of Israel and the Jewish people.

Beerman always stood apart when it came to Israel. He loved Israel, even yearned for it, but declared, "To love does not mean . . . that we pretend away the imperfections we find in the one we love." He was deeply distrustful of any nationalism, and reluctant to identity as a Zionist. In 1947, he supported the "moral dignity" of the bi-nationalism of Martin Buber and Judah Magnus, even as he later acknowledged it as politically unrealistic. And in the immediate aftermath of the Six-Day War he was one of the few American Jewish leaders who agonized over what control over millions of Arabs—whose right and connection to the land he understood to be just as valid as those of the Jewish people—would mean for Israel's democracy, future, and soul. It was characteristic of Leonard that, decades later, he took no pleasure in being proved right.

34

CCAR Breira Statement

1977

The two documents below, which are discussed in Professor Michael Meyer's commentary, relate to Breira, an organization with which Leonard Beerman was closely associated. It arose in 1973 as an "alternative" (the English word for breira*) to the existing policies of Jewish organizations toward the Israeli-Palestinian conflict. Founded by the Chicago-based Reform rabbi Arnold J. Wolf, the organization was devoted to a two-state solution well before that idea, as Professor Meyer notes, became a mainstream principle in the American Jewish community. As a result, it was cast as a radical deviation from Jewish communal norms and was widely criticized in the community.*

Accustomed to and undaunted by the adoption of controversial positions, Beerman worked with his friend and colleague Rabbi Richard Levy to establish a presence for Breira in Los Angeles. They worked with Yoav Peled, an Israeli graduate student at UCLA and later political scientist at Tel Aviv University, to bring together progressive Jews, including Rabbis David Berner, Laura Geller, Sandy Ragins, and Chaim Seidler-Feller, to support the cause of Breira, which ceased to exist in 1977.

COMMENTARY BY PROFESSOR MICHAEL A. MEYER

The failure of the Israeli government to recognize the existence of a Palestinian entity and the expanding settlement in the West Bank led in the mid-1970s to the formation of a Jewish organization known as Breira (Alternative). It included a considerable proportion of non-Orthodox rabbis, who were committed to the Jewish state but critical of its current policies. The organization was ahead of its

The Rabbinate and the Middle East:

DISSENT IN THE JEWISH COMMUNITY

The undersigned CCAR colleagues active in Breira
invite you to join in a discussion of the nature of
Breira's proposals for peace in the Middle East pro-
pounded both by Breira and by Israeli groups headed by
such figures as Arie Lova Eliav and Maj. General Mattityahu Peled. The problem of sharing such views in the
American Jewish and non-Jewish community will be discussed
with the hope of broadening the understanding of both the
aims of Breira and even more importantly of the steps
needed to end the Arab-Israeli conflict.

Leonard I. Beerman
Steven Jacobs
Douglas E. Krantz
Richard Levy
Michael Robinson
David Saperstein
Martin J. Zion

MONDAY AFTERNOON   4:30 PM

COLONIAL ROOM

FIGURE 19. CCAR letter on Breira (1977).

time in coming out strongly for a two-state solution when that was still strictly a minority view among American Jews.

The Jewish establishment soon took aim at Breira, claiming that its views were damaging to the State of Israel. The organization was demonized, and its members, including myself, for a time suffered ostracism. Nonetheless, during a period of

BREIRA—A "Choice" for Shared Responsibility Between Israel and the Diaspora
200 PARK AVENUE SOUTH—ROOM 1315
NEW YORK, NEW YORK 10003 (212) 674-5533

EXECUTIVE COMMITTEE

Chairperson
Rabbi Arnold Jacob Wolf (New Haven)

Vice Chairpersons
Rabbi David Wolf Silverman (New York)
Rabbi Max Ticktin (Washington, D.C.)
David Tulin (Philadelphia)

Treasurer
Inge Lederer Gibel (New York)

Secretary
John Ruskay (New York)

Executive Director
Robert Loeb

Rabbi Balfour Brickner (New York)
Nancy Fuchs-Kreimer (New Haven)
Mike Masch (Philadelphia)
Arthur Waskow (Washington, D.C.)

BOARD OF DIRECTORS

NEW YORK
Edya Arzt
Ross Brann
Peter Geffen
Rabbi Doug Krantz
Rabbi Chuck Lippman
Prof. Sidney Morgenbesser
Rabbi Michael Robinson
Rabbi Gerry Serotta
Dr. Morton Siegel
David Szonyi

New Jersey
Rabbi Israel Dresner

Philadelphia
Rabbi Louis Bogage
Peter Braun
Rosalie Riechman
Rabbi Ya'akov Rosenberg

Northeast
Martha Ackelsberg
Rabbi Al Axelrad
Rabbi Stanley Kessler
Hillel Levine
Prof. Jacob Neusner
William Novak
Prof. Don Peretz

District of Columbia
Rabbi David Saperstein

Midwest
Prof. Michael Meyer

South
Rabby Stanley Ringler
Rabbi Steven Schatz

West Coast
Rabbi Leonard Beerman
Rabbi Richard Levy

Canada
Gershon Hundert

STAFF
Dan Gillon, Associate Director
Faye Ginsburg, National Co-Ordinator
Arthur Samuelson, Editor, interChange

Breira means alternative

January 31, 1977

Dear Leonard and Richard:

The steering committee of Breira requests
you, as members of the Breira board, to
choose other members of Los Angeles Breira
to select a candidate for West Coast Field
Worker, to be housed in Los Angeles but
with regional responsibilities, who will be hired
by Breira's national office at $300 per month
for ten months, with the following duties:

    developing and organizing of local
    programming

    co-ordinating activities on the West
    Coast with national office

    developing local outreach into Jewish
    community, local press, etc.

We should like you to select a candidate for
our approval no later than February 1, so
that the person may participate in the national
conference, to which we shall endeavor to
send you some scholarship money to ensure
Los Angeles representation.

                        Yours sincerely,

                        Arnold Jacob Wolf
                        Chairman, Breira

AJW:hsa

FIGURE 20. Breira letterhead (1977).

about half a decade, Breira was able to publicize its views both within and outside
the Jewish community.

It is not surprising that Rabbi Leonard Beerman should have associated himself
with Breira. He had shown his commitment to Zionism when, as a rabbinical student, he joined the Haganah, the pre-state Jewish military, in 1947. He continued

to be a lover of Israel, but a moral critic of its policies, even as, in various areas, he criticized policies of the United States. The brief undated document, which he signed together with other Reform rabbis, indicates that he sought to bring the message of Breira to his rabbinical colleagues in the Central Conference of American Rabbis, most likely at its convention in June 1977. The second document, a letter to Leonard and Richard Levy dated January 31, 1977, shows the Breira letterhead.

35

Yom Kippur Morning

October 11, 1978

Rabbi Beerman's Yom Kippur sermon was delivered eleven months after Egyptian president Anwar Sadat came to Jerusalem in a bold gesture of peace and spoke in the Knesset, Israel's parliament, on November 20, 1977. It also came a month after the historic Camp David Accords were signed by Israel and Egypt on September 6, 1978, with the active mediation of US president Jimmy Carter.

In the midst of the euphoria about this historic moment in which the Jewish state and its largest Arab neighbor made peace, Beerman assumed his prophetic voice and issued a cautionary note: over the course of their long history, Jews have not been especially good at either statecraft or making war. Their real excellence—and true calling— lay in struggling for "the realization of truth and justice in the fullness of everyday life." Consistent with that theme, Beerman cut through the excitement of the day and focused with laser-like attention on what he saw as the heart of the problem. "Only through peace with the Palestinian people," he declared, "can the final goal of peace be realized." Already during his first visit to Israel in 1947, he apprehended the abiding challenge of how a Jewish majority must deal with an Arab minority. Following 1967, when Israel came to occupy the West Bank and Gaza Strip, the problem became more acute. Beerman never lost his sense of the critical importance of the Palestinian issue throughout his career. He returned to it again and again, seeing its resolution as a measure of "the realization of truth and justice" that was the Jewish vocation.

There is a picture on my desk at home of my father as a very young man. He is dressed in a World War I khaki uniform with a tight-fitting collar, and he is wearing one of those campaign or doughboy hats with a broad brim all around; and he is standing with two other soldiers, one of them his cousin Alex. The photograph is of the time when my father served in the United States Army Ambulance Corps. He was stationed in Italy. There are other pictures I used to look at as a boy; they are all in a photo album, which seemed always to be old and which is still in my parents' home. There were even a few colored postcards of places my father visited when he was a soldier. I remember the one I liked best of all and I thought to be most beautiful. It was a picture of the Bay of Kator along the Dalmatian Coast. There were other places he loved to speak of in Montenegro, along the Adriatic, and in Italy itself.

When I was very young, it used to bother me that my father was in the ambulance corps. Playing in the gravel-covered park of the small Pennsylvania town of my early boyhood, where we used to throw stones at each other, hiding behind the large cannons set there, replicas of the war, I wished my father had been in the infantry, a fighting man, not condemned (so it seemed to me) to bring comfort and healing to the wounded. To a small boy, that didn't seem very military at all. Nothing like the 03 Rifle and the big Mauser automatic pistol he had brought home from the war, and which we used to keep in the attic. That automatic was so heavy; as long as it was around I never developed sufficient strength to pull the trigger.

It was some years later, when I first learned about the Great War and began to think about it and raise questions about it, and even much later than that when I first read Hemingway's *A Farewell to Arms* (Hemingway had also served in the ambulance corps in Italy), it was then that I began to think that if one had to be in such a horrible war, it was a sign of honor not to be among those who killed. I came to understand, also, that my father's military service was really an expression of his basic character, a reflection of ideals and principles which were an integral part of his thought and behavior as a man, of his whole system of values. Compassion for those who were hurt was not something he put on and took off like a uniform, for a temporary period of his life. That was to be a life-long profession of his. Until a year or so ago, he used to spend a day a week helping out at the Veterans Hospital in Long Beach. Caring about the injured, the poor, the lonely, those who labored in the factories and those who stood outside of them in the long depression years, somehow making society a better place for all, and especially for the least of its people, that has always been a passion of my father's. It permeated his business life as well, his treatment of his employees and his customers. It went everywhere with him, and it still does—although today, sporting a patch over one eye, he looks a little like Moshe Dayan, or at least like Moshe Dayan ten or fifteen years from now.

I was very slow to grow when I was a boy, and in some ways I still am. I had to grow a lot in mind and sensitivity to come close to my father's stature. I finally understood that the essence of my father's strength was really the essence of the strength of our people, the Jewish people. For the strength of our people has always been in the power of its spirit and its sensitivity, in the deep commitment to the ideals set in the center of its being, the commitment to act out of love, and to be willing to bear the suffering that decent human beings must inevitably bear in a world such as ours. That is the strength that accounted for our tenacity, our fierce determination to live; that is the incredible power within us that made for our survival. Yes, the strength of our people has always been in that power. Some of us have been able to learn that from our parents. I have. Some of us are teaching it to our children. I hope you are.

Oh, I know that through most of our history we Jews have done a lot of fighting and struggling. But our greatest struggles, as Heine once said, were on the battlefield of human thought. It was there, in the realm of spiritual warfare, in that relentless restlessness of our people's spirit, it was there [that] we won our great medals, it was there [that] we found our greatest greatness.

For very early there had entered into our people's spirit a ferment that would give it no rest. In the midst of the pagan world, so magnificent in the grandeur of its material achievement, one people questioned what was universally accepted by those who lorded their power and their majesty over them. When all about them the great nations of the world worshipped gods of stone and mountain, one people alone refused. For this people had come to believe of itself that it had been called to prepare this earth as a kingdom for God through the realization of justice. That just as there was the One who "had set the sun in the sky," Buber taught us, "so did they believe that there was a Lord of being and coming to be who had set a commandment of truth and justice above the heads of the human race." The great duty set before our people was the realization of truth and justice in the fullness of everyday life.

This command, this expectation, has always been difficult, too difficult for our people. It always set upon us the painful requirement that we be different, that we seek a special dignity, a special refinement, that we separate ourselves from the manners and the values of the nations amongst whom we lived, where those values violated the essential principle of our civilization. The way was too hard, and from the earliest times our people rebelled against it. They preferred a visible god to the invisible One of whom Moses taught them. They were forever to be seduced by the idols of power and wealth, of comfort and ease. The Bible describes in excruciating detail how this happened, what cruel punishments were visited upon the people, culminating in their destruction and exile. But not only the Bible, the whole of Jewish history is a record of struggle against all those forces, within and without, that would divert a people from the truth of its being, from the essential principle of its civilization, which is, I repeat, the realization of truth and justice in the fullness of everyday life.

The same forces beset us today, only this time more powerful, more seductive than ever before. But I believe the strength of our people to reckon with those forces is still in the power of its spirit, in its capacity to act out of love on behalf of the ideals set in the center of our being.

I am very much aware that I speak these words on the fifth anniversary of the Yom Kippur war, and in the thirtieth year of the establishment of the State of

Israel—a reminder not only of the incredible achievements of Israel but also of its remarkable military accomplishments as well, the tremendous courage it has displayed in its wars of survival.

It may be uncomfortable to remember, but surely it is well known to all of you, that from the most ancient times the Jewish people has demonstrated no particular gifts at making war. Nor have we been particularly good at maintaining a nation. None of the battles of our ancestors, the ancient Israelites, has ever been recorded in military annals. Great military geniuses we have never produced. Before the mighty armies of the ancient Near East, Israel always fell to defeat: Assyria, Babylonia, Egypt, the Greeks, the Romans—it was always the same story. In works of fiction, we won military victories. In the Book of Esther, which we read every Purim, although we carefully manage to skip this part of it—there we are able to slay 75,000 Persians, and glory in it. The Maccabees had a brief experience of victory over the Syrian Greeks, but the independence they achieved quickly gave way to inner Jewish corruption; soon, Jews were once again a subject people.

Israel became what it was to be for most of its history as a national entity, and what it is today—a vassal state, dominated always by someone else's purposes. So we were to Greece and even to Rome, until Rome became impatient with the rebelliousness and the pretensions to power of the Jewish zealots, mystical hooligans. So the Romans finally did to the Jews what they could have done at any time—they destroyed the Temple; they destroyed the nation. Yet our people lived on because the rabbis of that time helped them understand that the foundation of their being as a people was not in a cult centered in a temple, but in something sacred to be realized in the fullness of their everyday life. If they could hallow themselves and their lives, they could outlive any conqueror. And so they did.

Yet it has been our historic fate to dwell always in the shadow of the power of others. So it was then; so it is today, for Israel, for Jews everywhere. It is in the light of this uncomfortable truth that we consider the events which have culminated in the dramatic achievement at Camp David.

Eleven months ago I was in Jerusalem, dancing in the street with the crowd gathered there, as I saw President Sadat enter the King David Hotel. The next day, along with every Israeli and millions of people throughout the world I heard the leader of Egypt, the most powerful Arab nation, speak these words: "You want to live with us in this part of the world. In all sincerity I tell you we welcome you among us with full security and safety. What is peace for Israel? It means that Israel lives in the region with her Arab neighbors in security and safety. To such logic, I say yes. It means that Israel lives within her borders, secure against any aggression. To such logic, I say yes. It means for Israel all kinds of guarantees that insure these two factors. To this demand, I say yes."

With this dramatic and courageous initiative, unparalleled in diplomatic history, the Egyptian president at great personal danger changed the situation in the Middle East, made a total break with Arab policies of the past thirty years, a break with that deeply imbedded rejection of Israel's right to exist as a sovereign nation ("No negotiation, no recognition, no reconciliation").[1] It was clear that Egypt was determined to achieve peace even at the terrible risk of a deep rift in the Arab world. It seemed so certain that a peace settlement was within reach, and that it could be a real peace in the full meaning of the word, not just a truce between opposing nations growling fiercely at each other.

So I wanted to believe last November, and so I did. Here was an opportunity to put an end to the conflict that had brought untold misery and bloodshed—the terrible waste of life, resources—the mental anguish. I was overwhelmed by the euphoria of that moment, grateful that I could have been in that place in that historic time. Thirty years before that November, in November 1947, Martha and I had been in the same Jerusalem rejoicing at the news that had come from Lake Success in New York, announcing that the United Nations had voted to partition Palestine into two states: One Jewish, One Arab. That decision permitted Israel to come into being six months later, in May of 1948. But the joy of November 1947 gave way to the fierce and terrible events of Israel's War of Independence. Would the joy of November 1977 vanish as quickly as it had come into being? Such, unfortunately, was to be the case. The drama of November, the exchange of visits, the ecstasy that swept over Egyptians and Israelis soon gave way to a war of words and a new gloom.

We have been rescued from that gloom because the President of the United States and his advisors seized the initiative, indicated to both parties what they thought was right for the Middle East, invited Egypt and Israel to Camp David to negotiate based on this plan, and then provided the necessary "nudging" to help bring about the agreement.

For the central factor in the Middle East since 1973 has been the emergence of the United States as the dominant power in the region. As Professor Stanley Hoffman of Harvard's Center for European Studies has pointed out, and it is his words I now bring to you, our country is now involved in a complex web of relationships in the Middle East. America is engaged with its Arab clients, especially Saudi-Arabia, in a relationship such that it is sometimes difficult to determine who is the real client, who manipulates whom. We need the oil; they need our weapons and technology. We want them to turn to us rather than to the Europeans or the Japanese, to invest their money in the United States, to keep OPEC from raising oil prices to levels our allies and many developing nations could not afford, to cooperate with us in managing an increasingly acrobatic world financial system. United States policy now has two imperatives, Professor Hoffman argues: Arab power must be used in ways favorable to American interests. There must be no war between the Arabs and Israel, since such a war would present America with impossible choices and could provoke new strains between the United States, Western Europe, and Japan.

The second imperative is for a movement toward a settlement of the Arab-Israeli conflict, for a settlement of the Arab-Israeli conflict is the only way to maintain

American dominance in the area and to prevent a new Soviet penetration into the area. The Arab-Israeli conflict is therefore obsolete, from the American point of view; it is an obstacle to the pursuit of the long-range interests of all the parties. A peace settlement, Professor Hoffman insists, is absolutely imperative for the United States and for Israel and the Arab states, the nations within the American orbit of influence.

The achievement at Camp David is a tribute to all of the participants in it, and surely to the reason and the flexibility demonstrated by President Sadat and Prime Minister Begin. Still it must be remembered that peace has not been accomplished, but only a framework within which peace can be achieved. The agreement is very fragile. It leaves so very much to be thrashed out. And it is fraught with areas of danger, and the areas of danger are precisely the areas of the agreement that are vague.

The agreement is particularly vague with regard to what lies at the very heart of the Israeli-Arab conflict—the problem of the Palestinians and the future of the West Bank. Only through peace with the Palestinian people can the final goal of peace be realized; only through a generous and respectful recognition of the right of the Palestinians to define themselves, their identity, to have their sovereignty over the portion of Palestine promised to them and agreed to by every Israeli government, prior to this one, and not to have a definition imposed upon them by the PLO, by Jordan, by the Israelis, by anyone but themselves—only thus can there be peace.

Whoever would still deny to Israel or the Palestinian Arabs the right to build a life of their own is an enemy of peace. Within the Arab world, the PLO and the so-called radical Arab states are still sworn to war. But among Jews there are those who are enemies of peace and security as well. Those religious zealots who claim the land by divine mandate, whose battle cry is "not an inch," "all or nothing," are a grave danger to the hope for peace. Wherever they are, they are as dangerous to life and to Israel as their equivalents among the Arab rejectionists and terrorists. Those who advocate more settlements on the West Bank are in the same category.

As for us American Jews, it is time for us to seize the hope engendered at Camp David and to join the peacemakers; to open our minds and hearts to the justice due our enemies. And to join those tiny forces in the world that insist that the continued reliance on military power is an ill-breeding of the mind that perverts every possibility for the ennoblement of the human enterprise.

And it is time for us, long overdue, to think seriously again about the quality of our lives as American Jews, for the quality of our lives has suffered immeasurably because of the mentality of being under siege, a mentality which has held us captive over these thirty years. Our sense of perspective has become totally distorted. A single anti-Semite opens his stupid mouth and ten thousand American Jews summon up images of a new holocaust. The spectacle of 5,000 Jews in Chicago, marching in protest before twenty-six puny American Nazis, is a symbol of the idiocy to which otherwise intelligent people can descend. The hyperventilated response to the Scheer articles is of the same order.[2] There is a great deal about us Jews that calls for celebration, and there is much about us for which we should be ashamed, not the least of which is our exaggerated self-pity and self-righteousness, the rising cultic tribalism—and a new phenomenon—the Jewish Archie Bunkers among us, only nobody is laughing.

There is much work of healing that needs to be done, to bind up our wounds, to renew the vision of our true strength, to take up again the ideals set in the center of our people's being. For that is our strength, that is our power. Wherever we act out of love to help diminish the store of human anguish, we assert our power as Jews . . . but this is another sermon, one that will be continued throughout the year.

Do the children still play in the gravel-covered park of my birthplace? Do the boys throw stones, hiding behind the cannons set there, replicas of my father's war? Do they imagine their fathers brave in battle, wielding their rifles and bayonets and pistols? Will they grow to be strong in their power, to be tender human beings, loving themselves, loving life, nurturing it?

"See I have set before thee this day life and death and blessing and curse, therefore choose life, that thou mayest live."

COMMENTARY BY MILTON VIORST

Leonard Beerman delivered this sermon barely a decade after the Six-Day War, and five years after the Yom Kippur War, which together transformed Israel's relationship with its Arab neighbors and the international community. It was a lament for where he perceived Israel was heading. His warning did not make him more popular among his congregants, but Leonard was always more committed to truth than to popularity. Since then, the Arab-Israeli conflict has grown more heated, global society more remote, prospects for peace more elusive. Today Leonard's sermon of four decades ago is no less relevant, and were he with us, he could deliver it again.

In the sermon, Leonard lauds the refusal of the early Jews to follow the era's great powers in worshipping the gods of stone and mountain, seeking instead to establish a kingdom of God through the realization of social justice. It was a severe challenge, which many Jews found too difficult to embrace. It did not, furthermore, endear the Jews to the peoples among whom they lived, and over the centuries they paid heavily for their differences. When Herzl founded Zionism as a refuge from the pains inflicted on them by their enemies, Vienna's Chief Rabbi implored him to beware that a Jewish state built on cannons and bayonets risked emulating Europe's warrior powers. Herzl scoffed, but time, vindicating the rabbi's admonition, has seriously deformed Herzl's dream.

I came to know Leonard because we both believed Jews could best be served by giving their allegiance to another, more humane Zionism. He alluded to it not just in this, but in nearly all his sermons. It is a cause for which he will long be remembered. I am proud to have been his friend.

36

Yom Kippur Eve

September 26, 1982

When Rabbi Beerman took the pulpit on the eve of Yom Kippur in 1982, it was barely a week after the massacre of hundreds (and perhaps thousands) of Palestinian refugees by Christian Phalangist militia men in the Sabra and Shatila camps in Beirut on September 16–18. The Phalangists were operating in the camps under the general command of Israeli forces that had taken control of Beirut as a result of intense fighting in the summer of 1982.

Beerman did not miss the opportunity to peer into his soul and that of his fellow Jews, to engage in the work of heshbon ha-nefesh *(moral accounting) that Jewish tradition encourages on Yom Kippur. The day, he declared, "has always been a call to conscience." And he, as the spiritual shepherd of his well-heeled congregation, felt a particular obligation to issue and answer that call.*

Beerman numbered himself among the few American Jews—and surely rabbis—to deem the first Lebanon War "a moral and political failure" from its first day. He lamented the fact that virtually every national Jewish organization lined up in unwavering support of the decision of the Israeli government to invade Lebanon. And yet, the Lebanon War proved to be enormously divisive. In Israel, it was called the first war to lack a national consensus and prompted widespread protest by antiwar activists. Abroad, the early stages of the war began to create "troubled consciences" among Diaspora Jews, as the New York Times *reported.*[1]

For Beerman, the Lebanon War represented a gross violation of the prophetic impulse to seek out justice and righteousness. It was a case in which the once powerless not only had become powerful, but were also corrupted by the power they assumed. The scale of destruction wrought by the Israeli invasion was vast and was the result of "arrogance and self-destructive impulses." The hour demanded a new "declaration of independence" for Diaspora Jews, who must unmoor themselves from silent complicity, assert their consciences, and embark on the path of repentance that Yom Kippur demanded.

These are the words we read in our service every Rosh Hashanah morning, the words of Paul Kornfeld, born 1889 in Prague, died in Lodz concentration camp, 1942:

> Everything on this earth follows the age-old rules.
> When spring comes, the ice melts . . .
> And when someone is enraged he does evil.
> Yet no rule or law can keep us from dreaming
> that one day all this travail will turn to ashes,
> and that You, oh my Lord, playful and senseless,
> great and powerful,
> will cause a new rule to blossom forth under your breath,
> and the miracle will spread across the earth.
> How glorious it would be, were Your will written
> throughout the world through Your deeds.
> See!—the world is a dark pit,
> and men haltingly stumble and falter from abyss to abyss,
> from battle to battle . . .
> They aim for the good and commit the evil,
> they do evil and regret it . . .
> They think about what they have wrought and tear their
> own flesh.
> And they are full of errors and full of lies. . . .
> And everything has its reason and its cause.
> Also the evil has its cause . . .
> Also the lie has its cause . . .
> And the errors have their cause.
> And everything goes its way according to the age-old
> rules and laws . . .

Last week, at the close of the service on Rosh Hashanah eve, as Rabbi Ragins, Cantor Sharlin, and I stood wishing members of the congregation a good year, one of our members, a veteran of many differences with me over the many years of our friendship, greeted me warmly and said, somewhat impishly: "I'm so grateful you didn't speak about the war in Lebanon tonight, and that you will be addressing that subject on Yom Kippur. Because I won't be here on Yom Kippur; I'll be on my way to India."

Oh, I wish I might be with him tonight, wherever he is, and I have colleagues throughout the land who feel the same. Their hearts are heavy, full of anguish, and yet they know, as I do, that it is their responsibility to attempt to provide some guidance, some understanding of the events that have shaken the conscience of every Jew. And what is a more appropriate time for this than the Day of Atonement?

Yom Kippur has always been a call to conscience. It has always urged us to acknowledge a simple truth—that we are human, and therefore subject to error, transgression; that by our deeds of omission or commission we may have added to the store of indecency in the world. Yom Kippur tells us that we should turn away from the way we have been going and choose another way, a way of justice and love, a way that leads to our fellow human beings. The sins we confess this day are meant to encompass every domain of our lives, the personal and the collective, wherever we have negated by word or deed the ideals we cherish. Yes, Yom Kippur is a call to conscience, an annual reminder of the distance that separates our ideals from our conduct. Yom Kippur is a celebration, a celebration of moral failure.

We all shrink from this responsibility. It implies, with Cassius, that the fault is not in our stars but in ourselves, that we are not the persons we pretend to be or wish to be. In Judaism, Leo Baeck once taught us, the highest possible standard is imposed upon us. "The ethical command with its ceaseless, thou shalt, stands before us and demands our life. Our ethical consciousness is the consciousness of an unending task. If we can feel a reverence toward this task, then we can feel a reverence toward ourselves."

So we are challenged not to blunt the conscience but to awaken it. Not to pretensions of virtue, but to the acknowledgment of moral failure.

The contemporary rabbi who ventures to lead his congregation up this path is aware that he is engaged in a dangerous mission. For the rabbi is the bearer of a dark secret. He knows he is the servant of a religion which rarely developed any passion for the dilemmas of the privileged. The calf worshippers of old, who stood at the foot of Sinai, sincerely believed that they were worshipping the God of Israel.

The rabbi who serves a congregation as fashionable and respectable as this one feels too often like an Aaron, the brother of Moses, who took the gold, fashioned the calf, and gave the people exactly what they wanted. The rabbi who serves the enlightened and the affluent knows that he is the bearer of a religious tradition whose God pants after the disinherited, the lonely, the abandoned, the homeless. Its God is the god of the hunted, not the hunter; of the defeated, not the victor.

How does the teacher, the rabbi, how does any knowledgeable Jew, take this tradition with its literature of tragedy and loneliness and the joy that flowers from it, how does one take a religion of the insulted and the injured, and guide his congregation on the path that leads to the acknowledgment of moral failure, the awakening of conscience, the path that leads to the repentance that this day calls for?

I do not know that I can do it. I certainly cannot do it alone. I need your help, as never before.

> Everything has its reason and its cause
> Also the evil has its cause

Also the lie has its cause
And everything goes its way according to
the age-old rules . . .

I confess to you: I am one of that minority of rabbis, and that minority of Jews here and in Israel who believed, from the first day, that the war in Lebanon, the war of Begin and Sharon, was doomed to be a moral and political failure. I confess to you, I was full of shame and horror and despair from the very first moment of the Israeli invasion of the Lebanese border. And yet I prayed that I was wrong. I prayed that some blessing might be wrested from the destruction and the loss of life this invasion, or, as Menachem Begin insists on calling it, this "incursion," might bring.

I listened to the news with dread. I read every piece of information, particularly those issued by the major Jewish organizations: ADL, the AJC, the CRC, the Federation Council, which without exception celebrated and justified the Israeli action. Then I began to see some of the material from the Israeli press. There was that story of Col. Eli Geva, an armored brigade commander who created a sensation in Israel by asking to be relieved from his command rather than lead an assault on Beirut. The Israeli newspapers reported an exchange between Prime Minister Begin and Col. Geva. Begin, who hoped to persuade the young colonel to change his mind, asked why the colonel, the youngest brigade commander in Israeli history, wanted to be relieved of his command. Geva replied that when he looked through his binoculars into West Beirut he could see children playing. "Did you receive an order to kill the children?" Begin asked him. "No," Geva replied. "Then what are you complaining about?" the Prime Minister is reported to have said.

Then there was Mattityahu Shmuelevitz, Director General of the Prime Minister's office, who told the following story: "Three men, one an Israeli, are captured by cannibals, and while the cauldron of water is heating they are each granted a final wish. After the others' conventional wishes are met, the Israeli makes his request—that the cannibal chieftain kick him in the behind. The wish fulfilled, the Israeli pulls his Uzi sub- machine gun from under his shirt, kills his tormentors and sets his companions free. 'But why did you ask him to kick you?' they asked. 'Because, otherwise, no matter how justified my shooting him, I will still be accused of aggression,' the Israeli replied. So we take into account that we shall be accused of aggression even when the water to cook us is already boiling," said Mr. Shmuelevitz, as he launched into his analysis of negative world reaction to the Israeli invasion.

Eliyahu Ben Elissar, Israel's first ambassador to Egypt, and now chairman of the Foreign Affairs and Defense Committee of the Knesset, Israel's parliament, explained international hostility in these terms: "The free Christian world has still a long way to go to get used to a new type of Jew," he said. "We are a very normal people. No nation would allow its citizens to be killed with impunity, but somehow, people take it for granted that Jews have always been killed throughout their history. While Americans or French or others would never let it happen, we have always been asked to behave otherwise. But we are not the Jews of the Diaspora. We will show the nations that we are not that kind of Jew."

Statement by Robert Alter, distinguished professor at the University of California, Berkeley, from an old issue of COMMENTARY in the bottom of my desk drawer, to be taken out whenever I become too moralistic: "Morality on the subject of Israel comes cheap to an American Jew, because he is not directly confronted with the responsibilities of power, the naked needs of survival . . . "

Letter to the Editor of the American Jewish periodical SHMA: "God bless our Jewish intellectual liberals [the rabbis among them]. God bless them with their Jewish consciences and their Jewish sympathy for the hurt and suffering of all people. God bless them and keep them far from positions of responsibility. We need their prophetic reminders of who we are and how we should act, but we would have disappeared off the face of the earth many generations ago if we had let them make the practical decisions of daily existence."

From the Israeli newspapers: Israeli actress Hannah Meron, whose leg was blown off several years ago by a PLO terrorist bomb, speaking at a rally in Jerusalem, said: "I met two wounded Lebanese children. Both had their legs amputated. I came to cheer them up. I do not have to tell you how hard it was for me to look into their eyes. For the first time in my life I feel that I am an accomplice to an act with which my conscience cannot live."

> Zion will be redeemed with justice.
> I will break the bow and the sword and the battle out of the land . . .
> They shall beat their swords into plowshares . . .
> Everything has its reason and its cause
> And everything goes its way according to the
> age-old rules and laws.

The stated purpose of the war: To secure peace for the Galilee. Prime Minister Begin solemnly promised that "when we reach the 40 kilometer limit the fighting will cease." It soon became clear that that was a lie. It should have been obvious. It was well known to Israeli military correspondents that Israel had been looking for a pretext to push itself into a full-scale war in Lebanon in order to liquidate once and for all the PLO, thus securing Israel's northern border and bringing to submission the Palestinian population of the occupied West Bank and Gaza, having deprived them of their national leadership.

The purpose of the war: To destroy the PLO, but in truth, if anything may have been destroyed it is the moral stature of the State of Israel. The massive use of military force, including the total destruction of refugee camps, not only caused death and destruction for the civilian population; it also supplied credibility to the hostile propaganda that presents Israel as an aggressive state, bent on expansion and annexation, while trampling on the rights of the Palestinian people. It permitted every closet anti-Semite to come out into the open.

The purpose of the war: To destroy the PLO. It may have been destroyed as a military force, but the war of Begin and Sharon achieved the very opposite of destroying the PLO: It has raised the PLO to a more important factor in international relations and has made the Palestinian issue the decisive one. The Pope would never have received Yasir Arafat had it not been for this war. Yes, the PLO's brutality is well known. Yes, its deeds of terror have brought death to the innocent, but "it never constituted a threat to Israeli security," Abba Eban declared. "This war," Eban said, "has been a dark age in the moral history of the Jewish people."

To "crush" the PLO, to "eradicate," to "liquidate," to "fumigate," to "wipe out," this was the new Jewish lexicon of Menachem Begin. And as he said in a June letter to President Reagan, "we are marching to Berlin to liquidate Hitler."

Jews who were opposed to this war were not complete fools or zealots or ideologues. We knew how much the people of Lebanon had suffered from the presence of the PLO in their midst, and the tremendous loss of life, greater than under the Israeli invasion. We were fully cognizant of the PLO's tactics, its politics of negation: NO, to the State of Israel; NO, to the Sadat initiative; NO, to the Israeli peace forces which had sought dialogue with them. The stubborn, rigid, reckless, brutal policies of the PLO betrayed the possibilities of a just solution for both Israelis and the Palestinian people. Yet the suffering of the Palestinians is sorrowful and painful and real. The terrible blunders of the PLO did not diminish the hope that something constructive might emerge from their midst; that they might create a leadership that would be able to respond positively.

For the PLO was the leadership of the Palestinian people; it was a bad leadership but a leadership nonetheless. It was a leadership that should have been dealt with, with selective military force but also (as A. B. Yehoshua said) "by reasonable and honorable proposals that would have challenged it to change its stand, alternatives whose moral test would lie in the fact that Israelis would be able to say in all honesty that if they were in the position of the Palestinians, they would be prepared to accept this as a final compromise proposal."

This was not the path chosen by successive Israeli governments, culminating in the excrescence of this one. So while Israeli soldiers fell in the Lebanese war and their obituaries appeared in the Israeli newspapers, there appeared continuously advertisements for housing on the West Bank at extremely low prices seeking to attract more and more Jews to the area.

The war has been fought. The dead have died, and the latest massacre adds to the toll. The Israeli radio report of the provisional estimate of the losses: 340 Israeli soldiers dead; 2,078 wounded. 17,000 Lebanese Palestinians killed; 30,000 wounded. About 50,000 people altogether, not to mention the 100,000? 200,000? 300,000? homeless. What kinds of Jews are these who kill and injure so many thousands and cause such massive destruction as a reasonable technique for carrying out policy? As the defeated Palestinians strengthen their national will by weaving heroic tales and creating a new martyrology, thousands upon thousands of Israeli citizens (over 300,000 of them) and Jews throughout the world are expressing their shock and shame—a tribute to the true Jewish spirit, a clear demonstration that it still breathes.[2]

The Israeli government cannot end the Palestinian will for nationhood. Will the world permit another wandering people to be driven forth with no place to go? We Jews are the one people of the world who should have known what it was like to be unwanted, to be homeless. No one wanted Jews—not America, not Britain, not Europe—there was only one place to go, and that was home, and Israel came into being for that purpose. There is one, one place for the Palestinians to go—home—and it is time long overdue for Israel to declare that it does not wish to rule over the Palestinian people and to annex their territories, that it is ready to negotiate with them on their right to self-determination and independence, if they in turn will give up the option of military struggle.

Thus far, not one Israeli government—not the labor governments of Golda Meir, Rabin, nor that of Menachem Begin—not one of them has been willing to make this declaration. There is no hope for Israel—no hope for peace in the Middle East unless this offer is at least attempted, and unless this reality is confronted.

"I, the Lord, will put my law within them: I will write it upon their hearts: and I will be their God and they will be My people," said the prophet Jeremiah.

"Your hands are full of blood, your fingers with guilt. Your lips have spoken lies, and your tongues mutter wicked things. No one calls for justice, no one pleads his case with integrity. They rely on empty arguments and speak lies, and your tongues mutter wicked things. No one calls for justice, no one pleads his case with integrity. They rely on empty arguments and speak lies: they conceive trouble and give birth to evil . . . acts of violence are in their hands . . . they are swift to shed innocent blood. The way of peace they do not know: there is no justice in their paths," said the prophet Isaiah.

Let us choose Jeremiah, not Begin and Sharon (as my friend Rabbi Jerome Grollman has said).[3]

Let us choose Isaiah, not any of the governments of Israel.

This is not the first time in Jewish history that our people has succumbed to arrogance and self-destructive impulses. In the least fertile periods of Jewish history, the vehemence of religious feeling and mystical pretensions of power led to excesses of Jewish dogmatism and fanaticism and the betrayal of all that lay at the center of the moral purpose and vision of our religious civilization. The Bible records it in shame. Thus Israel fell to the Assyrians. Judah was destroyed by the Babylonians. The descendants of the Maccabees became corrupt and ruthless with power, and Israel's independence was taken away. A band of mystical religious zealots thought that they could take on the mighty armies of Rome in the second century. Israel was destroyed, a million and a half Jews were killed, and in some incomparable vulgarity, these Jewish hooligans, some rabbis among them, were elevated to the status of heroes among the Jewish people, especially in Israel.

"This is a critical hour in the history of Israel and the Jewish people. The great problem for Israel is the problem of being powerful." With incredible foresight, the distinguished Jewish leader Nahum Goldmann, who died a month ago, saw this when he said: "For two thousand years we were powerless as a people, and without power we learned how to be the best visionaries, the best dreamers, the best idealists. But without power we could not implement our visions. Now the powerless have become powerful. We have an army and flags and a state and victories, and in America Jews are well organized and wealthy, but we have not yet learned how to use our power in the service of our visions. To place our reliance on power is our greatest weakness. The survival of the Jewish people is more in danger today than ever before. There can be no survival without peace."

This is a critical hour in the history of Israel and the Jewish people—There can be no survival without peace, peace between the great powers, peace between Israel and her rejecting Arab neighbors. And this, it seems to me, is where we enter the picture. For if this is a critical hour, it is also an hour full of promise if it brings us to contrition, to some humility, some acknowledgment of our own culpability.

It is easy to find culprits: Get the rascals out! That is the language of politics. Contrition is not the American style; finding culprits is. But contrition is the purpose of this Holyday, of Yom Kippur. It is our weapons that have killed all of the combatants in this futile war, those massacred by the Christian Phalangists at the Shatila Camp in Beirut—our American-made aircraft bombed the cities of Lebanon; even the PLO had American weapons courtesy of one of our major allies, Saudi Arabia; weapons provided by every American government, Democratic and Republican.

It is the great powers, we and the Soviet Union, who have set the pattern to be emulated by the rest of the world. When faced by an adversary one must be willing to sacrifice everything in the search for military superiority. The great powers have declared their willingness to destroy life everywhere on this earth, if need be. The race to nuclear armaments does not provide security; it poisons the total atmosphere of human discourse and aspiration; it provides the moral context for the violence taken up by the tiny nations of the world.

The nuclear technicians in the highest offices who conceive and prepare for limited or protracted nuclear wars with acceptable risks of millions upon millions of casualties, all the makers of those sadistic scenarios, are they not the real assassins? We cannot remain silent as those assassins go about their grizzly work of preparation, any more than we would have wanted those Israeli soldiers and their commanders to have been silent as the Christian Phalangists prepared and then executed their massacre in the Shatila refugee camp.

The possession of nuclear weapons and the very planning of their use is an offense against God and against humanity, against all that is holy in Judaism. This is not a time to be silent; we must join the peacemakers. And we have a modest but most significant opportunity to send a stirring and vital message to our own government and to the Soviet Union through Proposition 12 on our November ballots—the call for a Bilateral Nuclear Weapons Freeze. This is a time not only to vote ourselves, but also to encourage others to do so. We cannot permit ourselves any longer to succumb to the crime of silence, for we are responsible for everything against which we do not protest.

Our country is not at the center of the planet; nor is the Soviet Union. This is not the American Century nor the Russian Century. This is the human century, and the first order of human business, as my friend William Sloane Coffin has said, is to freeze nuclear weapons before we are all burned by them.

Yes, time to confess our own culpability at this judgment season. Let us confess that we, and the leaders of the Jewish community and all of their agencies, have neglected our moral tasks by failing to protest each step that led Israel deeper and deeper into the whirlpool of Lebanese hatreds.

Let us confess that by adhering to the view that American Jews should not oppose decisions of the Israeli government, we emboldened those who see enmity and endless militancy as the only future, and we failed to encourage those in Israel who saw more clearly that this was a moral tragedy, an insult to the noblest impulses of our Jewish heritage.

This is a time then for a clear declaration from us, a declaration of independence. We will not abdicate our conscience to anyone. We will not abdicate our conscience to the decisions of our own government or to any Israeli government or to any Jewish organization. We will demand a full and open accounting. We will insist on the presentation of options, a debate of alternatives.

Let us resolve to begin our repentance by a renewed commitment to Israel and the Jewish people by urging Israel to renew the search for peace, accepting the American initiative as a start for serious negotiations that could both lead to a resolution of the issues of Israeli security and Palestinian homelessness, and help to bring the tragic cycle of death and destruction to an end. At this judgment season, this time of the affliction of our souls, for the love of our people we can do no less. "For Zion's sake, we may no longer keep silent; for Jerusalem's sake, we may not be still."

"Everything on this earth follows the age-old rules" . . . must it be so? "The world is a dark pit and men stumble and falter; they aim for the good and commit the evil . . . they are full of errors and full of lies, and everything has its reason and its cause . . . Yet I pray for a miracle, many miracles, a rain, a storm of miracles that will sweep down over mankind. May at last the evil one's hand, as he lifts it to beat another, be paralyzed. May at last the man who opens his mouth to speak an evil word . . . may he be stricken with silence . . . I am so tired of the age-old rules and laws."

What does it all mean? What is it we want, my friends? What is it do you suppose that every person yearns for: Jew, non-Jew, American, Russian, Chinese,

Lebanese, Israeli, Palestinian? Only this, I believe, something stated poignantly by Lillian Hellman:

"It no longer matters whose fault it is. It matters that this game be stopped . . . We want to declare that there are still men and women in the world who do not think it is dangerous or radical to declare themselves for the continuation of life . . . we place ourselves among those who wish to live, think, and breathe, to eat and play and raise their children, among the millions who want to be a little use, and have a little pleasure, and bear a little sorrow, and die a little death, close to someone who has loved them, in decency and in peace."

(For some of the above thoughts on Israel, I am indebted to my Israeli friends Simha Flapan and David Shaham.)

COMMENTARY BY CONNIE BRUCK

I did not know Leonard until many years after he delivered this sermon, in 1982. Reading it, though, I see hallmarks of the Yom Kippur sermons I treasured, in the last decade of his life. He often began with self-deprecating humor, and an acknowledgement that he knew some congregants would much prefer not to hear what he was about to say. He would try hard to reach them, though, with his warmth, empathy, eloquence, and inspired allusions to literature and to Jewish teachings. He would often speak about Israelis who opposed their government's policy toward the Palestinians—thus demonstrating that what was almost taboo in the organized Jewish world, here, was frequently expressed, there. As he recounted in this sermon, being the rabbi of a congregation "as fashionable and respectable as this one" was inherently challenging, for he was "the bearer of a religious tradition whose God pants after the disinherited, the lonely, the abandoned, the homeless."

Despite that challenge, Leonard never tailored his message. In his sermons, he may have started off disarmingly, but he built his argument steadily, meticulously, and inexorably, until he had earned the right to articulate what he fully believed. When he delivered this sermon, the massacre at Sabra and Shatila had taken place just ten days earlier. He had opposed the Lebanon War from the start, though he said he had prayed his fears would prove unfounded. Now, he excoriated Menachem Begin and Ariel Sharon for their actions; later investigations showed how right Leonard was. As he said of that war, "What kinds of Jews are these who kill and injure so many thousands and cause such massive destruction as a reasonable technique for carrying out policy?" But he found some solace in the fact that "thousands upon thousands of Israeli citizens (over 300,000 of them) and Jews throughout the world are expressing their shock and shame—a tribute to the true Jewish spirit, a clear demonstration that it still breathes." Tragically for the Israel Leonard loved, he was far-sighted not only about the Lebanon War but about so much else that the government of Israel has undertaken.

37

Visions of Peace in the Middle East

For the Cousins' Club of Orange County,
October 31, 1992

Rabbi Beerman's speech, based on some fragmentary notes below, came at an event-
ful moment in the history of the Israeli-Arab conflict. Yitzhak Rabin had been elected
prime minister four months earlier. He quickly signaled his willingness to reignite
negotiations with the Arab states, especially after the Madrid peace conference of
1991, convened by Spain, the United States and the USSR, did not yield any break-
throughs. Unbeknownst to the world, the Rabin government also initiated secret
back-channel discussions with Palestinians in Norway in the summer of 1992. It was
on the basis of those conversations that Rabin, Israeli foreign minister Shimon Peres,
and Palestinian leader Yasser Arafat signed the Oslo Accords on the South Lawn of
the White House on September 13, 1993.

Beerman did not know of the secret Norwegian negotiations in 1992. But he had
a good sense of the key issues. He recalls in this speech the origins of his own deep
connection to the land, when on his first visit in 1947 he was struck by the beauty of
the land, the dynamism of the Zionist settlers, and the dangers of chauvinism. He
then moved on in his remarks to a clear-headed analysis of some of the key problems
at the center of the conflict. The Israeli settlement project in the West Bank, he noted,
would be a serious obstacle. At the time of the speech, there were 100,000 Israeli set-
tlers; today, there are nearly a half million, whose presence renders difficult the idea
of a territorially viable Palestinian state.

Mindful of the decades of enmity between Jews and Arabs, Beerman was sensi-
tive to the fact that the Palestinians had not yet received much tangible benefit from
peace negotiations. The Camp David Accords promised them a limited form of local
autonomy that was never realized. And despite his support for the Oslo peace process,
Prime Minister Rabin never affirmed publicly the right of the Palestinians to a state

of their own. Beerman understood that concrete and meaningful gestures had to be made by the Israelis in order to make the Palestinians recognize the value of peace. This was not only a matter of strategic wisdom, but—in typical Beerman form—of moral necessity. As a whole, the speech below contains an interesting mix of autobiographical insight, prophetic remonstration, and prescient realism.

The Negotiations—historic is an overused word, yet for the first time in the history of the conflict, we have negotiations between Palestinians, the Arab States, and the Israelis, with all sides agreeing on the principle of exchanging land for peace (i.e., they agree that Resolution 242 applies to the West Bank and the Golan Heights).

There is reason for some optimism. While Yitzhak Shamir intended, by his own admission, to stall the autonomy negotiations and thought it possible to drag them out for ten years, Rabin has stated his desire to conclude them in nine months. With the new Israeli government it is possible to believe that someday this conflict will end; someday there will be real peace.

Still there are reasons to be cautious. The issues that separate the Israeli government from the Palestinian negotiators are fundamental. (E.g., 1. the Israeli government is opposed to the emergence of a Palestinian state, while for the Palestinians this is the basis on which they are prepared to make lasting peace with Israel. 2. Israeli and Palestinian politics are unstable. It will take many years to resolve the conflict; the Israeli right wing will have opportunities to return to power. On the Palestinian side, the centrists who are committed to negotiations will be under constant pressure from more radical nationalists who oppose these negotiations and from the fundamentalists who oppose any negotiations.)

There are many obstacles ahead. Each side views these negotiations as laying precedents that will bear powerfully on the final status that will only begin during the third year of the autonomy period. Thus even though these are negotiations over "interim" arrangements, they are vested with great importance—e.g., although Jerusalem is not a substantive topic now, any election plan will have to deal with [the] question of whether or not Palestinians living in East Jerusalem will be able to vote and run for office.

The U.S. will continue to be a major factor. Not just a question of U.S. policy, but also a question of the priority that the next President will give to the negotiations. The next Administration will be focusing on domestic issues, and its foreign policy concerns may give minimum attention to the Middle East.

SETTLEMENTS—Rabin announced that he will complete approximately 10,000 units of housing in the West Bank. These units [are] in various stages of construction. Some finished, others merely a hole in the ground. Will not go ahead with 7,000 planned by Shamir government. 10,000 units equals about 50,000 people over the 100,000 already there.

Once upon a time, forty-five and a half years ago in the summer of 1947, bored by my studies at rabbinical school, and stimulated by a charismatic teacher, a world-renowned archaeologist with a passionate love for what was then called Palestine, I decided to spend a year of study at the Hebrew U in Jerusalem. For $250 I was able to make the fifteen-day voyage by ship from New York to Haifa, with a stop in Beirut, where the Jews onboard were forbidden to leave ship. It was a most glorious time to come, one that would profoundly shape my life and my thinking forever.

I was swept away by the beauty of the land and by the incredible dynamism of my Jewish brothers and sisters who had come there to build it and to be built by it. It was a most peaceful time and not a day was without its violence. British tanks patrolled the streets. Etzel and Lehi, Irgun and Stern Gang whose prominent leaders were Begin and Shamir, were at work, bombs; into cafes frequented by British soldiers, or at army installations. The walls everywhere marked with graffiti—*al Habritim hakovshim, zohi artzenu*—British invaders, out of our country—a rifle cut through a map of Palestine that included both sides of the Jordan, with the inscription *rak kach*—only in this way, with the rifle, with force.

My teacher had provided me with an introduction to Judah Magnes, President of the Hebrew University. He and Martin Buber had proposed the idea of a binational state of Jews and Arabs as the only reasonable and equitable solution to what was called "the problem of Palestine." I easily came under their influence. That year, 1947, the University opened on October 31. Magnes gave the address to the assembled faculty and student body on Mt. Scopus, passionately warning of the danger of the rising tide of Jewish nationalism. I sat there as the students roared their disapproval in a loud chorus of boos.

Meanwhile, at what was then called Lake Success in New York, the UN was debating the future of Palestine. On Nov. 29 the UN arrived at its historic decision—that the land should be partitioned into two separate states, one Jewish, one Arab. There was great joy—for everyone, except for those rejectionists in the Irgun and the Stern Gang, and the Arabs, who the very next day erupted in acts of violence, and began their war against the decision, against us.

All the rest is familiar history: The creation of Israel in May of 1948, the departure of the British, the invasion of Arab armies, the flight of the Arabs, and for Jews the great victory, the great valor. The goal of the Zionist movement, it had always seemed to me, was the liberation of the Jewish people. Young and old died to create a Jewish society, just and equitable, at peace with its neighbors, secure in its own nation, on part of the historic Jewish homeland. Partition of the territory between Jordan and the Mediterranean into two states was accepted by the overwhelming majority of the Zionist movement as a necessary condition for maintaining Israel's particular Jewish vision. It was the principle of compromise through that partition that alone provided the basis for the broad international recognition of the legitimacy of Israel's 1948–1967 borders despite the implacable opposition of the Arab nations and the Palestinians.

The hope of generations of Jews was repeatedly threatened by the relentlessness of Arab hostility. But following the Six-Day War in 1967 it would come to be threatened by something else: The hidden contradictions within Israel itself— the desire to reach a settlement, certainly, but also territorial ambitions. The will to compromise, but also the belief in a particular and decisive right to the land of Israel.

In the years since 1967, the moral credibility of the Jewish people would come to be tested in the occupied or administered territories, particularly in the last year (depending on which locution you prefer). "Was the wonder of our renewal as a people," Abba Eban would come to ask, "the ability to take a language, a land and a people separated for centuries, and to have brought them back together again in a new birth of independent life in the land of our ancestors, was that rebirth meant so that we might produce another nation state, like all of the others, living by the gun? Was it to create a homeland out of the energy of so much will and courage and sacrifice and imagination, so that Jews could have a land where children were beaten as a matter of routine? Where an enemy, however dangerous, could be buried alive? Where books were censored, dissidents imprisoned or sent into exile." Could a Jew, I wondered, a *Jew,* be at home in such a land?

The goal of the Zionist moment, which created Israel, was the normalization of the Jewish people. The bitter fruits of normalization in Israel made it possible for us to produce our farmers and scientists, our artists and writers, and always our courageous soldiers, and now our own share of sadists.

How could Jews permit their souls to be annexed by the territories they occupied?

When the Kahan Commission, which investigated the Sabra and Shatila massacres, charged General Arik Sharon with "indirect responsibility" for the murders, it quoted a passage from the Talmud, saying: "A basis for 'indirect responsibility' may be found in the outlook of our ancestors . . . 'It is said in Deuteronomy (21:6f) that the elders of the city, who were near a slain victim who had been found (when it was not known who had struck him down), would wash their hands over the (victim) and state: 'Our hands did not shed this blood and our eyes did not see . . . '"

Ours, as American Jews, we who loved Israel, we who fought for it, supported it, believed in it, ours, I believed, was surely the responsibility, at least the indirect responsibility—all of us, those who approved, those who were silent, those who joined the Israelis who criticized the policies of their government. The common wisdom had always declared that we who live outside of Israel owe deference to the Israelis because they and their children have fought the wars of Israel, and bear the risks of living in Israel, while we have merely provided money and political support. That it is our duty to accommodate to Israel's prevailing government and persuade our government to do the same. Those who are still charitably called American Jewish leaders have dutifully been willing to do that, regardless of their private feelings.

Now all of this is taking place against the backdrop of the opening of the peace talks. The prospects for peace are surely threatened by the settlements, since a peace inevitably will mean some sort of territorial compromise.

There is a real possibility to move forward toward peace, as never before in the past forty-four years. But whether the Israelis will turn the wish for peace into a decision to compromise on land is yet to be seen.

An October 1992 article in *The Economist* recounts that in 1937 Jabotinsky visited Britain's House of Lords to press the case for a Jewish state. He said he understood the desire of the Arabs to set up their state in Palestine, but that it had to be balanced against the disaster awaiting the Jews of Europe. The Arabs already had several states: When the Arab's claim for another one in Palestine was confronted with the Jewish claim to be saved, it was like "the claims of appetite vs. the claims of starvation."

Within a few years, Hitler had proved him tragically right. But that was one-half century ago. Today we Jews have our sanctuary. The whole world is ready to accept Israel's permanence and legitimacy within legally defined borders. For Israel to demand the West Bank as well, on top of the territories gained in 1948, has become a claim of appetite. It is the claim of the Palestinians that is now the claim of starvation. Unless it is met, there will be no peace.

Over the past several months, there had been a marked decline in the incidence of popular violence, and there was a return to a more upbeat mood. Palestinians were holding large wedding celebrations, going out to rest. Israel had announced a cutback in the number of troops allotted to the territories, and as a gesture, had released some 800 prisoners, relatively low grade intifada offenders being held in detention camps.

Even today some 12,000 political prisoners are serving sentences—7,000 in IDF detention camps, 5,000 in security wings of [the] Israeli prison system. On September 27, these latter went on a hunger strike for better conditions.

Palestinians have little to show from the negotiating process. Their leaders have requested that Israel ease the tax burden, and travel restrictions, or release all prisoners—[the] Rabin government has not responded. Nor would Rabin agree that Israel reveal its plan for final settlement regarding the territories.

There are some positive signs. Latest Israeli proposal states that Administrative Council will be responsible to Palestinians. There is, for the first time, no reference to Judea and Samaria. Palestinians, of course, have asked that Israel state that 242 will apply to final settlement, that nothing will be done in the interim agreements to prejudice [an] ultimate solution.

Palestinians need to be promised something real after autonomy. U.S. is important!

COMMENTARY BY SALAM AL-MARAYATI

In reading Leonard's analysis of the Palestinian-Israeli peace process, I saw one who was on a spiritual quest to transcend religious nationalism. He critiqued his own: "How could Jews permit their souls to be annexed by the territories they occupied?" He believed that religion has no value if it is imprisoned by power and is violating the rights of others. That's what I admired about Leonard the most—he was not a religious leader who clung to his own community at all costs (whether you are a rabbi or an imam or a priest); he added to the richness and to the complexity and to his sophistication, because he was both religious and spiritual—a rare combination in any individual. He moved beyond the dogma to uphold what is ethical. He exemplified what we find in our scripture: "O you who believe, stand up for equity and be witnesses to God even if you have to testify against yourself, your family, or your community . . . " (Quran 4:135). It made him question himself, his congregation, and all of us on how to find truth and adhere to justice in our interactions and struggles. That's what made him stand out as a great Jewish leader, one who could be consistent with his stands on social justice, whether addressing Los Angeles or the Middle East. He helped me find my spirituality as a religious leader. He helped me see him as a brother in faith.

38

A Sermon for Yom Kippur Morning

October 1, 2006
(On the 24th anniversary of the 1982 war)

As he took the pulpit on the morning of Yom Kippur in 2006, Rabbi Beerman felt an ominous sense of familiarity. Twenty-four years earlier, he had given a sermon about the grave dangers lurking in Israel's first Lebanon War. His fears were not unfounded. That conflict lasted, in one form or another, for eighteen long and difficult years, during which time Lebanon devolved into civil war and the reputation of the Israeli army and state suffered.

In what would become a recurrent and haunting phrase that Beerman would utter from the Leo Baeck pulpit, he said, "Here we are again," referring not only to Yom Kippur, but also to another Israeli military engagement in Lebanon. A little more than two months earlier, on July 12, Israel responded to a rocket attack and the abduction of two of its soldiers by the Lebanese militia group Hezbollah with punishing aerial attacks and a ground incursion into southern Lebanon. Israel's aims were twofold: to attempt to degrade the offensive capacity of Hezbollah, which would send thousands of rockets during July and August into northern Israel (generating deep fear and even panic among its citizens); and to attack the civilian infrastructure of Lebanon, including Beirut, in order to pressure the government to bring Hezbollah to heel.

In seeking to fulfill these aims, the second Lebanon engagement became, according to Beerman, "but a new chapter for Barbara Tuchman's March of Folly," *the 1984 book that explored the constant impulse of governments, from antiquity to the present, to act against their interests in undertaking military actions. Even more damaging than the conflict on the battlefield was the internal struggle—within Israel, the Diaspora community, and the Jewish soul. Beerman feared, as he had earlier, that the Jews, in Israel and beyond, had lost their moral compass. In his own immediate environs, he sharply criticized the Jewish communal organizations that condemned the decision of the Los Angeles County Human Rights Commission to bestow an award in September 1982 on his close friend the Muslim leader Dr. Maher Hathout. The groups believed that Dr. Hathout was too extreme in his criticism of Israel—including his assertion that the country was an apartheid state—a claim that Beerman sought to parry by referring to similar comments by Israeli public officials themselves.*

These are the words of Nobel Laureate Pablo Neruda:

> Now we will count to twelve
> and we will all keep still.
> For once on the face of the earth
> let's not speak in any language,
> let's stop for one second
> and not move our arms so much.
> It would be an exotic moment
> without rush, without engines,
> we would all be together
> in a sudden strangeness.
> . . . If we were not so single-minded
> about keeping our lives moving,
> and for once could do nothing,
> perhaps a huge silence / might interrupt this sadness
> of never understanding ourselves.
> Perhaps the earth can teach us /
> as when everything seems dead
> and then proves to be alive.
> Now I'll count up to twelve
> and you keep quiet and I will go.

One—two—three—Maybe that's all this sermon requires, that and a deep breath. Maybe. But—you know how it is with rabbis, and especially on Yom Kippur.

When this day is over. When the gates of Yom Kippur are closed for another year. When the prayers and the music and the words spoken have fallen silent, we will all be, once again, alone, alone to face ourselves, to return again to what our lives are, and perhaps, to wonder what they mean. When I try to think of what my life is and was, when I wonder what it meant, the sad days passing, the dog sick and still waiting to be fed, the closeness of my wife sleeping, presences of our grown children and grandchildren, blessing them one by one on the Shabbat, listening as they sing with the guitar, or the youngest of them screaming as they chase one another through the house, "the sun, the smell of the air just now, each physical moment passing, passing," as the poet Robert Creeley once said, "it's what it always is or ever was, just then, just there."

Have you felt that? Or is it just old people like me? Each physical moment passing, passing, just then, just there.

Here we are again, you and I, come to greet another year, another Yom Kippur,
nestled here in Bel-Air, just below the Getty, privileged by our geography and
by the distinction of our membership. Fences, security guards, several security
guards, just for us, we could well live out our lives as a guarded gated community
of Jews, absorbed in our own spiritual needs and dedicated solely to the advancement of Jewish learning and religious observance for ourselves and our children
and acknowledging our responsibility for the security and well-being of our fellow
Jews in Israel, everywhere. Is that what it's all about? Is that what it means to be a
Jew, to be a Jew in the twenty-first century? To be absorbed primarily in our needs
as Jews? No (it hardly needs be said), that's surely not enough for the Leo Baeck
Temple whose spiritual leader is Ken Chasen, and Sandy Ragins before him. Just
take a look at this month's Temple Bulletin to see again that the Jewish hearts in
this synagogue clearly have a place of significant value for something beyond our
Jewish selves.

It's a hard thing talking to you this year. Such a tumult is the world, brimming
with anger and adversaries and terror and hatred and fear, great fear everywhere.
Why, unlike you and me, does everybody else and everything in this world have
to be so complicated? It is confusing. To live in this world, in this irrational time,
when the values that we Jews have always affirmed are daily being coarsened,
mutilated even, by our own country, even by Jews, is to be confused and angry
and frightened. Confusion, anger, and fear seem to me to be thoroughly rational
responses to an irrational situation.

Exactly twenty-four years ago, 1982—that was the year that Israel invaded
Lebanon—I gave a sermon for Rosh Hashanah evening in the course of which
I said that I would be speaking about the war in Lebanon on Yom Kippur. As I
stood at the door to greet our members as they left, a good friend of mine, the
late Norman Tyre, approached me. Norman frequently had had serious problems
with some of the views expressed in my sermons (would you believe that?) [and]
never failed to communicate his distress with me, but that in no way impinged on
our affection for one another. This time he said: "I'm so glad to hear that you will
be talking about the war in Lebanon on Yom Kippur, because I'm gong to be in
India." (I have a feeling that some of you might wish to be somewhere else by the
time this sermon is done.)

Now in those days I used to keep in my desk drawer a statement by Robert
Alter, distinguished professor at Berkeley, which I would take out whenever I felt
like being critical of Israel. "Morality on the subject of Israel comes cheap to an
American Jew, because he is not directly confronted with the responsibilities of
power, the naked needs of survival."

Back then—this will hardly surprise you—I was one of that minority of Jews
here who believed, from the very first day, that the war in Lebanon, the war of

Menachem Begin and General Ariel Sharon, was doomed to be a moral and political failure. About rabbis like me there was a letter written to the American Jewish
periodical *SH'MA*. "God bless our Jewish intellectual liberals (the rabbis among
them). God bless them with their Jewish consciences and their Jewish sympathy
for the hurt and suffering of all people. God bless them—and keep them far from
positions of responsibility. We need their prophetic reminders of who we are and
how we should act, but we would have disappeared from the face of the earth if we
had let them make the practical decisions of daily existence."

The purpose of that war, Prime Minister Begin solemnly declared, was "to secure
peace in the Galilee and when we reach the forty kilometer limit, the fighting will
cease." It soon became clear as the Israeli army marched closer to Beirut, that this
was a lie. It was well known that Israel had been looking for a pretext for a full-scale
war in Lebanon in order to create a new order in Lebanon and to liquidate once and
for all the PLO, thus securing Israel's northern border and bringing to submission
the Palestinian population of the West Bank and Gaza, having deprived them of
their leadership. "To crush, to eradicate, to liquidate, to fumigate, to wipe out"—
this was the lexicon of Menachem Begin, and as he said in a letter to President
Reagan, "we are marching to Berlin to liquidate Hitler." The war did succeed in
driving Hitler (Arafat) and the PLO from Lebanon, but it was not the PLO that was
destroyed; it was the moral stature of the state of Israel. The massive use of military
force, the massacres at the refugee camps at Sabra and Shatila as the Israeli troops
stood idly by, not only brought untold suffering to the civilian population; it also
supplied credibility to the hostile propaganda that presented Israel as an aggressive state bent on expansion and annexation while trampling on the rights of the
Palestinian people. But the war was fought, and the dead died. And the defeated
Palestinians strengthened their national will by creating a new martyrology, and
300,000 Israelis would rally in protest in the streets of Tel Aviv, expressing their
shock and shame. Abba Eban, once Israel's Ambassador to the United States would
say, "This war has been a dark age in the moral history of the Jewish people." The
government of Menachem Begin would fall; Begin would disappear from public
life. Ariel Sharon was disciplined and prohibited from ever becoming Defense
Minister again. (Obviously that didn't apply to becoming Prime Minister.) Eleven
years later in this month of September 1993, the defeated Arafat would be standing
on the White House lawn with Prime Minster Yitzhak Rabin and President Clinton.

And, as you remember, out of that 1982 war in Lebanon there arose a small
extremist organization called The Party of God, Hizbollah, dedicated to the
destruction of Israel.

What does our prayer book say? "The Torah has taught us to put our trust not
in force and violence, not in aggression and domination, but in justice and truth,
in kindness and compassion." How naïve. How naïve.

This new ugly thirty-four-day war in Lebanon has now been fought. Hizbollah
crossed the Israeli border, captured (or, if you prefer the locution, kidnapped) two

Israeli soldiers, killed three others. Israel responded not many days later with a massive attack against the whole of Lebanon. The chief of staff of Israel's army, Dan Halutz, declared that "for every rocket fired by Hizbollah a ten story building will be destroyed. We'll set the country back fifty years. Everything is a target." Most Israelis gave their full support for this war. There were some protesters. Even those who had previously been identified with the peace movement in Israel, intellectual leaders among them, fully supported the war, at least in its initial stage.

Hizbollah, according to Israel and confirmed by Human Rights Watch and Amnesty International, committed war crimes in deliberately targeting civilians with its rockets. But these ruthless acts, which brought death and suffering to Israelis in the north, did not go unmatched by the Israeli army. Although there were indeed occasions when Hizbollah was embedded among civilians, Human Rights Watch and Amnesty insisted that Israel committed war crimes in being indifferent to the lives of civilians in towns and villages where there were no Hizbollah fighters nearby, and in dropping hundreds of thousands of cluster bombs in the closing days of the war, many of which lie still unexploded.

This war, as brutal as it was, trumpeted and believed in by so many Israelis and American Jews as being full of high cause, as an existential threat to Israel, was, in my view, but a new chapter for Barbara Tuchman's *March of Folly*, one that could comfortably and logically follow our country's folly, its ill-fated war in Iraq, not so strange since Israel and the United States are linked to each other's sometimes poorly considered militant purposes. Or the war could be seen simply as another bloody chapter in the many tragedies in the Middle East, many of which might have been avoided with creative diplomacy and political vision instead of the insistent assertion of military power. Jacques Derrida, one of the outstanding philosophers of our era, wrote of the "autoimmunity crisis" he found rampant in the United States and other countries of the West after 9/11, whereby the defensive system devised to keep out infection (the enemy that is) actually invites it and works against itself.

But the real struggle for Israel's survival, as Zeev Maoz has pointed out, is not the one against Israel's many enemies such as those heard spewing forth in the ranting of Hamas, Hassan Nasrallah of Lebanon, and Mahmoud Ahmadinejad of Iran. The real struggle is one taking place within Israel and within us as American Jews. It is a struggle for the heart and soul, one that has been taking place in Israel from its very beginning, and certainly since 1967, when it conquered all of the territory between the Jordan and the sea. So it has become a struggle about the future of Israel as a moral state. But it is also a struggle about our purpose as American Jews, whether we are just to be Jews, to be supporters of Israel, and our fellow Jews, since all Jews are responsible for one another, to be Jews and to continue to be what we have been, a monument to endurance; or whether we are in any way, more importantly, to be Jews, and to become bearers of a great moral aspiration. Yes, to be responsible for our fellow Jews and especially Israel, reveling in its remarkable accomplishments, to be responsible, but not always in the way these members of our Jewish family choose to define themselves, not in ways that bring destruction to others or to themselves.

I shall never forget the words I heard spoken almost thirty years ago by the great Jewish leader Nahum Goldmann, when he said at a meeting I attended in Tel Aviv: "This is a critical hour in the history of Israel and the Jewish people. The great problem for Israel is the problem of being powerful. For two thousand years we were powerless as a people, and without power we learned how to be the best visionaries, the best dreamers, the best idealists. Now the powerless have become powerful. We have an army and flags and a state and victories." (He could have gone on to say, and an air force and nuclear weapons and sophisticated technology, the envy of many nations in the world.) "And in America, Jews are well organized and wealthy and highly placed in all of the realms of political, cultural and economic life. But we have not yet learned how to use our power in the service of our visions. To place our reliance on power is our greatest weakness. The survival of the Jewish people is more in danger today than ever before."

I think we must be on guard against those in the Jewish community whose definition of policy is the assertion of military power. That leads to a shrill militancy in reckoning with anyone with whom we differ, viewing them as enemies of the good, enemies of Israel, anti-Semites. We had a pathetic example of that here in Los Angeles recently, when a group of our respected Jewish organizations, led by the American Jewish Committee and the JFC [Jewish Federation Council of Los Angeles], engaged in a public campaign of vilification and humiliation of one of the most respected leaders of the Muslim community, Dr. Maher Hathout, my friend of almost twenty years, who had been named to receive an honor from the Los Angeles County Human Relations Commission. Why? Because he had been critical of Israel, because he had said some outrageous things about Israel and therefore, they insisted, he had been masquerading as a moderate. He had dared to call Israel an apartheid state. Dr. Hathout should have simply read aloud the words of Michael Ben-Yair, Israel's Attorney General from 1993 [to] 1996, who wrote: "After the 1967 war we enthusiastically chose to become a colonial society, ignoring international treaties, expropriating lands, transferring settlers from Israel to the Occupied Territories . . . Passionately desiring to keep these territories, we developed two judicial systems: one—progressive, liberal—in Israel; and the other—cruel, injurious—in the Occupied Territories. In effect, we established an apartheid regime in those territories."

This being a day for acknowledging our sins it is a day to be reminded that there is one sin (as my friend the late William Sloane Coffin once said) that locks people up in all other sins, and fastens them more tightly than ever in their predicaments. It's the sin of self-righteousness. Self-righteousness is trouble enough in a single human being, but when it afflicts a nation, it spells enormous danger. Hope for a different kind of world is not to be found in an America or an Israel that will stand tall. No, it is to be found in the capacity to yield a little of our self-righteousness, repenting, just a little, for the cruelties brought to the innocent. Bill Coffin said it so well: "If only we wouldn't go on using the conspicuous wrong-doing of our adversaries as a means of nourishing our own self-righteousness, instead of permitting the wrongs to deepen our awareness that we are all in need of some repentance, some humility."

We need some humility, but we also need a far greater, wider, brighter vision of what it can mean to be a Jew. Israel's first Chief Rabbi, Abraham Isaac Kook, once said that there are many rungs in the ladder of perfection which must be climbed before the height of a truly universal human being is reached. "There are those who sing the song of life and in themselves find everything. There are others who sing the songs of their people. They leave the circle of private existence for they do not find it broad enough . . . they attach themselves with tender love to the whole of Israel, sing her songs, grieve her afflictions and probe the content of her inner essence. Then there are those whose spirit extends beyond the boundary of Israel to sing the song of humanity and this is the life source from which they draw their thoughts and their yearnings and visions. But there are those who rise even higher, uniting themselves with the whole of existence, with all creatures, all worlds. It is of such that the tradition has said that whosoever sings a portion of this universal song each day is assured a life in the world to come."

This is Yom Kippur, and the spirit of Yom Kippur has no boundaries. It sees repentance as the most creative force in the universe. It comes to tell us that life can be a time that we throw off our helplessness and that we can be the bearers of love and forgiveness, of compassion and hope.

Listen, my friends. One—two—three—each physical moment passing, passing, just then, just there. We can't make time stand still. The mind will be paralyzed that tries to make time stand still. But what will sustain us is to uphold an image of hope and beauty. The sun is here. Life and the earth in all their complexity are here. And before us the great mystery before which we all stand equally. I see the people standing in Tyre, Sidon, and Beirut; I see them in Kiryat Shemona and Jerusalem; I see them in Ramallah, and in Kalkilya, in Isfahan and Teheran, in Baghdad; I see them in Watts and here in Bel-Air, all standing equally before the great mystery, in awe and in ignorance. In this ultimate humility the human spirit can find a home, a place of safety.

Al tira, do not be afraid. Al tira, the commandment that appears more frequently in our Bible than any other. Al tira, do not be afraid.

One—two—three—each physical moment—just then—just there.

AMEN

COMMENTARY BY RABBI BRANT ROSEN

In this sermon and subsequent exchange, we can clearly see Rabbi Beerman's unique ability to combine an unwavering insistence on justice with a deep and abiding empathy.

In 2006, this rabbi stood before his congregation on Yom Kippur and agreed with a human rights organization's claim that Israel had committed war crimes. Even as I write these words ten years later, it is fair to say that most rabbis would never be able to say such things and keep their jobs—even if they believed such things to be true. Those who knew Rabbi Beerman know well that he was able to say such things because of the trust he had for the members of his congregation.

There can be no better evidence of this trust than the final paragraphs of his sermon. This was not, in the end, a sermon about Israel's actions in Lebanon. It was, in Rabbi Beerman's own words, a sermon about humility, love, forgiveness, compassion, and hope. Thus even a congregant who violently disagreed with Rabbi Beerman's views was still able to respond to his words with "unconditional love."

According to a famous midrash, when God created the world, God said, "If I create the world with the attribute of compassion alone, its sins will be too many; if with justice alone, how could the world be expected to endure? So I will create it with both justice and mercy, and it may endure!"

Rabbi Leonard Beerman was that unique moral leader who was able to combine justice and compassion. And this is why his rabbinate endured.

39
_____

Exchange of Letters with Bruce Ramer

October 2006–January 2007

The exchange of letters between Leonard Beerman and Bruce Ramer was an annual ritual. Ramer is a prominent Beverly Hills lawyer with deep involvement in the Jewish and non-Jewish communities. He was also a member of Leo Baeck Temple who admired Leonard Beerman greatly and considered him a good friend. That said, the two held to very different political views, especially on Israel. Typically, Ramer would attend the rabbi's Yom Kippur sermon and then write a letter filled with criticism, but also containing an affirmation of his love and admiration. Beerman would respond in kind.

Below is an exchange that took place after Beerman's 2006 Yom Kippur sermon. It begins with Beerman's response to Ramer, which contains an elaboration of the rabbi's support for his friend, Dr. Hathout. Ramer followed suit some three months later with a point-by-point response. The exchange exemplified the kind of serious, candid, and civil debate that Beerman valued.

October 11, 2006

Dear Bruce,

That is indeed true friendship. You have given me the better deal. I get your love, respect, and adoration to the end of your time, and you get all of the same from me (at 85) to the end of my time. Whatever—we will both be able to indulge in some mischief along the way.

Maybe it's the white Yom Kippur robe, or that I'm standing elevated above the congregation, but I am more of a creature of doubt than you may imagine, well aware, along with you, that everything human is complex and especially everything Jewish. That nothing Jewish can ever be simple is a principle inserted into the process of creation at that suspended moment between the end of the sixth day when God completed the work, and the beginning of the seventh when God rested. Your letter said this in a different and certainly more concise way, but start with the premise that all things human are flawed—you and I, Hathout, AJC, Human Rights Watch, Israel, America, Steve Emerson and Lawrence Rose, even the *Wall Street Journal,* which I was reading every morning when I began this letter, and you have at least the beginning of some humility. I think we both could use a little more of that, and so too, the causes we represent.

You are troubled with my views and my friends. Where to begin? I had read the Lawrence Rose correspondence some time ago, and actually was expecting to attend a meeting with him and some Human Rights Watch people; but the meeting was cancelled. I thought he made some interesting points, but fuelled as they were with so much zeal to undo the findings, I didn't find them persuasive. One must begin these discussions with the understanding that no one engaged in them will live long enough to know the truth about this war in Lebanon. After all, we are just learning new truths about Washington, Jefferson, and Lincoln—and the Bible, and the Mona Lisa, and Pluto, not to mention the weapons of mass destruction in Iraq. The horrors perpetrated by Israel are indeed pale and puny compared to the outrages of other nations, but they are nonetheless real. Yet I had been impressed that HRW [Human Rights Watch] had had the courage to issue its report on the war crimes of Israel and Hizbollah. I dread the revelations still to come. These little wars are great for testing out new weapons.

As for Steve Emerson, I have always been skeptical of his reliability. I remember his utter certainty on CNN that Muslim terrorists were responsible for the Oklahoma City bombing. But if you, the AJC, and the *New Republic* can forgive Emerson, why not my friend Maher Hathout? Maher was also a friend of my colleague Rabbi Alfred Wolf, and was one of two non-Jews (Msgr. Royale Vatakin, the other) invited by Alfred's family to speak at his Wilshire Boulevard Temple funeral. Is it only the AJC, the JFC, the ZOA, and the JDL that have not been duped by him?[1] Hathout is not a Jew, and he is not a Zionist, so his views can never be fully at one with ours, and have on occasion been offensive, but this much is a certainty: Every single outrageous word he has ever spoken about Israel has been uttered by Israelis themselves.

This is the place I reached on October 21. I no longer remember what rose up to block me from going further. I do know that we traveled to New York, saw the new Tom Stoppard play, *The Coast of Utopia,* the first of a nine-hour trilogy, based on the life and thought of some of the great Russian intellectuals of the mid-nineteenth century. Stoppard was stimulated to take up this subject by reading Isaiah Berlin's *Russian Thinkers,* which has long been one of my favorites.

There is a quotation that appears in the introduction to the book; it's from an author Berlin did not identify. In some way I would like to think it applies to you and me, maybe to you and me at our very best: *"To realize the relative validity of one's convictions and yet stand for them unflinchingly, is what distinguishes a civilized man from a barbarian."*

I'll leave you here, hoping that we will continue this discussion ad meah v'esrim (to 120), and knowing that our friendship will always accompany us along the way.

With love,
Leonard

January 2, 2007

Dear Leonard:

It may be the difference between being a Rabbi and being a lawyer.

Either way, I truly enjoyed and, more importantly, respect your response of October 11, whenever completed.

Let me respond, however, very briefly:

1. Quite accurately, the love, respect, and adoration is, as you say, mutual and forever (in the context of human life).
2. Life, Jewish and otherwise, is complex and perhaps too often perplexing.
3. Lawrence Rose made more than some interesting points.[2]
    His first letter did it well enough. But the abject failure of the Executive Director of Human Rights Watch, who wrote a long, empty, and non-responsive letter, prompted Mr. Rose's second letter. Between them, he seriously devastated the processes, procedure, and credibility of HRW, at least in this report (and by implication, since they defended their procedures, others). HRW does some good work, but this was not it. Lawrence did not set out with "zeal to undo the findings." Indeed, he has been a long and active supporter of HRW and was deeply distressed by what he read in their report on Israel-Hezbollah. Any court or unbiased reader would have agreed with him.
4. I have a great deal of respect for Steve Emerson, his longstanding concerns, his objectivity, and his methodology. He was not alone, indeed nearly the entire country believed that Muslim terrorists were responsible for the Oklahoma City bombing. The next day, when he and most others discovered otherwise, he said so.
    In this instance, while I could not find it to send to you, he had undercover tapes of Mr. Hathout, so his credibility is certainly not an issue in this instance. I also question your contention that "every single outrageous word he has ever spoken about Israel has been uttered by Israelis themselves," although I suppose one can find anybody anyplace to say anything about anyone. He certainly, at least in the view of many of us, did not deserve recognition of a Human Rights Award, whether from LA County or anyone else.

5. I unconditionally love the final three paragraphs of your letter—. You never cease to amaze me with the depth of your knowledge and your thinking.

With love,
Bruce

COMMENTARY BY BRUCE RAMER

Leonard Beerman was unique. Yes, an icon but a unique one. Rarely does one find a person with total intellectual integrity, an advocate par excellence, with opinions and positions, some easy, most difficult, held and voiced by him with passion and conviction. My disputes with him (actually honest debates)—the rabbi and the lawyer—were serious but enjoyable, fiercely held by each of us and similarly advocated, and embraced by each of us to the end.

Debates with Leonard were always substantive, authentic, respectful, and civil. Leonard had a rare gift. Taking a page from his lifelong love of tennis, you had to be on your best game with him. Our debates were not discussions. They were spirited challenges, each to the other. Leonard was living proof that the most important words in a democracy are, I disagree.

But always with great love, admiration, and respect for the other—at least mine for Leonard. He was a rare and beloved community treasure. I shall forever miss our exchanges, whether written or over lunch. As we get to say once in a while, they don't make them like that anymore.

40

———

A Sermon for Yom Kippur Morning

October 4, 2014

"And here we are again, you and I. Another Yom Kippur." With these words, Leonard Beerman launched into his last sermon at Leo Baeck Temple, his last cri de coeur after sixty-six years of teaching, admonishing, and inspiring his congregation. Leonard Beerman knew that the end was approaching, but he would not surrender the opportunity to use this final Yom Kippur as a call to conscience. As usual, there was plenty on his mind, and it had to do with Israel.

The focus of his attention was no longer Lebanon, but rather the Gaza Strip. Following the disengagement of Israeli settlers from Gaza in 2005, tensions escalated between Israel and the ruling party there, the militant Islamist group Hamas. The first major round of fighting between the two came in 2006 after the kidnapping of Israeli soldier Gilad Shalit, to which Israel responded with air and ground assaults. In subsequent years, Hamas sought to demonstrate its capacity to unnerve Israel by sending locally produced Qassam rockets into southern Israel. Israel responded in late 2008–early 2009 with a major air and ground offensive (Operation Cast Lead) that wrought vast destruction and considerable loss of life. The cycle of Hamas rockets and a large-scale Israeli response was repeated in 2012 (Operation Pillar of Defense) and then again in 2014 (Operation Protective Edge).

These rounds of violence, in which Israel's huge military advantage led to disproportionate and massive damage on the Palestinian side, weighed heavily on Beerman. As a committed pacifist, he had spent a lifetime warning against the excesses of military power—and against the replacement of the Jews' moral compass with a willingness to engage in violence. In 2014, at the end of his life, he was heartbroken at the death of so many children in Gaza, to the point that he considered calling the Israeli attack on them slaughter. To the last, Beerman was prepared to defy convention and provoke to the point of anger in order to restore the ethical imperative of the Jews.

Although he understood that the overwhelming majority of the Israeli public and organized American Jewish community stood in solidarity with the war effort, Beerman was not alone. He belonged to a group of LA-based rabbis, scholars, and activists who had been meeting periodically since the later stages of the second Palestinian Intifada (2005) under the banner "One Community, Many Voices." The group gathered anew after the destructive summer of 2014, forging a statement of principles that Beerman quoted in this sermon. Whenever that group convened, Beerman was the unquestioned moral authority. And so too he was for his congregants at Leo Baeck. Summoning all his psychic energy and literary prowess one last time, he mixed references to poets and writers with a weary refrain: "Another Yom Kippur. Another war in Gaza." When he came to the end of his sermon, admirers and critics alike rose in appreciation, recognizing that this might well be their last encounter with their leader, whose powers of empathy and desire to do good in the world had shaped their community.

In 1947, two years before I became a rabbi, the poet Auden wrote a long poem entitled "The Age of Anxiety." There was a refrain in it which haunted me when I first read it, and has haunted me ever since. "It is getting late. Is there no one to ask for us? Are we simply not wanted at all?"[1]

Everyone wants to be wanted and needed. Everyone wants to matter. As I contemplated giving this sermon, some part of me, still a child, wanted the words I would speak, gently to be heard, kindly to be judged by you.

When the blast of the war in Gaza rang in my ears this past July, I became totally absorbed, enmeshed, obsessed with feelings of sorrow and pity, with disappointment and despair, and anger, and even with shame. I knew that this mixture of feelings might not be the proper stuff out of which to fashion a sermon for today, and surely, if this were to be the last Yom Kippur morning sermon I would ever give, I would not want it to be that. But nonetheless, here it is.

And, here we are again, you and I. Another Yom Kippur. Another time to reflect on our lives and consider again who it is that we are and what we have become. Another Yom Kippur, another time to think seriously about whether there is anything in the way we are living that needs to be mended.

Another Yom Kippur. Another war in Gaza. The outrages perpetrated by Hamas, the thousands of rockets deployed, thousands of Israelis rushing for shelters, living in fear, the many Hamas tunnels burrowing their way into the borders of Israel.

Another Yom Kippur. Another 500 children of Gaza killed by the Israel Defense Forces, with callous disregard for their lives. I had thought about using the word "slaughtered" for what I was really feeling, and I lingered over it, wondering whether it was too provocative. And then I remembered Ari Shavit, Israeli journalist, and his much celebrated book, *My Jerusalem, the Triumph and Tragedy of Israel.*[2] Three of us, Chasen, Ragins, and Beerman, reviewed it here at the Temple. The most closely examined chapter in that book was entitled "Lydda." It told the story of the all-Arab city of Lydda located near the center of Palestine, a short distance from the international airport. As Israeli military forces began to take over the city in the summer of 1948, 200 Arab citizens took refuge in a small mosque. The military forces killed every one of them. A massacre, Shavit described it. Which set me to thinking: if the killing of 200 Arabs in July of 1948 was a massacre, what about 500 children in 50 days of the summer of 2014. Is that not also a massacre? Massacre, slaughter, callous disregard for life—does it really make any difference?

My friend George Regas once said that the first priority of any civilization is the care of its children—to prevent needless suffering among the most vulnerable and blameless. A Gaza mother sits amidst the rubble of what was once her home. If she knew the words of Nurit Peled-Elhanan, an Israeli mother whose 13-year-old daughter was killed by a suicide bomber in Jerusalem some years before, she might want to use Peled's words and say to us: "We are the only ones who can tell you that there is no civilized killing of innocent, or barbaric killing of the innocent, there is only criminal killing of the innocent." And remembering the last time she saw her little boy or girl, again using Peled's words she would say: "After the death of a child there is no other. No one can avenge the blood of a child because a child takes into her small grave, with her small bones, the past and the future and the reason for war and its consequences."

Another Yom Kippur, another war in Gaza. A few weeks after the Gaza war five years ago, in 2009, the Jerusalem prize, Israel's most celebrated literary award, was given to Haruki Murakami, the distinguished Japanese novelist. There was great protest in Japan and in the literary world when it was announced that Murakami would receive this award. They threatened that if Murakami were to accept this Jerusalem prize, they would boycott his work as a response to Israel's massive attack in Gaza and the terrible number of those who had died there. In his own kind of protest, after apologetically stating that it was his nature to do the opposite of what other people were telling him to do, here he did do the opposite. He went to Jerusalem, even though everyone was saying, "Don't get involved. Don't go there."

Now this is some of what he said in Jerusalem in February 2009:

> I do not intend to stand before you today delivering a direct political message. Please do however allow me to deliver one very personal message. It is something that I always keep in mind when I am writing fiction. I have never gone so far as to write it on a piece of paper and paste it to the wall: Rather, it is carved into the wall of my mind, and it goes something like this:
>
> Between a high solid wall and an egg that breaks against it, I will always stand on the side of the egg. Yes, no matter how right the wall may be and how wrong the egg,

I will stand with the egg. Someone else will have to decide what is right and what is wrong.

What is the meaning of this metaphor? In some cases it is all too simple and clear. Bombers and tanks and shells are that high solid wall. The eggs are the unarmed civilians who are crushed and shot by them. This is one meaning of the metaphor.

This is not all, though. It carries a deeper meaning. Think of it this way. Each of us is, more or less, an egg. Each of us is a unique, irreplaceable soul enclosed in a fragile shell . . . And each of us, to a greater or lesser degree, is confronting a high solid wall. The wall has a name. It is the System. The System is supposed to protect us, but sometimes it takes on a life of its own, and then it begins to kill us and cause us to kill others—coldly, efficiently, systematically.

I have only one idea, to believe in the utter uniqueness and irreplaceability of our own and other's souls, and in the warmth we gain by joining souls together.

The System did not make us. We made the System. We must not allow the System to exploit us.

Another Yom Kippur, another war in Gaza. A huge percentage of Israelis gave their full support to the war. In 1982, Israel invaded Lebanon with massive force, and marched on ready to begin the siege of Beirut. Israeli newspapers carried the story of a Col. Eli Geva, an armored brigade commander who created a sensation in Israel by asking to be relieved from his command rather than lead an assault on Beirut. The papers reported an exchange between Prime Minister Menachem Begin and Col. Geva. Begin hoped to persuade the young colonel to change his mind and asked why the colonel, the youngest brigade commander in Israeli history, wanted to be relieved of his command. Geva replied that when he looked through his binoculars into West Beirut he could see children playing.

This time, so far as we know, there was no Eli Geva. Oh, there were indeed Israelis who protested. In the middle of the war, 10,000 Israelis demonstrated in the Rabin Square in Tel Aviv. Standing and speaking there would be David Grossman, one of Israel's most celebrated writers, to criticize the war, certainly differing with his distinguished colleague Amos Oz, about whom Ken spoke in his Rosh Hashanah sermon. But those in Rabin Square constituted a small minority.

And here, it seemed that American Jews were speaking in one voice. Every major Jewish organization rallied to the cause, rabbis among them, expressing their solidarity, the absolute necessity to continue the attack on Hamas and the people of Gaza. "Israel has a right to defend itself," a principle that must have first been developed by the Neanderthals, was all the justification needed. It was unassailable. It could cover every doubt, if there was doubt about Israel's conduct of the war, the horror of it. Hardly a word found its way out of a Jewish mouth to express the slightest concern about the way Israel was exercising its right to defend itself, the appalling human suffering being visited upon the people of Gaza.

Although there was a rabbi, a certain Chasen, in Bel-Air who, breaking ranks from this rank indifference, wrote this to his congregation: "The past three weeks have undeniably been among the most agonizing in the modern state of Israel's 66-year history. While the aerial bombardment in Gaza and Israel has been carried on relentlessly, our eyes and spirits have been bombarded with an endless stream of heartbreaking images—dozens of Israeli soldiers falling at the hands of Hamas' terrorists . . . countless battered and bloodied children trapped in the middle of Gaza's warfare, so many of whom are dying . . . most of Israel's civilian population living in fear as air raid sirens force them into bomb shelters every day . . . a growing destruction of life in Gaza that will take enormous time and commitment from the world to reverse." Those were Ken's words.

As for me, it seemed clear that somewhere on the way to Gaza Israel had lost its moral compass; it was the very moral compass that had brought such glory to the people of Israel, the high ideals that had gone into its making, the passion for justice for all, the yearning for peace, the wonderful, warm, human decency that could be found among its people. And now Israel had risen up and said that it needed, as they put it, "to mow the lawn" again in Gaza. Seduced by the lure to war and filled with the desire for revenge, and with the passion of utter rightness, cheered on by Jews everywhere who wanted to demonstrate their solidarity, no one but a very few questioned whether this might possibly lead to a strategic failure and a moral defeat.

Here in Los Angles an assorted group of Jewish academics and a sprinkling of rabbis met to speak of our anguish and sorrow over the loss of life and scale of destruction and decided to give expression to the idea that this is one community with many voices, not just one. I suppose that in some way we were striving to give expression to the dignity of difference. And we produced a statement of principles that would come to bear, along with many others, the signatures of four rabbis associated with Leo Baeck Temple, Lewis Barth, William Cutter with Georgie, Sandy Ragins, and Leonard and Joan Beerman.[3]

(The following is an abbreviated version of the Statement of Principles.) "Love thy neighbor as thyself. One community, many voices." This was the epigraph for our statement. "We, members of the Los Angeles Jewish community write to express our anguish and sorrow over the loss of life and scale of destruction in the conflict between Israel and Gaza. We condemn Hamas' war time tactics and at the same time are acutely aware of the destruction inflicted by Israel. In thinking of the violence, we affirm the ancient wisdom of the Mishna that 'whoever destroys a single life, it is as if he or she had destroyed an entire world' (Sanhedrin 4:5).

"Hovering about all, above all questions of tactics and strategy—are the dead children, nearly 500 Palestinians and one Israeli. The loss of one innocent life is intolerable. The loss of many hundreds of innocent lives demands a moral accounting . . . Especially as we enter into the season of Teshuvah, repentance, it is imperative that we look into our souls and not rest quiet until we understand how this massive loss of innocent lives could have taken place. We insist that it not happen again. As deeply as we are connected to Israel, we reject the demand that we support Israeli policy without dissent. We believe it is an obligation of all Jews to contribute humanitarian relief in both Israel and Gaza as a reflection of our commitment to our own people and to the neighbors with whom we must find a way to live together in peace. And we urge our friends and colleagues and above all rabbis in our community to undertake a profound rethinking of the way they manifest 'support' for Israel. Unreflective support perpetuates the myopia that leaves too many of us insensitive to the suffering of our Palestinian neighbors and cousins. At the same time, the kind of unreflective support on display in the latest Gaza war does not serve Israel's best interests, but rather reinforces the extremist tendencies that threaten to undermine Israel's democratic core.

"We believe that the blockade that Israel has imposed on Gaza since 2007 has contributed to an intolerable economic, health and humanitarian situation that should be removed with appropriate supervision to ensure that the materials brought in be for civilian use only."

Another Yom Kippur. In the summer of 1936, in the heart of the great depression, Henry Luce, publisher of *Time and Life* and more recently of *Fortune,* must have discovered that there was indeed a depression, and he sent off James Agee and the photographer Walker Evans to explore the daily lives of tenant farmers in southern Alabama. It was an extraordinary collaboration. Agee wrote a report of 30,000 words, submitted it with the instruction that not one word of it could be changed. Luce rejected Agee's work, leading Agee to rework the material and to create five years later *Let Us Now Praise Famous Men,* which has come to be considered one of the most influential books of the twentieth century.

There is a paragraph in the original rejected article which is a ringing testament of Agee's beliefs, and at the same time will lead us to understand why Luce would not feel it was appropriate for his *Fortune* magazine and its readership. "A civilization which for any reason puts a human life at a disadvantage, or a civilization which can exist only by putting life at a disadvantage, is worthy neither of the name nor of continuance. And a human being whose life is nurtured in an advantage which has accrued from the disadvantage of other human beings and who prefers that this should remain as it is, is a human being by definition only, having much more in common with the bedbug, the tapeworm, the cancer and the scavengers of the deep." We could apply that to our own country, with its gross inequalities. Or we could remember that for forty-seven years the Palestinian people has lived under Israeli occupation and suffered the humiliations, great and small, that come with being an occupied people, severely restricting their freedoms in every aspect of their lives, while Israeli lives are nurtured in an advantage which has accrued from the disadvantage which has been imposed upon the Palestinians.

Well, enough of this raucous stuff, some of you may be thinking. Is this what Yom Kippur is all about? Yes, Yom Kippur calls us to account for who we are as Jews, to remind us that we can never fulfill ourselves in an inhuman world. We can never fulfill ourselves until we become dedicated to each other's fulfillment.

If Judaism has any continuing relevance it is because it has always been to grapple with the character and destiny of Jews and all humanity. And the distinctive quality of our faith as Jews is its will to sanctify life because of the sacredness of every human being. So it is that we have come here again to affirm our identity as Jews, and to assert for all to hear that there is a people in the world that has suffered all of the outrages of history, that has been victimized by thousands of lies and deceptions, a people whose bodies were trampled, whose spirits were mutilated in every era of human history, and yet that people persisted in believing in the infinite task of sanctifying human life.

Another Yom Kippur. It has come to us to remind us that our world, you and I, need desperately to be mended. Our world needs troubled people, Jews even, men and women who care, men and women who are not ashamed to be sensitive and tender. And our world needs men and women who have the courage to be afraid, afraid of all those forces which have removed our own humanity. And we need men and women who can resist all those, friends and enemies, who seek to prevent us from seeing the utter uniqueness and irreplaceability of our own and others' souls, and in the warmth we gain in joining souls together.

It is to such a challenge that this New Year comes in all of its brightness, in all of its persistent hope.

COMMENTARY BY PROFESSOR
NOMI M. STOLZENBERG

Leonard's last summer was a difficult time. On July 8, 2014, responding to rocket fire from Hamas, Israel invaded Gaza. Over 2,000 people were killed in the ensuing weeks, including 66 Israeli soldiers, 5 Israeli civilians, and somewhere between 2,100 and 2,300 Palestinians.

Like many of us, Leonard was anguished by the Gaza war. Unlike many of us, Leonard found a way to put that anguish into words. I was not among those who had the privilege of attending his last Yom Kippur sermon. But if there was any consolation, it was that I got to hear him practice it and to discuss it with him over the months leading up to Yom Kippur. Leonard said it was his habit never to discuss his sermons before delivering them. But this year was different. This year he worried over every word, weighing each one. The words he was ruminating over came tumbling out over the dining tables over which we met, as he rehearsed his text, testing it, seeking our response.

One word in particular caught all of our attention, and that was the word "slaughter." One member of our party argued vociferously against it, contending it did not accurately describe the IDF's motivations. Even if the IDF deserved blame, Leonard's interlocutor argued, it did not deserve blame for *slaughter,* which implies the *intent* to bring about mass killing. Leonard conceded the point, agreeing there was no proof of a desire for the deaths on the part of the IDF. Eventually we came up with "callous disregard" as an alternative. Yet Leonard refused to completely let go of his original word choice. For him, no passive, agent-less language, no "mistakes were made," would do. And if the only choice was between language that implies responsibility for slaughter and language that evaded Israel's moral agency, he was going to go with "slaughter."

Sayings of Leonard I. Beerman

(Left on the desk of his study)

1. We should know above all that war and the threat of war aggravate tyranny and provide the soil in which it thrives, while every effort made in the direction of peace relaxes not only international tension, but produces great liberty within each nation.
2. For . . . years we have sacrificed upon the altar of war and its preparation the greatest gifts of this nation, the gifts of mind and of technique; and in so doing, we have demonstrated a total contempt for man.
3. For . . . years, the angel of death has hovered over our civilization, fending off any serious endeavor to re-cultivate the waste places, to make a serious assault upon the problems of human anguish . . . The result of all this cannot adequately be measured, but we know it in the form of greater frustration and estrangement for us and greater poverty for the poor; for it is upon the poverty of multitudes that the unswerving, irresponsible dedication to defense and war is built.
4. Belief in the intelligent use of violence is the arrogance that bestrides the world . . . the nation shivers with insecurity; very few of us have any confidence that the political parties currently available to us have the leadership or the imagination and courage to liberate us from more of the same. Violence and the threat of violence abroad . . . violence and the threat of violence at home . . . the kind of violence that is shaking profoundly the inner life of all of us, as we see the traditional morality, the old religion, and the structure of family life, the relations between the generations crumbling.
5. We must not permit the terrible complexity of the problems of our society, or the resistance of confusion and fear, to deter us from our will to work for

the achievement of full and equal human rights for all. Nor can we permit our confidence in the ultimate goal to shrink before the difficulties that attend its achievement.

6. It is a common responsibility of all Americans to bring an end to the discrimination and exploitation which have for so long enmeshed the life of the Blacks in a tangle of pathology. We must not let ourselves be driven from this quest, either by the bitter rejection of some Blacks or by the renewed and intensified resistance of Whites.

7. Guilt . . . is the mark of a grand, profound struggle. It is the residue of the struggle between the conflicting forces of good and evil within us. It is the sign of our dignity as human beings, even as it is the mark of our failure to achieve the divine potential within us. To experience the awareness of our moral failure is, paradoxically, to experience the dignity of our own humanity.

8. We need those who have the courage to be ashamed, who have the muscle to care. And more than caring . . . we need those who will preserve and cultivate an enduring vision of the good, who will maintain a vision of the future as a permanent possibility in the present.

9. Not a day must go by without some expression of tenderness to those who are near and to those who are far off. Not a day must go by until we have used it to communicate our reverence for the despised, the humiliated, the unwanted. Not a day must go by unless it is good enough to be our last.

10. The fulfillment of the task, the fulfillment of life is in the here and now. The solutions will not be found in heaven. They will be found here on earth. And the message of religion is not designed to make us comfortable but to make us alive to our responsibility.

11. One either collaborates with the enemy, with whatever it is, with whatever is miserable or inhumane, with whatever is unjust, with whatever demeans the life of any of God's children, or one joins the resistance.

12. What does it mean to be human? To be human is to love; but the other side of love, we know, is hate. That, too, is human. It is human to make mistakes and to involve others in our mistakes. It is human to be ignorant and to achieve wisdom slowly and painfully, to be humbled by our experiences. It is human to be confused and bewildered by the turmoil and complexity of life. And it is human to be distressed by one's own inadequacy. It is human to face the future with deep uncertainty and not to be able to see very far ahead. It is human to hurt and to be hurt. It is for us to keep alive our faith that man can be human, that he can glorify the earth.

13. We will find ourselves not in solitude, not in escape, not in reliance upon myths of our own superiority, but by our capacity for compassion, our ability to care, our ability to develop a conscience broad enough to leap

across the barriers of the little, little environment in which all of us live.

14. Isn't it a perversion of everything that is morally precious in our religious tradition to permit the military to set the priorities for our country and the world? How can we pursue human goals, how can we reckon with the decay of our cities, how can we care for the poor and the hungry and the abandoned, how can we pretend to revere the dignity that is present in every human being, when our ultimate commitment is not to what is humane, not to God, but to this super Moloch in whose nuclear temple we have been prepared to sacrifice our children?

15. How can we profess our faith and continue to depend upon nuclear weapons to save us? How can we erect a religious commitment on a foundation of the believable threat to kill a hundred million of God's children? . . . Is there any religious doctrine in any faith that can justify a nuclear war?

16. The way to give meaning to our life is to do what we can to abate its misery, to heal its wounds, to be comrades in the only war worth fighting: the battle to extend the domain of love and reconciliation and justice in the world, and thus to declare ourselves for the continuation of life.

17. Nothing is so hard to overcome as the will to be enslaved by our own moral inertia. Yet we know there is another power within us, a power that enables us to say no to the forces that have ruled over our thinking and feeling. It is the power of our own critical intelligence, or our own decency; the power of the human spirit; it is that spiritual power present in every person—and it can be actualized.

18. The earth is too small and life is too short for anything to be more important than the quest for peace.

19. Human social systems with their human beings, anxious, insecure, swollen with pride, driven by the will to power, corrupted by self-intoxication and self-deception, sooner or later sin against the laws of proportion and harmony and plunge into decay and self-destruction . . . Now our civilization may be in the process of making the same mistake.

20. We hold life to be sacred, do we not? We have been taught to do so by the heritage of our tradition and even our nation; yet, paradoxically, we patiently accept our roles as victims and perpetrators of mass slaughter, and by what we do, by what we prepare, we convey the steady message that life is worthless, it is not sacred at all.

21. To achieve national security by the threatened annihilation of whole populations is an evil I cannot believe any serious Jew, any serious Christian can countenance.

22. Human existence is coexistence. Before I can realize my own freedom, my independence, my humanity, I must join the fellowship of others, my people, humankind.

23. From where, if not from this place, will come the call for peace? And the peace that we seek can never be the imposition of our wills on each other, but rather, the activating in each other of those forces which make for a common identity. Not by might and not by power, not by force and not by conquest can we transcend the dangerous, destructive imagery of victory and defeat that has been our human heritage.

24. We must understand the importance of a sense of dependence. And if we fail to celebrate this sense of dependence, no matter how far we reach into outer space, there can be no significant human life on earth. If we cannot cultivate a passion for what one human being owes to another, what are we?

NOTES

INTRODUCTION

1. See Michael A. Meyer's discussion of the role of the progressive and Christian social gospel movements in the formation of a social justice imperative in American Reform Judaism in *Response to Modernity: A History of the Reform Movement in Judaism* (New York and Oxford: Oxford University Press, 1988), 287.

2. See Jonathan D. Sarna, *American Judaism: A History* (New Haven: Yale University Press, 2004), 308–309.

3. See the commentary by Rev. Lawson on "The Legacy of MLK," January 15, 1982.

4. The rabbi and scholar David Polish has discussed the balancing act between universal and particular tendencies in Reform rabbis in "The Changing and the Constant in the Reform Rabbinate," in Jacob Rader Marcus and Abraham J. Peck, eds., *The American Rabbinate: A Century of Continuity and Change, 1883–1983* (Hoboken, NJ: Ktav, 1985), 173–251.

5. "Why the Prophets Are Important," May 20, 1983.

6. "Chapel Sermon," October 30, 1948, italics added. This image of the "eternal dissident" echoes the long-standing Christian myth of the "wandering Jew," who was destined to wander the world after rejecting Jesus Christ. On this mythic personality, see Richard I. Cohen, "The 'Wandering Jew' from Medieval Legend to Modern Metaphor," in Barbara Kirshenblatt-Gimblett and Jonathan Karp, eds., *The Art of Being Jewish in Modern Times* (Philadelphia: University of Pennsylvania Press, 2007), 147–175.

7. The grandparents wrote a touching note, in their immigrants' English, expressing the hope that their grandson remain true to his faith on the occasion of his *brit milah*. Leonard Beerman kept the note in a frame in his study.

4/16, 1921   Altoona, Pa

My Dear Grandson,
Enclose you will find a smole [*sic*] gift Presented to you by your Grandparents on the day that you became a member, according to the law of Moses, to the most glorious religion on the face of this earth. We therefore Bestow our Blessing upon you. May you be the Sunshine of your Parents and a healing Balm to the People of Israel and to all mankind, a good American and a good Jew, and a servant to the God of Israel, the soul of this Great universe.

And when you will mature to that age that you will be able to understand these few words then we will ask of you to tell your darling Mother to read this letter to you often.

Save this letter for many years so that you will be able to read it to your own children.

We remain,
Your Grand Parents
Jacob I. And Rose Grossman

8. Beerman often punned that like his father, he too was a purveyor of "notions," intending not the wares that his father sold, but the ideas that he sought to disseminate.

9. Leonard I. Beerman, interview by author, July 11, 2013. Although outliers in Owosso, the Beermans belonged to a large majority of American Jews who held to liberal views and were strong Roosevelt supporters. On this pronounced Jewish political disposition, see Marc Dollinger, *Quest for Inclusion: Jews and Liberalism in Modern America* (Princeton: Princeton University Press, 2000).

10. See Donald Warren, *Radio Priest: Charles Coughlin, the Father of Hate Radio* (New York: The Free Press, 1996).

11. Beerman, interview, July 11, 2013.

12. Ibid.

13. Ibid.

14. Leonard I. Beerman, interview by author, August 15, 2013.

15. Beerman's transcript from the Pennsylvania State College is found in the Central Archives of the Hebrew University (CAHU). Thanks to Michael Vinegrad of the CAHU for his assistance in retrieving the Penn State, and HUC transcripts.

16. Beerman, interview, July 11, 2013.

17. Ibid.

18. Ibid.

19. Ibid. As a reflection of his growing sense of Jewishness, Leonard performed a decidedly Jewish act in the AC spark plug factory. While putting the finishing touches on the .50 caliber rifles on the assembly line, he would chisel a six-pointed Star of David on the barrel.

20. Beerman, interview, August 15, 2013.

21. Ibid. Spinoza was the favored philosopher of many modern Jewish iconoclasts, for whom he represented a rare example of intellectual courage and integrity. Daniel B. Schwartz has chronicled the wide range of modern Jewish admirers of Spinoza in *The First Modern Jew: Spinoza and the History of an Image* (Princeton: Princeton University Press, 2012).

22. Beerman, interview, July 11, 2013. He recalled that his decision to enlist was motivated by his desire "to show that I wasn't afraid. I wasn't afraid of what I've been. I'd always been afraid of fighting, physical conflict."

23. Beerman, interview, August 15, 2013.

24. Ibid.

25. His transcript from HUC covering the period 1943–1947 reveals that Leonard was a fine student, but also that grade inflation was not present at the college in that period. For example, he was not only awarded a number of "Goods" during his time there (the letter equivalent of 80–85), but he also received one in his favored subject of philosophy in 1945–1946. One course in which he always received the highest grade of E (95–100) was public speaking. His transcript is found in the CAHU.

26. Beerman, interview, August 15, 2013. Cronbach laid out his views on war and peace in *The Quest for Peace* (Cincinnati: Sinai Press, 1937).

27. The Hebrew word *kavanah* denotes intense spiritual intention and refers here to those rabbinical students who were most intent on enhancing their Jewish spiritual experience, as opposed to the academic study of theology or engaging in social justice activity.

28. Beerman, interview, August 15, 2013.

29. The CAHU contains Beerman's transcripts from Penn State and HUC, but no trace of classes taken at the Hebrew University. This suggests that he applied for admission, but never formally registered for classes in Jerusalem.

30. Quoted in "Students and Revisionists Hiss Magnes at Opening of Hebrew University," *Jewish Telegraphic Agency*, November 20, 1929, accessed at http://www.jta.org/1929/11/20/archive/students-and-revisionists-hiss-magnes-at-opening-of-hebrew-university, on September 5, 2016.

31. Daniel P. Kotzin, *Judah L. Magnes: An American Jewish Nonconformist* (Syracuse: Syracuse University Press, 2010).

32. On the various iterations of the binational idea in Palestine, see Susan Lee Hattis, *The Bi-national Idea in Mandatory Palestine* (Haifa: Shikmona, 1970), as well as Benny Morris, *One State, Two States: Resolving the Israel/Palestine Conflict* (New Haven: Yale University Press, 2009).

33. For a fuller account of the experience of an HUC student in Palestine and in the Haganah in 1947–1948, see Ezra Spicehandler's remarks in *Alumni and Faculty Reflections on Israel*, accessed at http://huc.edu/sites/default/files/News-Events/Spicehandler-Reflec-tions%20of%20Israel.pdf.

34. "Beerman Holds British to Blame for Violence" (undated bulletin of the Penn State Hillel chapter).

35. Ibid.

36. For a helpful analysis of the ingredients that make up a successful sermon, including a discussion of a 1910 address by Judah Magnes, see Michael Marmur, "Contemporary Jewish Homiletics: Some Key Components," *International Journal of Homiletics* 1 (2016): 52–70.

37. "Chapel Sermon," October 30, 1948.

38. Ibid.

39. Beerman had in mind the Swiss theologian Karl Barth, one of the leading representatives of the Protestant neo-orthodox movement. For a brief, but helpful explication, see Mark Galli, "Neo-Orthodoxy: Karl Barth," *Christianity Today* 65 (2000), accessed at http://www.christianitytoday.com/history/issues/issue-65/neo-orthodoxy-karl-barth.html on June 7, 2017.

40. "Chapel Sermon," October 30, 1948.

41. "A Dissident Rabbi Speaks Out about Lebanon," *LA Weekly,* July 30–August 6, 1982, cover, 10–12.

42. "Our History," Leo Baeck Temple (website), http://www.leobaecktemple.org/who-are-we/history/our-history/. On Baeck, see Michael A. Meyer, "The Thought of Leo Baeck: A Religious Philosophy for Our Time," *Modern Judaism* 19 (May 1999): 107–117.

43. "The Kindest Use a Knife," October 16, 1953.

44. Prinz's speech can be found at "Civil Rights," Joachim Prinz (website), http://www.joachimprinz.com/civilrights.htm, accessed on June 7, 2017.

45. "Notes for Symposium on Black Power," January 6, 1967.

46. Rev. James Lawson, interview by author, October 31, 2016. Lawson explained his encounter with Gandhi and his approach to nonviolence at https://www.youtube.com/watch?v = Q8K4HLMo3dw, accessed on June 7, 2017.

47. For an early case study based in Queens, New York, see Kurt Lang and Gladys Engel Lang, "Resistance to School Desegregation: A Case Study of Backlash among Jews," *Sociological Inquiry* 35 (January 1965): 94–106. See also the conversation between Hyman Bookbinder, an official of the American Jewish Committee, and Eleanor Holmes Norton, the well-known scholar and public official, in "Blacks and Jews: Affirmative Action and Civil Rights," originally printed in *Washington Jewish Week,* July 2, 1987, and accessed at http://www.bjpa.org/Publications/downloadFile.cfm?FileID = 13372 on June 7, 2017.

48. In addition, the two clergymen frequently preached in each other's institution. On one occasion in 1988, Leonard preached a sermon on Easter at All Saints Church's service at the Hollywood Bowl. See John Dart, "Rabbi to Participate in Hollywood Bowl Easter Sunrise Service; Organizer Seeks Involvement of All Communities, Religions," *Los Angeles Times,* March 19, 1988.

49. "Letter to President Lyndon Johnson," April 13, 1967.

50. "Rosh Hashanah Eve," September 30, 1970 (5731).

51. Another indication of his popularity in the face of controversy was the fact that he was solicited for a number of rabbinic positions over the course of his career, including by Rodef Shalom in Pittsburgh (1966) and Central Synagogue in New York City (1971). Letters attesting to this interest are in the Beerman Archive. In addition, he was invited by the faculty of HUC in Cincinnati to be a candidate for the position of dean. See his letter to his good friend Prof. Eugene Mihaly, declining the offer, January 1, 1979, Beerman Archive.

52. Meyer, *Response to Modernity,* 372.

53. "How I Lost the Election in St. Louis," July 9, 1971.

54. Members of the delegation included Bishop James Armstrong, Robert McAfee Brown, Harvey Cox, Bishop Robert DeWitt, Sister Mary Luke Tobin, and Leonard. The trip itinerary and rationale are included in the Beerman Archive. See also "World Clergy Unites against Vietnam War," *Stanford Daily,* January 15, 1973, accessed at http://stanforddaily archive.com on November 2, 2016.

55. See "CCAR Breira Statement," 1977. For a brief history of Breira, see Alex Klein, "J Street's Forerunners," *Tablet,* March 23, 2012, accessed at http://www.tabletmag.com/jewish-news-and-politics/94906/j-streets-forerunner on June 7, 2017.

56. In fact, in his last years, Beerman served as a member of the rabbinical council of Jewish Voice for Peace (JVP), the left-wing group known for its support of the Boycott, Divestment, and Sanctions (BDS) movement. Although he did not support a global boycott of Israel (as opposed to a boycott of products produced in Jewish settlements in the

West Bank), Beerman embraced his JVP affiliation. See the extended conversation between between him and Brant Rosen, cofounder of the JVP rabbinical council on April 28, 2014, in Westwood, at https://www.youtube.com/watch?v = C7opr1iHG20&t = 2734s, accessed on June 7, 2017.

57. "Rector, Rabbi Join in Dialogue," *Los Angeles Times*, February 17, 1975.

58. "2-Day Conference on 'Reversing Arms Race' Set," *Los Angeles Times*, October 20, 1979.

59. In the tribute booklet honoring Leonard Beerman in 1986, the Interfaith Center described its goal as "bring[ing] an end to the nuclear arms race and the threat of mass nuclear destruction."

60. "Jews Urged to Oppose Nuclear Weapons Race," *New York Times*, April 26, 1982. See also Dov Waxman, *Trouble in the Tribe: The American Jewish Conflict over Israel* (Princeton: Princeton University Press, 2016), 42.

61. "Yom Kippur Eve," September 26, 1982.

62. Ibid.

63. Proverbs 30:22. Perhaps the most compelling use of the phrase from Proverbs in this context was made by Simon Rawidowicz in a hard-hitting, though unpublished meditation on Arab refugees from Israel written in the early 1950s. See D.N. Myers, *Between Jew and Arab: The Lost Voice of Simon Rawidowicz* (Hanover, NH and London: Brandeis University Press, 2008), 99, 103.

64. See his reflections in "Time in Israel, Part II," November 1967.

65. The call for "an American Jewish Intifada" can be found in the manifesto of the Jewish Committee on the Middle East from 1988, accessed at http://jcome.org/jcometestimony.pdf.

66. "A Sermon for Yom Kippur Morning," October 1, 2006.

67. Ibid.

68. Emmanuel Levinas, *Entre Nous*, trans. M. B. Smith and B. Harshav (New York: Columbia University Press, 1998).

69. The year of the meeting that was reported in various accounts of Leonard's life was 1983, although a photograph of a visiting delegation of Americans meeting with Arafat in Amman is from 1985. The photograph appears in the Jordanian daily newspaper *Al Ra'i*, June 24, 1985, which is found in the Beerman Archive.

70. For example, Beerman's mix of openness and tireless defense of the rights of others won him an award from the ACLU of Southern California in 1981. The letter of invitation made reference to "the enormous contributions you have made in preserving constitutional rights and freedoms." See the letter of invitation from Ramona Ripston, executive director of the ACLU of Southern California, February 19, 1981, Beerman Archive. Over the course of his career, Leonard received awards from the American Friends Service Committee, Death Penalty Focus, the Muslim Public Affairs Council, Physicians for Social Responsibility, the Human Relations Commission of Los Angeles, the Jewish War Veterans, the Union of American Hebrew Congregations, the Levantine Cultural Center, and the Liberty Hill Foundation, among others.

71. Commendation from the 2007 commencement ceremony, Washington & Jefferson College, Beerman Archive.

72. Leonard Beerman kept this quote at hand on his desk. For the quote, see the prologue to Bertrand Russell, *Autobiography*, intro. Michael Foot (London and New York: Routledge, 1998), 9.

73. The original members of the group were Beerman, Gunther, Nicholas, Willens, and Sheinbaum, along with Paul Schrade, Ralph Carson, Jack Roberts, Stanley Gortikov, Albert Wells, and Bob Powsner. Subsequent additions included George Regas, Mike Farrell, Arthur Greenberg, and David Rintels. This roster comes from a brief history of the group written by Fred Nicholas, November 18, 2014.

74. "A Sermon for Yom Kippur Morning," October 4, 2014.

75. This statement of principles, crafted by a group of about fifteen scholars, rabbis, and activists in a private home, was published as "Love They Neighbor as Thyself," *Jewish Journal,* September 5, 2014, http://jewishjournal.com/opinion/133057/.

76. Drawn from saying 12 of Leonard Beerman's favorite sayings; see "Sayings of Leonard I. Beerman" in this volume.

77. "A Sermon for Yom Kippur Morning," October 4, 2014.

78. Kurt Streeter, "At 93, Leonard Beerman Still Stirs Passions with Pacifist Views," *Los Angeles Times,* November 26, 2014, accessed at http://www.latimes.com/local/great-reads/la-me-c1-rabbi-beerman-20141126-story.html.

79. Rabbi Beerman's sermons and other writings were often works in progress; as such, they contained occasional mistakes of punctuation, which, for the sake of clarity, have been corrected in the selections presented in this volume.

1. CHAPEL SERMON, OCTOBER 30, 1948

1. Genesis 3:7.

2. SIGMUND FREUD, MAY 11, 1956

1. On this phenomenon, see Andrew R. Heinze, *Jews and the American Soul: Human Nature in the Twentieth Century* (Princeton: Princeton University Press, 2004).

2. Yosef Hayim Yerushalmi, *Freud's Moses: Judaism Terminable and Interminable* (New Haven: Yale University Press, 1991).

3. The typescript text contains these words on a line between paragraphs.

4. Typescript text is incomplete.

5. THE LEGACY OF MLK, JANUARY 15, 1982

1. The boycott lasted from December 1, 1955, until January 17, 1956—381 days.

2. M.K. Gandhi, *Non-violence in Peace and War* (Ahmendabad: Navajivan Publishing House, 1942), 113ff.

6. FIRST ENCOUNTER WITH GEORGE (REGAS), APRIL 13, 2005

1. Regas and Beerman met in 1967, not 1971.

11. FROM THE DIARY OF A LEO BAECK TEMPLE
RABBI, FEBRUARY 5, 1971

1. Adapted from T. S. Eliot, "The Love Song of J. Alfred Prufrock."
2. Adapted from T. S. Eliot, "The Love Song of J. Alfred Prufrock."

15. MY TROUBLES WITH GOD; GOD'S TROUBLES
WITH ME, FEBRUARY 9, 1979

1. The two paragraphs above appear typed on a piece of paper just before the sermon below, which begins with Rabbi Beerman's handwritten words "Rough copy, Unedited, Not for Distribution."

2. Rabbi Baeck was deported to Theresienstadt in 1943, but survived his time there and lived until 1956; he also taught at Hebrew Union College, as Beerman knew.

20. UCLA TEACH-IN ON VIETNAM WAR, MARCH 24, 1966

1. Ed.: Rabbi Beerman concluded here, it appears, with a prose poem by Mark Twain called "The War Prayer" (1904) that he often invoked. "The War Prayer" reflected Twain's deep skepticism that one could summon God to support one's own war effort: "The burden of its supplication was, that an ever-merciful and benignant Father of us all would watch over our noble young soldiers, and aid, comfort, and encourage them in their patriotic work; bless them, shield them in the day of battle and the hour of peril, bear them in His mighty hand, make them strong and confident, invincible in the bloody onset; help them crush the foe, grant to them and to their flag and country imperishable honor and glory."

26. SURVIVAL IN A NUCLEAR AGE, FEBRUARY 17, 1984

1. Ed.: Beerman originally wrote "guns" in the typed version of the text, but crossed it out and wrote in pen "m.r. nw," the last two letters of which might signify "nuclear weapons."

29. A VISION FOR A BEWILDERING TIME, MAY 18, 2007

1. Ann Lauterbach, *American Poetry Review,* April/May/June 1996.

33. TIME IN ISRAEL, PARTS I AND II, NOVEMBER 1967

1. Ed.: The preceding sentence was inserted by pen in the text, with the last portion unreadable.
2. The word here is illegible.
3. Ed.: family.

35. YOM KIPPUR MORNING, OCTOBER 11, 1978

1. This is a reference to the famous "Three No's" of the Khartoum Resolution issued by the Arab League at its summit on September 1, 1967. The actual formulation from that resolution was "no peace, no recognition of Israel, no negotiations."

2. Beerman is referring to the hostile reaction within the Jewish community to a lengthy and probing profile of Los Angeles Jews that appeared in the *Los Angeles Times* January 29–31, 1978, written by Beerman's friend the journalist Robert Scheer. The profile is reprinted in Robert Scheer, *Thinking Tuna Fish, Talking Death: Essays on the Pornography of Power* (New York: Hill and Wang, 1988), 27–55.

36. YOM KIPPUR EVE, SEPTEMBER 26, 1982

1. Anthony Lewis, "At Home Abroad: The Consensus Cracks," *New York Times*, July 1, 1982.

2. Estimates are that the demonstration in central Tel Aviv on September 25, 1982, drew some 400,000 participants.

3. The reference is to Beerman's friend and fellow Reform rabbi Jerome Grollman (1922–2008), who served for sixty years at United Hebrew Congregation in St. Louis.

38. A SERMON FOR YOM KIPPUR MORNING, OCTOBER 4, 2014

1. The poem reads somewhat differently from what Beerman quoted: "It is getting late. Shall we ever be asked for? Are we simply / Not wanted at all?" W. H. Auden, *The Age of Anxiety: A Baroque Eclogue,* ed. Alan Jacobs (Princeton: Princeton University Press, 2011), 34.

2. The book's correct title is *My Promised Land: The Triumph and Tragedy of Israel* (New York: Spiegel & Grau, 2013).

3. See the Statement of Principles from September 5, 2014, at http://www.jewishjournal. com/opinion/article/statement_of_principles_ve_ahavta_le_reacha_kamocha_love_thy_ neighbor_as_th, accessed on November 21, 2016.

CONTRIBUTORS

RACHEL ADLER is the David Ellenson Professor of Modern Jewish Thought at the Los Angeles campus of the Hebrew Union College-Jewish Institute of Religion.

J. EDWIN BACON recently retired from a twenty-one-year tenure as Rector of All Saints Church, Pasadena, authored the book *8 Habits of Love,* and now lives with his wife, Hope, near their grandchildren in Birmingham, Alabama, continuing to write, preach, and teach.

JOAN WILLENS BEERMAN, PhD, is a practicing clinical psychologist who was blissfully married to Leonard Beerman for nearly twenty-seven years.

SHARON BROUS is the senior and founding rabbi of IKAR and is involved in multifaith justice work in Los Angeles and around the country.

CONNIE BRUCK is a longtime staff writer at the *New Yorker.*

KENNETH CHASEN is Senior Rabbi at Leo Baeck Temple in Los Angeles, California.

ARYEH COHEN is Professor of Rabbinic Literature at the Ziegler School of Rabbinic Studies of the American Jewish University and Rabbi-in-Residence at Bend the Arc: A Jewish Partnership for Justice.

WILLIAM (BILL) CUTTER is Professor of Literature and Human Relations emeritus at Hebrew Union College and has been an active member of Leo Baeck Temple for over fifty years.

DAVID ELLENSON is Director of the Schusterman Center for Israel Studies at Brandeis University and served as President of Hebrew Union College-Jewish Institute of Religion from 2001 to 2013.

MIKE FARRELL is an actor and a human rights and social justice advocate.

SAUL FRIEDLANDER is the 1939 Club Professor of Holocaust Studies emeritus at UCLA.

JONATHAN D. GREENBERG is Scholar-in-Residence at the Daniel Martin Gould Center for Conflict Resolution at Stanford Law School.

AZIZA HASAN has been with NewGround: A Muslim Jewish Partnership for Change for well over a decade and currently serves as the organization's executive director.

SAMUEL KARFF is Rabbi Emeritus of Congregation Beth Israel in Houston, the author of numerous books, and the former president of the Central Conference of American Rabbis.

ZOË KLEIN is Senior Rabbi of Temple Isaiah in Los Angeles and the author of a number of books of fiction and poetry.

JAMES M. LAWSON JR. is a theologian and activist, who introduced the principles of nonviolent resistance to the civil rights movement upon his return from India in 1955; he served for twenty-five years as Pastor of Holman United Methodist Church.

NORMAN LEAR is a television producer and writer who founded People for the American Way in 1991.

MEL LEVINE is a lawyer in Los Angeles and represented the West Los Angeles, Santa Monica, and South Bay areas in the US Congress between 1983 and 1993.

RICHARD LEVY is a former Assistant Rabbi at Leo Baeck Temple and a past President of the Central Conference of American Rabbis.

PETER LOEWENBERG is Professor of History emeritus at UCLA, as well as Training and Supervising Analyst at the New Center for Psychoanalysis and an elected member of the Board of the International Psychoanalytic Association.

SALAM AL-MARAYATI is President of the Muslim Public Affairs Council and has worked on Abrahamic peacemaking since meeting Leonard Beerman in 1991.

MICHAEL A. MEYER is the Adolph S. Ochs Professor of Jewish History emeritus at the Hebrew Union College-Jewish Institute of Religion in Cincinnati, Ohio.

JACK MILES, the author of *God: A Biography* and other works, is Professor emeritus at the University of California, Irvine.

DAVID N. MYERS is the Sady and Ludwig Kahn Professor of Jewish History at UCLA.

JANE OLSON cofounded in 1979 and for a decade chaired the Interfaith Center to Reverse the Arms Race with Rabbi Leonard Beerman and Dr. George Regas, an experience that led to her leadership of Human Rights Watch, Landmine Survivors Network, and the Women's Refugee Commission.

SANFORD RAGINS, PhD, is Senior Rabbi emeritus of Leo Baeck Temple, where he served as Leonard Beerman's assistant, associate, and successor.

BRUCE RAMER is an entertainment lawyer who has had the privilege of doing what he loves for over fifty years with a small firm—Gang, Tyre, Ramer & Brown—which he also loves.

GEORGE F. REGAS is Rector emeritus of All Saints Church, Pasadena, a past Chair of the Desmond Tutu Peace Foundation, New York, and founder of Interfaith Communities United for Justice and Peace (ICUJP).

DAVID RINTELS is a writer in theater and television and, for more than thirty years, was a member of the Tuesday Knights with Leonard Beerman.

STEPHEN ROHDE, a constitutional lawyer, writer, and political activist, is author of two books, *American Words of Freedom* and *Freedom of Assembly*; served with Rabbi Beerman on the board of Death Penalty Focus for twenty years; and is National Chair of Bend the Arc: A Jewish Partnership for Justice.

BRANT ROSEN is the founding rabbi of the congregation Tzedek Chicago and the Midwest Regional Director of the American Friends Service Committee.

JOHN L. ROSOVE is Senior Rabbi at Temple Israel of Hollywood and serves as National Board Chair of the Association of Reform Zionists of America (ARZA).

STEVEN J. ROSS is Professor of History at the University of Southern California and Director of the Casden Institute for the Study of the Jewish Role in American Life.

CHAIM SEIDLER-FELLER is Director emeritus at UCLA Hillel and Director of the Hartman Fellowship for Campus Professionals.

DANIEL SOKATCH is CEO of the New Israel Fund, the leading organization working for democracy and equality for all Israelis.

NOMI M. STOLZENBERG is the Nathan and Lily Shapell Chair at the USC Law School and Co-director of the USC Center for Law, History, and Culture.

RACHEL TIMONER is Senior Rabbi at Congregation Beth Elohim in Brooklyn and had the privilege of learning from Leonard Beerman for eight years at Leo Baeck Temple.

JUDITH VIORST is the author of many books for children and adults, including *Alexander and the Terrible, Horrible, No Good, Very Bad Day* and *Necessary Losses.*

MILTON VIORST has been writing on the Middle East for a half century as a journalist and scholar and is the author most recently of *Zionism: The Birth and Transformation of an Ideal.*

INDEX

"Releasing Powerful Armies of Moral Strength," interview by John Whiteley, Association for Counselor Education and Supervision, 1984 (29 minutes). Beerman clearly articulates his philosophy of activism and struggle against moral inertia, as well as his activism with the Interfaith Center to Reverse the Arms Race. https://www.youtube.com/watch?v = EWtI6OHLx8c.

Interview by Ed Hummel, 1997 (74 minutes), California Social Welfare Archive. This extended autobiographical survey follows key stations of Beerman's life. https://www.youtube.com/watch?v = QQIiIoNQxvc.

Audio tribute on the occasion of receiving an award from CLUE (Clergy and Laity United for Equality), 2009 (4 minutes). Beerman discusses the deep roots of his commitment to social justice, which is based on the biblical injunction to manifest concern for the widow and orphan, as well as his own experience during the Depression. https://www.youtube.com/watch?v = 4TfbbHmr124.

Interview on the occasion of receiving the Courageous Peacemaker Award from the ICUJP (Interfaith Communities United for Justice and Peace), 2013 (14 minutes). Beerman discusses his antiwar activism and commitment to interfaith work, which is based on the unending quest to recognize the sacredness of human existence. He also articulates the view that religion is, of necessity, political. https://www.youtube.com/watch?v = edXP8qqjLtI&t = 5s.

"Progressive Politics from the Pulpit," conversation with Rabbi Brant Rosen, February 2014 (67 minutes). Beerman discusses the roots and evolution of his views about Israel, including reflections on strategies to effect change in the present. https://www.youtube.com/watch?v = C70pr1iHG20.

Interviews with Rabbi Leonard I. Beerman, by David N. Myers

Interview, July 11, 2013 (49 minutes). Beerman discusses his life.
DOI: https://doi.org/10.1525/luminos.50.1.

Interview, August 15, 2013, Brentwood, CA (52 minutes). Beerman discusses key episodes in his life.
DOI: https://doi.org/10.1525/luminos.50.2.

CPSIA information can be obtained
at www.ICGtesting.com
Printed in the USA
LVHW01s1923240418
574734LV00001B/1/P